♠ ♣ ♥ ♦

Winning Poker Tournaments

One Hand at a Time

Volume I

♠ ♣ ♥ ♦

By

Jon "PearlJammer" Turner
Eric "Rizen" Lynch
Jon "Apestyles" Van Fleet

Foreword and Introduction by Matthew Hilger

Dimat Enterprises, Inc.
www.InternetTexasHoldem.com

Winning Poker Tournaments One Hand at a Time Volume 1
Copyright © 2008 by Eric Lynch, Jon Turner, and Jon Van Fleet
Published by Dimat Enterprises, Inc.

Cover Illustration: Craig Ditman
Cover photo of Eric Lynch and Jon Turner courtesy of Cardplayer.com
Book Design and Graphics: Andrew and Eva Kuczynski

ISBN 978-0-9741502-7-7

♠ ♣ ♥ ♦

About the Authors

Eric "Rizen" Lynch

Eric "Rizen" Lynch is recognized as one of the top tournament players in the world in both live and Internet play. In just two years at the World Series of Poker, he has seven cashes, including a 2nd and 3rd place finish. He finished 26th in the 2006 main event, winning $494,000, his biggest prize so far. His lifetime total for cash finishes in live tournaments is a little shy of $1 million.

Online, Eric has over 50 wins, made 300 final tables, and has won over $1.5 million. In 2007, he won one of the major Sunday tournaments, beating out thousands for a prize of $156K.

Eric writes a popular blog found at www.rizenpoker.com and is a columnist for Bluff magazine.

Jon "PearlJammer" Turner

Well-known for his online prowess, Jon "PearlJammer" Turner, who also plays online under the name PearlJammed, actually got his start playing live games in Raleigh, NC, and then later in Las Vegas. He won the 2007 Internet Player of the Year award, tracked by www.InternetPokerRankings.com, after a 3rd place finish in 2006. He consistently ranks in the top 10 players at www.PocketFives.com.

Over the last couple of years, PearlJammer has amassed an impressive online resume: He has over 100 wins, made 600 final tables, and won almost $2 million. In 2007, he placed second in one of the major Sunday tournaments to win his biggest online cash prize of $100,000.

Jon "Apestyles" Van Fleet

Jon "Apestyles" Van Fleet started playing professionally in 2004 after graduating from college, and quickly moved up the ranks in the online poker world. He ranked in the top 20 in both 2006 and 2007 at www.InternetPokerRankings.com. He consistently ranks highly at www.PocketFives.com and is a two-time winner of their Triple Crown award.

Jon has made close to $2 million playing in tournaments online, including over 350 final tables and 70 wins. His biggest online cash to date is $135K when he finished 2nd in a major Sunday tournament.

About Dimat Enterprises, Inc.

Dimat Enterprises, Inc., a publishing company founded by Matthew Hilger, specializes in books about poker strategy. Authors interested in being published can contact Matthew at his website, www.InternetTexasHoldem.com.

Books

Internet Texas Hold'em, by Matthew Hilger, published in 2003.

Texas Hold'em Odds and Probabilities: Limit, No-Limit, and Tournament Strategies, by Matthew Hilger, published in 2006.

The Poker Mindset: Essential Attitudes for Poker Success, by Ian Taylor and Matthew Hilger, published in 2007.

Winning Poker Tournaments One Hand at a Time: Volume I, by Eric "Rizen" Lynch, Jon 'PearlJammer" Turner, and Jon "Apestyles" Van Fleet, June 2008.

Upcoming

All About Limit Hold 'em by Matthew Hilger, Summer 2008

The World Poker Travel Guide, by Tanya Peck, Fall 2008.

Winning Poker Tournaments One Hand at a Time: Volume II, by Eric "Rizen" Lynch, Jon 'PearlJammer" Turner, and Jon "Apestyles" Van Fleet, early 2009.

No-Limit Tournament Strategy: Expert Strategies for Live and Online Poker, by Eric "Rizen" Lynch and Matthew Hilger, 2009.

A portion of the proceeds of Dimat Enterprise's books are donated to Colombianitos, a unique charity founded in Atlanta, Georgia that helps disadvantaged children in Colombia. Matthew is a member of the board of directors and encourages you to support the charity. Please visit www.colombianitos.org for further details about the charity's work and aims.

About Dimat Online, Inc.

Matthew started Dimat Online, Inc. to develop websites focused on poker strategy, content, and media. Its flagship site, www.InternetTexasHoldem.com, supports the books published by Dimat Enterprises and is one of the most popular poker content sites in the world.

www.InternetTexasHoldem.com, commonly known as ITH, receives thousands of daily visitors and is regarded as one of the best sites on the web to help improve your game. ITH contains a wide variety of information and resources including:

♥ **Forum** – A free poker discussion group where thousands of members discuss poker strategy, bonuses, and current events within the poker world.

♣ **Site Reviews and Bonuses** – A comprehensive analysis and evaluation of the major online poker sites and their most lucrative deposit bonuses.

♠ **The Poker Nutz Newsletter** – Our newsletter keeps you up-to-date with the best online poker bonuses, new articles published on ITH, Dimat Enterprises publishing schedule, and other events of interest for the ITH community.

♦ **Poker Odds Calculator** – The ITH poker odds calculator is the fastest on the web with the most features. It has lightning speed and calculates odds for every type of Hold'em situation including scenarios against random hands or against a range of hands.

♥ **Articles and Online News** – Unique articles written by some of the top online players in the world.

www.InternetPokerRankings.com, commonly know as IPR, is the first website dedicated to an objective ranking system of Internet players. Players are ranked based on money finishes in all of the major online tournaments. In 2008, IPR introduced the first ranking system for international players.

www.pokerwonks.com. The biggest and best collection of poker blogs on the net, including Matthew's blog, Poker and Life. All poker bloggers are invited to submit their blogs.

Acknowledgments

Eric Lynch

I would like to thank my beautiful wife Shauna and our two wonderful children, Corbin and Kira. I know the time and sacrifices they have made for both my profession and this book were numerous, and I appreciate their support more than they will ever know. Without their blessing this book could never have been completed. I would also like to thank the rest of my family for their constant words of support and encouragement throughout both the writing of this book and my life, as they have always believed in me and made sure I believed in myself. Also thanks to all the fellow poker players who have taken time out of their lives to discuss hands and situations with me, especially those I talk with every night (you know who you are). I hope that you all have learned half as much from me as I have from you. Finally, I would like to thank all of the fans out there (either of me or poker in general) who have made this book possible. The passion you all show for this simple card game we all love not only makes books like this possible, but helps keep those of us who are fortunate enough to be able to play it for a living reminded why we started playing in the first place, a fact that can easily be forgotten during the day to day grind of a being a professional poker player.

Jon Turner

Thanks to my parents who continue to support my passion for poker. Thanks to my friends, family, and especially my girlfriend, Tracey, who convinced me to take on this project and helped keep me motivated throughout the process.

Jon Van Fleet

I'd like to thank Danny Neylon, whose advice, ideas, and writing skills were essential in helping me put together my section of the book.

I also want to thank Stephen Chidwick who helped review my section and provided valuable feedback.

Matthew Hilger

I would like to thank several people who contributed to putting this book together:

Neil Myers and Julie Risinit for style and copyediting.

Andrew and Eva Kuczynski for typesetting and design.

Craig Ditman for the cover design and artwork.

Susan Myers for cover copy.

Also, thanks to all of the members of the Forum at www.InternetTexasHoldem.com. I wouldn't be nearly as successful as a player and poker author without all of your support.

Table of Contents

Foreword

by Matthew Hilger

Are you ready to take your game to an entirely new level? This book lays bare the inner workings of three of the brightest minds in poker today: Eric "Rizen" Lynch, Jon "PearlJammer" Turner, and Jon "Apestyles" Van Fleet. This book will show you exactly how three of the world's best poker players analyze and dissect a poker hand from start to finish.

What makes this book different from any other poker tournament book? First, you would be hard-pressed to find three poker players with more tournament experience under their belts. A professional playing only in live tournaments might play 100 tournaments a year. *These guys often play that many online tournaments in a week!* Collectively, they have played in over 35,000 tournaments, have made over 1,000 final tables, have logged over 200 major wins, and have cashed for more than six million dollars! Second, and most important, this book is about how to play a *poker hand.*

Theory and concepts are fundamental to becoming a good poker player, and there are many books that teach these, enabling you to establish a foundation of solid theoretical knowledge. Once you have established this foundation, you need to be able to put these theories into practice. This book guides you along the path to tournament success by putting you, as it were, inside the minds of some of the world's best players. You will see exactly how they analyze not only a hand, but a whole poker scenario.

The inspiration for the format of this book is *Middle Limit Hold 'em,* by Jim Brier and Bob Ciaffone, a book which contains hundreds of hand examples to illustrate how theory meets practice. I believe strongly in this format as a way of teaching and learning poker. For it to be successful, you need players with extensive experience. But experience alone doesn't make you a great teacher and author. What separates these experts from other good players is that all three of them are able to accurately describe their decision-making processes, articulating exactly *how* they think through individual hands.

I believe that this book is a unique addition to poker literature. Players who read and study these two volumes (volume two will be released in early 2009) will save themselves time, money, and years of frustration by learning from the wisdom of consistently successful tournament professionals.

Introduction: How this Book Was Created and What it Will Do for You

by Matthew Hilger

Early in 2007, I was looking to work on another joint project for the publishing company I founded. I had thoroughly enjoyed working with Ian Taylor, my co-author and the brains behind *The Poker Mindset: Essential Attitudes for Poker Success*. That book was well received in the marketplace, gaining a great deal of positive feedback from the poker world, and I really enjoyed the exchange of ideas that occurred while working with another poker player on a joint project. A book focused on hands played in poker tournaments seemed like a great next project, but only with the right experts with whom I could work.

Around the same time, I read an article by Rizen titled "Beyond Harrington". In that article, Eric taught the reader how to adapt to the ever-changing poker landscape. I was most impressed by Eric's clear writing style, and how he described new ideas and concepts.

Contacting Eric resulted in a fruitful meeting of minds, and this book (and others in the series) began to take shape. As Eric and I brainstormed the project, we discussed other potential coauthors for the book. Since I run the site www.InternetPokerRankings.com (IPR), it was logical that I start there to find some of the top-ranked players drawn from the site's Internet Player of the Year race. Players' rankings are based on their finishes in all of the major online tournaments. Those who, week on week, month on month, and year on year finish near the top of the leader board were clearly and consistently doing things that separated them from the rest of field.

One such player was Jon "PearlJammer" Turner. PearlJammer had finished 3rd in the 2006 Internet Player of the Year race, and won the race in 2007. Eric and Jon knew each other, and Eric thought he would be a great fit for the project. I called PearlJammer, and the next day he said he was on board—definitely someone who knows how to make a quick decision! I then asked PearlJammer and Eric to each create a short-list of other players who would be suitable co-authors. To my delight, the same player topped both their lists: Jon "Apestyles" Van Fleet.

PearlJammer has a style similar to my own: Early in a tournament, he focuses on managing the size of the pot to minimize his risk until he can set a trap for his opponents. He is willing to accept smaller pots early on for the sake of minimizing his risk. Later, he will start to open up his game in the right spots, but is generally a more conservative player than either Rizen or Apestyles. PearlJammer is always focused and rarely gets out of line during play.

Apestyles has a more aggressive approach and really turns up the heat on the bubble. He looks to build a stack quickly by taking an aggressive line against opponents who are more cautious in the early stages of a tournament. Apestyles is not afraid to take advantage of the smallest of edges. He also has a clear and carefully defined strategy on how to play against various stack sizes.

Rizen has more gears to his game than most. He is very focused on his image and his opponents' style of play, and then picks a style or strategy which is best for a specific situation, in that particular moment, against a particular opponent. Rizen plays a conservative sit-back approach at times, but he is willing to mix it up with you and take it to another level when game conditions demand it. Rizen takes risks, but generally only does so in low-risk, high-reward situations.

This book is the first volume in a two volume set. Volume 1 covers hands up until the money bubble. Volume II, will look at hands in the money, with a focus on final table play. Rizen and PearlJammer discuss 50 hands they have selected from their own play. Apestyles discusses 30 of his hands, and then another 24 hands devoted solely to a single tournament where he was on the bubble.

One of the goals of the book was to try to select players with different styles so that you, the reader, may observe contrasting styles in similar poker situations. To further illustrate these contrasts, I also selected 20 of my own hands, and asked all three authors to comment on how they would play the hand. Some of the hands were chosen to demonstrate consensus on important concepts, while other hands were chosen in the hope that they would generate discussion and debate. I was pleased when I would get a hand back and get three different answers! I also deliberately sent some hands that I felt I *did not* play correctly: it is instructive to see how top players would have played them differently.

Working with these top players has been a tremendous boost to my own game. I recently won a 750K guaranteed tournament for a prize of $132K. Can this book guarantee the same results for you? There are no guarantees, but there is no doubt in my mind that any player, from beginner to advanced, will be able to boost his or her game by learning from the poker wisdom offered here. These three players are the cream of the crop. They are the best of the best. How often does one get the chance to be coached by a top poker expert? Reading and studying this book is like attending a poker tournament master class.

Remember, poker is a fun game, but it is more fun when you win. Can you think of a better way to become a winner than by studying how the best in the world play?

Jon "PearlJammer" Turner

Hand 1

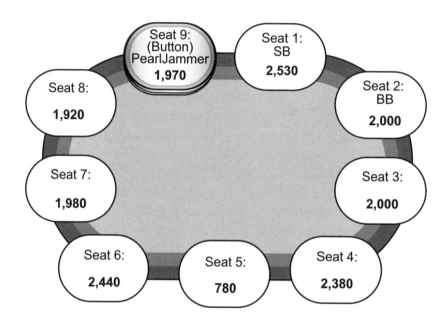

Setup: It is the first level of a $50, $50K guaranteed *freezeout*. The blinds are 10-20, and I have close to the $2K starting stack. I am some-what familiar with Seat 6 and perceive him as a solid player. The rest of the players are unknown.

 Pre-flop (30): Seat 3 limps in, and Seat 4 raises the minimum to 40. Seat 6 calls. The other players fold. I probably have the best hand now as the minimum raise does not usually indicate a lot of strength from an unknown player at this stage of a tournament. However, I do not want to reraise, creating a big pot pre-flop with such a vulnerable pocket pair when I am relatively deep stacked. There is not enough currently in the pot for me to risk a lot trying to take it down right now. I also have the type of hand where I want to see a flop, hoping to hit a set in position and win a big pot from an unsuspecting opponent. Also, I can use my position to make good post-flop decisions when I do *not* flop a set. I call, and Seat 3 also calls. I see the flop, and the pot is four-handed.

   Flop (190): Although I did not spike a 10, this is a very good flop for my hand. I have an overpair on a rather ragged board. A higher pocket pair is unlikely given the action pre-flop. My main worry is a possible set, but I can expect my tens to be good on this flop most of the time. Seat 3 checks, and Seat 4 leads out for 190, the size of the pot. Seat 6 then makes the call.

My hand looked very good on the flop, but now the action in front must be a concern. By making such a large bet, Seat 4, the pre-flop raiser, appears very confident in his hand, perhaps protecting an overpair. Seat 6, who I know to be a very solid player, should also recognize this, and therefore represents enormous strength by *cold-calling*. Given the action in front of me and no flush draw on the flop, I must be very wary of my opponents' hands. It is possible that Seat 4 is betting without a strong hand and Seat 6 is calling with a middle pocket pair such as 99 or 77; however, this is the best-case scenario. Most of the time in this spot, I should expect one, if not both, of my opponents to have me beaten. Another big problem with this hand is that in the unlikely scenario that I am in fact ahead, my hand will still be difficult to play on later streets. I take the safe route and fold. Seat 3 also folds.

 Turn (570): Seat 4 again bets the size of the pot, 570, and Seat 6 again calls.

 River (1,710): Seat 4 checks, and Seat 6 bets 700. Seat 4 then check-raises all-in for 1,580, and Seat 6 quickly calls, showing 33. Seat 4 shows a hopeless bluff, A-J.

Seat 6 flopped bottom set and slow-played it for all it was worth, and because he had a stubborn pre-flop raiser betting big into him, the slow-play certainly had merit. Seat 4's all-in check-raise on the river is indicative of an amateur player in a low buy-in tournament. He should have been well aware that he had run into a monster, yet he gave away all of his chips. Perhaps he was hopeful that Seat 6 had called him down with a straight draw and was attempting to steal the pot on the river. But if he can convince himself of this, his best play would be to just call the river bet, as he can beat a bluff with A-J. By the river, Seat 3's raise is also quite small, so even if he thinks his opponent would bet a pair on the river (which is unlikely), it is doubtful he could get his opponent to fold given the size of the pot and the small raise.

Hand 2

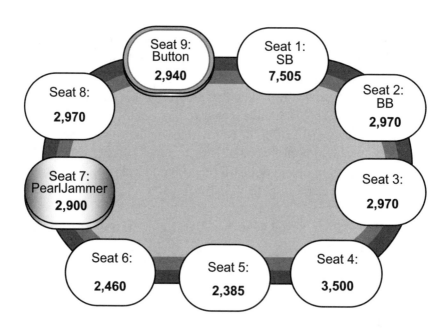

Setup: It is the first level of a $150, $100K guaranteed freezeout. The blinds are 10-20, and I am not familiar with any of my opponents.

Pre-flop (30): It would be standard and perfectly acceptable to open-raise with this hand, as I figure I have the best hand pre-flop. However, I am not interested in winning the 30 chips in the blinds. I am looking to make a big hand cheaply and perhaps break an unsuspecting opponent. By limping in, I am more than willing to release my hand on the flop without investing any more chips if I suspect that I am beaten. I call 20, the small blind completes, and the big blind checks.

   Flop (60): This is a dream flop! Not only have I made a well disguised, extremely strong hand, but if one of my opponents has a 6, I should be able to play a very large pot. My opponents both check. It is very tempting to check behind, giving my opponents a free card hopefully to improve their hand, like pairing an overcard. However, if I give them this opportunity and they hit, I am unlikely to get a lot of action as they would likely fear trips once I spring into action with a raise.

More important, if one of my opponents has checked a 6 on the flop, I would be missing out on my best chance to build the pot and perhaps give him reason to doubt the relative strength of his own hand on later streets. If I lead out on the flop with my full house, and one of my opponents has a 6, I am likely to take him for his whole stack. After all, he would expect me to check tens full on the flop, would he not? I bet 40, and Seat 1 calls.

 Turn (140): My opponent now leads out for 120. This is excellent news as it should mean that he has a 6 and is looking to build a pot! At worst, he would appear to have the case 10 and like his kicker enough to give me some action. Yet since I hold two of the tens, and he cold-called on the flop, I can safely assume that he has a 6. I should not slow-play, but raise for value now as any opponent with trip sixes would have a nearly impossible time folding his hand. I want to build a big enough pot that I can go for maximum value on the river as well. I raise approximately three times his bet to 340. My opponent calls.

River (820): My opponent leads for 420 into the pot of 820. He is certain to have a 6, and even if I move all-in, it would still be a very difficult fold for him. Therefore, I will go for maximum value and move all-in for 2,500. My opponent calls, showing 8♠ 6♣ for an inferior full house on the river.

Having my opponent fill up on the river was certainly fortunate for me as it made it impossible for him to fold. Perhaps he would have just checked and called my bet on the river if he had not filled up. If he had checked, I would have still moved all-in on the river even though it would have appeared to be quite an overbet. Although my opponent would have committed only 500 chips at this point and my all-in was for 2,500, I would still get this call almost 100% of the time. Even a very experienced opponent is going to have an extremely difficult time laying down trip sixes in this spot.

Hand 3

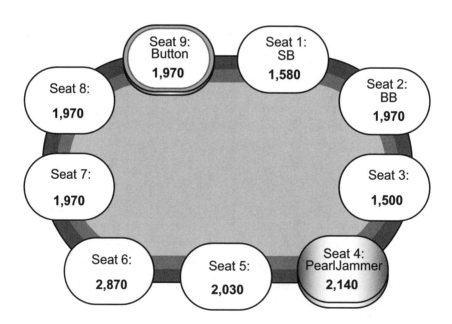

Setup: It is the very early stages of a $100 *satellite* to a $1,000 tournament. The blinds are 10-20, and I am not familiar with any players at my table.

Pre-flop (30): Seat 3 limps in under-the-gun. At such an early stage of a tournament, I prefer to make a slightly larger raise than normal with A-K, especially with a limper already in the hand. I will be playing the hand out of position if anyone calls behind, and this is not the type of hand I want to turn into a multiway pot. I want to discourage cold-callers by raising the full amount of the pot. I raise to 90. The players behind me all fold, but the small blind and the limper call.

   Flop (290): Both players check. Attempting a *continuation bet* would be quite risky given this board texture. Unless I can convince both of my opponents that I have an overpair, and neither of them has a strong enough hand or draw to continue, I have very little chance of winning this pot on the flop. I am content to take a free card in position, so I check.

 Turn (290): It always feels great to take a free card and then hit it! I now have top pair, top kicker, but the board texture is still dangerous. If my opponents both check, I would be content to see the river for free, thereby disguising the strength of my hand and setting up an easy value-betting situation if they check to me again on the river. I do not get this opportunity, though, as Seat 1 leads out for 290, the full size of the pot. If Seat 3 were to fold, I would probably just call, keeping the pot as small as possible. However, Seat 3 chooses to raise the minimum to 580! Given the action in front, I find it hard to believe my hand could be the best, so I fold.

Seat 1 calls the additional 290.

 River (1,450): Seat 1 checks, and Seat 3 bets 540. Seat 1 folds, and Seat 3 mucks his hand.

Although I will never know for sure, experience in similar situations tells me that Seat 3 probably flopped a set and hoped to trap me by check-raising on the flop. However, by playing the hand cautiously, I was able to get away from the hand without investing a single chip post-flop.

Hand 4

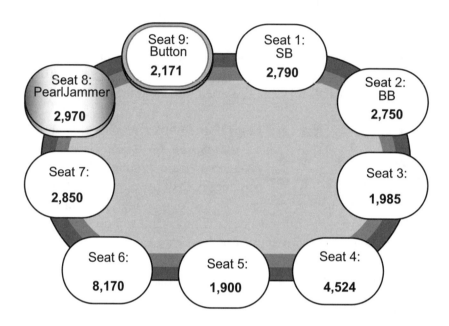

Setup: It is the early stages of a $300 freezeout with an excellent, slow structure. The blinds are 15-30. I know very little about the other players at the table apart from Seat 5, whom I know to be a very strong player.

  Pre-flop (45): Seat 3 opens under-the-gun for 90. The action folds to me. In the early stages of tournaments when the stacks are deep, I usually choose to call raises instead of reraising with pairs like JJ and TT. By treating them just as I would small pocket pairs, I keep the pot small pre-flop, letting me get away from the hand cheaply if overcards hit and I do not improve. Also, I encourage more callers, giving myself greater implied odds when I hit a set. If I reraise in this spot with JJ, I would probably drive out all hands besides QQ or better, or A-K. I call 90, Seat 9 also calls, and the blinds fold. I see the flop three-handed.

Flop (315): At first glance, this appears to be an excellent flop for my hand. I have an overpair, and because of the way I played the hand pre-flop, my strength is disguised. However, the flop's texture can be deceptive. It is hard to imagine being able to get all of my money in on this flop so early in a tournament with a good, slow structure, and getting action from a worse hand. I should play cautiously.

Seat 3 leads out for 180 into a pot of 315. This bet puts me in a difficult spot: If I raise and get action from Seat 9, I could be certain that I am behind and fold the hand without further analysis. If I raise, Seat 9 folds, and Seat 3 calls or comes back over the top, then I would have to lay down my hand to any further action, as a higher pocket pair or a set would be too likely.

However, Seat 3 could easily make this move with TT, 99, or 77, or even with complete air if he felt that I might be raising his continuation bet on a bluff. My raise could therefore cause me to make a big mistake by folding a dominating hand. If I choose to just call Seat 3's bet, I will have a better idea of where I stand on the turn from the next plays by Seat 3 and Seat 9. I also risk fewer chips in the process. The biggest potential downfall of this line would be giving Seat 3 a free card, but my position throughout the rest of the hand should negate this disadvantage. I call 180, and Seat 9 folds.

 Turn (675): My opponent checks. I have received the information I am looking for, as Seat 9 has gotten out of the way and Seat 3 seems to have given up on his hand. I should now be able to bet to confirm my suspicion of Seat 3's weakness and not allow any more free cards. A bet of about half the pot should accomplish my goals.

I bet 330, and my opponent check-raises to 1,080, leaving himself only 635 behind! It is time to reevaluate my assessment of my opponent's check. He has clearly committed himself to the pot, so I should treat his bet as if he had moved all-in. My opponent does not appear worried about my committing almost 600 chips to a pot on a relatively uncoordinated board at the 15-30 level of a high buy-in, deep-stacked tournament. He should know that I have a very strong hand (an overpair at the very least), yet he is still willing to risk his entire stack on his hand. I now realize that JJ is virtually never ahead here. My opponent is representing a higher pocket pair at the very least. The chances that my opponent is bluffing here are slim to none. I have represented a strong hand, and my opponent doesn't have enough chips in this situation to put a lot of pressure on me.

However, in the heat of the moment, I ignore the obvious signs and convince myself that I am up against TT or 99. I make a rash decision to move all-in and risk the majority of my stack on one pair that should never be good given the action. Shame on me! I move all-in, and my opponent calls with AA. The Q♣ hits the river, and I lose to a pair of aces.

Hand 5

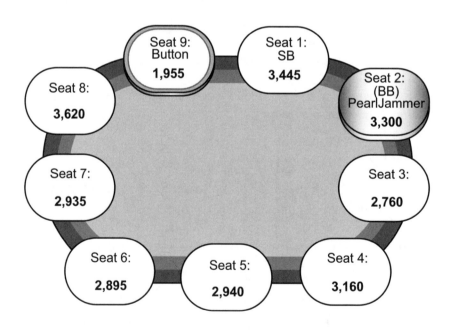

Setup: It is the early stages of a $300, $150K guaranteed freezeout with an excellent, slow structure. I am at a very tough table as I know Seats 1, 4, 5, 6, and 7 are all excellent players. The blinds are 15-30.

Pre-flop (45): Seat 4 opens in early position for 90. The action folds around to the small blind in Seat 1, who calls. Getting a good price with a strong suited connector, I decide to defend from the big blind. I call 60 and see the flop three-handed.

 Flop (270): Bingo! I flop a flush. However, I am vulnerable to a fourth heart hitting, and I am up against two excellent players. It may be difficult to get value out of the hand. Seat 1 checks, and the action is on me. In an unraised pot I usually lead out from the blinds when I flop a flush or a straight so as not to risk giving any free cards and to build a pot as quickly as possible. Leading out can also help disguise my hand, as most opponents do not expect me to lead out with such a strong hand. However, in raised pots, I generally like to check to the raiser, letting him take the lead. I check, but Seat 4 disappoints me by checking.

 Turn (270): This is an excellent card for me as it seems that neither of my opponents liked the flop, so they are very likely to have hands such as A-K or A-Q. Seat 1 checks. I could check again, hoping that Seat 1 will bet, as I believe he hit the ace. If Seat 1 were a weak player, I would do this. However, because I know him to be strong and he played the flop cautiously, I expect him to check the turn as well even if he has a hand as strong as A-K. Therefore, I figure the best action is to lead into him and not risk giving another free card to either opponent. I do not want to bet too strongly, as that may allow my opponents to get away from an ace. I lead out for 140, approximately half the pot. Seat 4 and Seat 1 both call.

 River (690): This is another excellent card, as I did not want to see another heart hit or the board pair. If my hand was good on the flop, it is still good on the river. With 690 in the pot, Seat 1 surprises me by leading out for 540! The action is on me.

I know Seat 1 to be a very strong, aggressive player, but also not one to get the least bit out of line in the early stages of a tournament. Before I get too excited with my flush and raise, I should reassess the situation. The 4 on the river puts a four-card straight on the board; however, it is very unlikely that Seat 1 has a straight. He might have called a raise pre-flop with 33, but he surely would have folded it on the turn to a bet and a call. It seems just as unlikely that he has 8-6, as he would not chase an open-ended straight with three hearts on the board, much less call a raise pre-flop from the small blind with this hand.

Because I do not expect Seat 1 to get out of line and fire such a strong bluff at this stage of the tournament, he seems to have either a set or a flush. It's very unlikely that he would have checked a set until the river and then made such a big bet with it. However, it's also doubtful that he would have taken the same action with a flush. Although I do beat some possible flushes, he would have been more likely to call the raise pre-flop with high hearts than with low hearts. The unusual action in the hand makes it very difficult to pinpoint his hand.

Perhaps a better question is, could I get value out of a raise? After making such a large river bet, would Seat 1 be capable of folding a low flush or a set, the two somewhat plausible hands that I beat? At this stage of the tournament, such a strong player should be capable of folding worse hands than mine to a raise. Thus, there is virtually no value in raising. Folding my hand seems out of the question given the action on each street. I call Seat 1's bet, and Seat 4 folds.

Seat 1 shows Q♥ J♥, winning the pot with a queen-high flush. Although I lost the hand, I am fortunate that my opponent didn't take a more aggressive line, as then I could have lost many more chips.

Hand 6

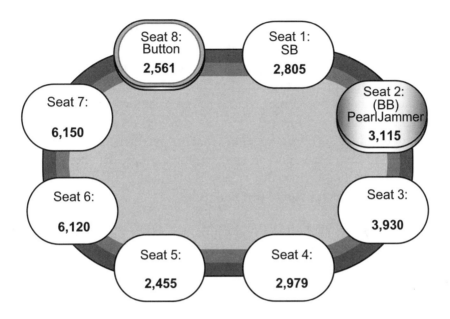

Setup: It is very early in a $150 freezeout with 20-40 blinds. The table is solid, and nobody is getting out of line.

 **Pre-flop** (60): The action folds to Seat 6, who puts in a standard raise of three times the big blind to 120. Two more players fold, and the small blind in Seat 1 reraises to 320. The action is now on me in the big blind.

This is a fairly standard trouble spot for many players. I have been dealt JJ, certainly a premium hand, yet the action in front puts me in a bind. I am very early in the tournament with a stack over 75 big blinds, and neither of my opponents is short-stacked. Seat 6 raised from the *hijack*, which could represent a wide range of hands, yet at this stage of the tournament, I am going to assume that he is not out of line. Seat 1 reraised from the small blind, out of position, and by reraising less than three times the initial raise, he appears to want action. Given his action at this early stage, I can confidently put him on a very narrow range of hands: AA, KK, QQ, or A-K almost every time.

Now that I have assigned Seat 1 this range, I must weigh my options. *Four-betting* is now out of the question, as I can safely assume that I am behind at least one of my opponents. I could call the 280. In that case, I would be playing only to flop a set, folding to any further action from Seat 1 if I do not hit. However, this course of action can put me in a tough situation when the flop comes all rags (all cards below jacks). If the flop brings three rags, and one of my opponents bet, it can sometimes be difficult to fold. I may want to believe that my opponent has missed with an A-K, and thus I may end up spewing more chips. Another problem with simply calling the pre-flop reraise is that Seat 6 still has the option to four-bet, to which I would certainly fold.

Even if I plan on folding if I don't hit a set, the implied pot odds are working against me. It costs me 280 to call, and I am about 7.5-to-1 to hit a set on the flop. This means that from an expectation perspective, I need to win at least 2,100 in chips simply to justify the cost of drawing to a set. Even though I have more than 3,000 in chips, and my opponents have me covered, there is no guarantee that they will put all of their chips in the pot.

For example, I would probably earn very little with a flop of A-J-x when my opponent holds KK or QQ. I might hit a full house on a flop of J-T-T, which might slow down the action if my opponents are afraid of trip tens. I must also realize that sometimes I will still lose even if I hit my set. The A-J-x flop is a prime example, as my opponent could be sitting on AA. Since there are no guarantees of getting fully paid off or even of winning when I flop a set, as a general rule of thumb I require implied pot odds of 15-to-1 to justify calling with pairs before the flop for their set value.

Therefore, the best option is just to fold the jacks, avoiding the trouble spot all together. JJ is a very pretty sight when you have been folding hand after hand in the early stages of a tournament, yet this hand can quickly shrivel up with a raise and a reraise before you. I take the safe route and fold.

Seat 6 also folds his hand, and Seat 1 wins the pot without a flop.

Hand 7

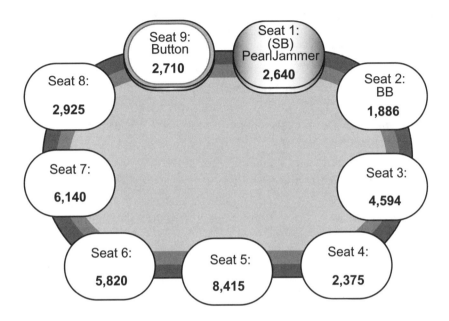

Setup: It is early in a $100 freezeout, and I have close to the starting stack of 3,000 and have not been involved in any big pots. The blinds are 25-50.

  Pre-flop (75): Seat 5 limps in middle position. The remaining players fold around to me. I raise five times the big blind to 250. At this point in the tournament, I could limp with JJ for pot control or I could raise to build a pot with what is very likely the best hand. Both are reasonable playing lines.

In this spot, seeing as I only have the middle-position limper and the big blind with which to contend, I choose to raise. From late position, I would have raised four times the big blind to 200, given that there was one limper in front (add one big blind to my standard raise for each limper). However, to account for my positional disadvantage in this hand, I increase my raise slightly. I find that it is very important to raise a higher amount than usual with my big hands pre-flop when I will be out of position post-flop. The big blind and the limper both call.

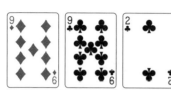 **Flop** (750): I flop an overpair to the board, yet it is somewhat dangerous as the board is paired. If either of my opponents has a 9, I am in big trouble. However, given that I raised five times the big blind pre-flop, I highly doubt either of my opponents has a 9. Their most likely hands are pocket pairs smaller than JJ, or *broadway* hands such as A-Q or K-Q. If I make a continuation bet, I can expect to get called or perhaps even raised by an opponent with a lower pocket pair than mine, as he would probably view this flop as very strong for his hand as well. I lead out for 400 into a 750 pot, enough to protect my hand against overcards on the turn, but not enough to scare away lower pocket pairs. Seat 2 raises the minimum to 800, and Seat 5 folds.

Although minimum raises can be scary as they often represent very strong hands, I should not be worried about being beaten here. Although my opponent would probably make this raise if he had a 9, he would also make the raise with lower pocket pairs, which I already determined were the more likely hands for him to have. If I run into a 9, then I would chalk it up to bad luck. My opponent has only 836 left after his raise, so he should be pot-committed. I reraise all-in, and my opponent calls off his last 836 chips, showing 44.

The 9♥ hits the turn, and the 9♠ hit the river. My jack kicker plays as we both make quad nines!

Hand 8

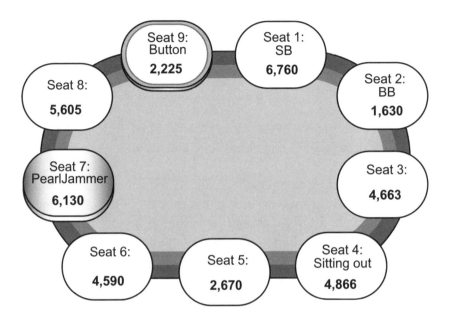

Setup: It is the early stages of a $150 buy-in, $100K guaranteed freeze-out with blinds of 25-50. I have already doubled up, so I am in good shape. I am unfamiliar with Seat 9, my opponent in this hand.

 Pre-flop (75): The action folds to me. In late position, first in the pot, I am almost always going to raise with K-Q, suited or not.

Generally, in the early stages of a tournament, my standard raise is three to four times the big blind. The blinds are so small at this point that I am not really interested in stealing them. Rather, I want to narrow the field a little to ensure I am not playing a multiway pot which can be quite dangerous. A slightly bigger pot pre-flop also gives my continuation bets more value after the flop and can help define my opponent's hands more clearly.

When the blinds increase to a point where they are more meaningful, generally around the 100-200 level, I like to lower my standard raise to about two-and-a-half times the big blind. At this point, stealing the blinds and antes becomes a key part of my strategy, and I want to achieve this with as little risk as possible. Also, I am interested in keeping the pots as small as possible to be able to use my post-flop skills to my advantage. If I were to build a bigger pot pre-flop, I would be in more difficult situations after the flop where a larger portion of my stack would be at risk.

I make my standard raise of three times the big blind, to 150. The button in Seat 9 reraises to 300. The blinds fold, and the action is back on me.

Seat 9's reraise was exceptionally small. At the current blind level, if I wanted to reraise from Seat 9, I would probably opt for an amount between 450 and 550. By making it only 300 to go, my opponent has priced me in with virtually any two cards. I am not thrilled to play K-Q suited out of position to a reraise, but I cannot fold for such a small price. I call 150 more and take the flop heads up.

 Flop (675): This is a seemingly excellent flop for my hand. I have top pair with a strong kicker on a relatively harmless board. On the other hand, if my opponent has me beaten, I am probably going to pay him off because of his short stack. Since my opponent took the lead with a reraise pre-flop, I should check to him as he is almost certain to fire a continuation bet on this flop. I check, and he bets 500 into the pot of 675.

After his bet, he has only 1,425 left. He is probably now pot-committed unless he has complete air; actually, I am absolutely certain that he is. The first question to consider is whether folding is even an option. I should be able to put my opponent on a fairly narrow range of hands, given his show of strength pre-flop at this stage of the tournament. AA, A-K, A-Q, KK, QQ, JJ, TT, and 99 are all likely, but it is possible that his range includes many more hands. If my opponent has AA or A-K, or the much less likely KK, I am in a world of trouble; however, once I hit this flop in a heads-up pot, I am going to take my chances against a short-stacked opponent. Folding is out of the question.

Should I reraise or just call? If I were to call my opponent's bet, there would be 1,675 in the pot, and my opponent would be left with just 1,425. Therefore, even if the only scare card, an ace, hits the turn, I would not consider folding if my opponent bet his remaining chips. I should go ahead and reraise, and given his short stack, I should reraise all-in. Along with the K, I could be representing a flush draw, and he most likely should feel committed with any pair. Of course, I may be up against AA or A-K, but that is a chance I must take. I reraise all-in, and my opponent calls, showing J♥ J♦.

The A♥ hits the turn and the 5♥ on the river. I win with a pair of kings, knocking my opponent out of the tournament.

Note that if I had just called my opponent's bet to see the turn card, even though I would have felt committed and called an all-in bet, my opponent might not have felt committed! He might have given up with his pair of jacks facing an ace and a king on the board. By going ahead and reraising all-in on the flop, I made sure that the board did not get too scary for my opponent, allowing him to save his remaining chips.

Hand 9

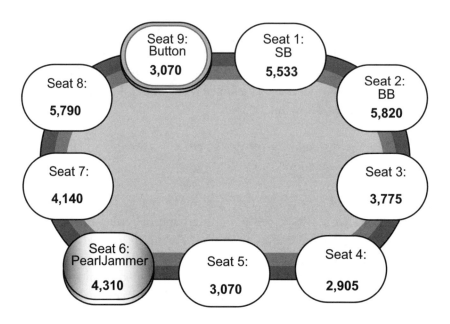

Setup: It is the early stages of a $100 buy-in, $25K guaranteed freezeout. The blinds are 25-50. I am only familiar with Seat 2, a tight, solid player who I believe views me as having a very similar style.

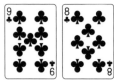 **Pre-flop** (75): It is folded to me. With suited connectors at this stage of the tournament, I would usually limp in behind limpers, but open-raise most of the time when given the chance. By mixing raises with suited connectors in with my premium hands, I ensure that I am not too predictable, and I am sometimes rewarded with great opportunities to double up when I connect strongly with the board. I raise three times the big blind to 150, and the action folds to Seat 2, who calls from the big blind.

Flop (325): I have flopped middle pair on an ace-high, rainbow flop. My opponent checks. I have a piece of the flop, but if I get action from my opponent, it means that I am probably behind. I could check and take a free card, and thereby get a better idea of my opponent's hand by his action on the turn. However, I then risk a K, Q, J, or T hitting on the turn, all cards likely to improve my opponent's hand.

If I had K-Q on an A-K-x flop, given the same action I would usually check, thus disguising my hand and keeping the pot small, as I am only risking being outdrawn by a gutshot straight hitting or a pocket pair spiking a set. However, 9-8 on an A-9-x flop is too vulnerable to allow a free card.

If I make a continuation bet at the pot at this early stage of the tournament, my opponent should give me credit for an ace. If he has an ace himself, he will probably just call as he may be concerned about his kicker. My position would then allow me to take a free river card if I do not improve on the turn. I expect my opponent will fold on the flop most of the time, though. His range should consist of any pocket pair, probably JJ or below, many high suited connectors such as Q-J or J-T, and only very strong A-x hands, probably A-J or better. As a tight, solid player, I expect him to fold a lot of weak suited and unsuited A-x hands pre-flop. I bet 200, a little less than two-thirds of the 325-chip pot. He calls.

 Turn (725): My opponent checks. Given his call on the flop, I feel very confident that he has A-K, A-Q, or A-J. At this early stage, given the information I have about my opponent, I believe he probably would have just called my raise with a hand as strong as A-K pre-flop instead of reraising out of position. It is possible that he is trapping with 99 or 33, but then he would usually lead out or check-raise with a set on the flop. Pocket nines is also not very likely, as I have one of the nines.

Now that I am confident that I have the best hand with my disguised two pair, I should value-bet. My bet should be slightly more than my usual half-pot bets as I am very confident that I have the best hand and that my opponent has a hand that is hard to fold. I bet 550 into a pot of 725, and he calls.

 River (1,825): My opponent checks again. Although this card puts a possible flush and straight on the board, it is not a very scary card for me. It would be very difficult for my opponent to have turned a calling hand on the flop into a flush or a straight on the river. If the suits of the A and 3 on the flop were reversed, then I would be somewhat concerned about my opponent having A-x of spades and making a *runner-runner* flush. However, even if this were the case, I still feel confident to value-bet on the river. I should not bet too much as my opponent will not expect me to fire a third shell on a bluff, and thus he might make a good fold with a hand like A-Q or A-J if bet too strongly on the river. I bet 850 into a pot of 1,825.

My opponent calls, winning the pot with 3♠ 3♣ for a set of threes! I am very surprised to see that my opponent flopped a set and then never chose to raise my bets the entire way. Perhaps his image of me as such a tight player saved me some chips, as I would have had a very hard time getting away from my hand on the turn if he had check-raised. He might have thought that if he check-raised the flop or turn, then I would probably not give him action with anything short of a set, an unlikely two pair, or A-K. Once a card hit that made a flush and a straight on the river, and I still bet, he might have feared a flush, a straight, or a higher set and chose to just call, as his hand was too strong to fold. Whatever his reasoning, I am lucky to have escaped with over half of my stack in a hand that could have ended my tournament life.

Hand 10

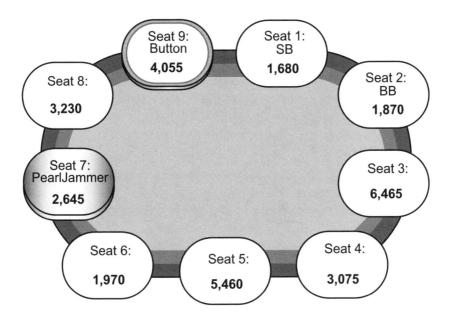

Setup: It is the early stages of a $300, $150K guaranteed freezeout. The blinds are 25-50. I am only familiar with Seats 2 and 6, but the table seems to be playing tight as this tournament has a very slow structure.

 Pre-flop (75): Seats 4 and 6 limp in from early position, and the action is on me. I could raise with TT as it is a reasonably strong hand; however, at this stage in the tournament, I usually choose to limp behind limpers to play the hand mostly for its set value. If I raise and get reraised, I would certainly have to fold. I would rather limp in, keep the pot small while disguising my hand, and reduce the risk of being bet out of the pot pre-flop. I call 50, the small blind completes, and the big blind checks. Five players see the flop.

 **Flop** (250): This is a good flop for me, as I have an overpair that is probably only beaten if one of the blinds has flopped two pair or someone has flopped a set. It is,

however, hard to imagine getting all of my money in on the flop and being up against a worse hand. I could be in a race against overcards with a flush draw, but even in that desirable situation, I would still be a slight underdog. If I manage to get all-in on this flop, most of the time I will be drawing very slim. The first limper, Seat 4, leads out for 100 into a pot of 250. Seat 6 calls, and the action is on me.

If Seat 4 had bet close to the size of the pot and Seat 6 called, I would lean toward folding my hand. One of those players, if not both, would usually be sitting on either a higher, limped-in pocket pair or on a set. However, with such a small (seemingly weak) bet and call, this appears to be a good spot for me to raise to better determine where I am in the hand. Also, because Seat 4's bet was so small, I am able to put in a reasonable raise without committing myself to the pot. I raise to 350. The blinds fold, Seat 4 calls, and Seat 6 folds. I see the turn heads up.

Turn (1,050): Ugh! This is a terrible card for my hand! Not only did the flush draw hit, but if my opponent limped in with T-9s, he just made the straight. I still beat A-8, 99, and 6-5, all possible calling hands on the flop, but only 99 seems reasonable given my opponent's early-position limp. It is much more likely that my opponent has made the flush with a hand like K♦ Q♦, has a higher pocket pair than mine, or just called me with a set on the flop. If my opponent leads out, I will fold my hand. But he checks, allowing me to check behind and take a free river card.

River (1,050): This is a rather harmless card, and my opponent leads out for 100 into a pot of 1,050. His bet is extremely small compared to the pot and could mean a couple of things. He might be acting like he has a weak hand, hoping to induce a bluff-raise while he is sitting on a strong hand. More likely, he is sitting on a mediocre hand, and the small bet is intended as a blocking bet. I could raise, but that basically turns my hand into a bluff, and it seems unlikely that I would be able to get a better hand to fold. With only 100 to call into a 1,150 pot, this is an easy call. I call and my opponent shows J♠ J♥ for a higher pair.

Hand 11

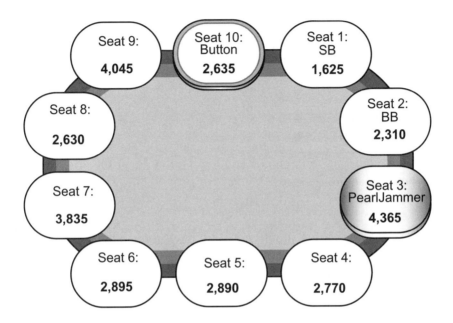

Setup: It is the early stages of a $120, $20K guaranteed freezeout. The blinds are 30-60. I am sitting comfortably with almost double the starting stack of 2,500. I am unfamiliar with most of the players at my table.

Pre-flop (90): With a deep stack and small blinds, I am comfortable either raising or limping with small pairs in early position. This tournament is ten-handed, so I am playing a bit more cautiously than usual and prefer to limp in. Note that if I were to raise and then get reraised, I might no longer get the correct implied odds that I need for hitting a set. However, I can certainly call a standard raise at this early stage of the tournament with small pairs as I have sufficient implied odds. I limp in for 60.

As discussed in a previous hand, I generally want to have at least 15-to-1 implied odds when calling a raise with a pocket pair. I will usually fold on the flop unless I hit a set. Up against a known weak opponent, I can cheat on the 15-to-1 rule and base calls on a 10-to-1 rule. I am much more likely to get paid off for my entire stack against weak opponents than strong ones.

Seat 6 limps in behind me, and Seat 8 raises to 180. I call 120 more, happy to see the flop cheaply. Seat 6 also calls.

   Flop (630): Oh, Judy! Leading out in this spot can often be profitable as it disguises my hand; my opponents would not expect me to lead out with such a strong hand. However, checking to the raiser and hoping that he or the other limper will bet is the more standard play. In this spot, I choose to take the standard route and check. Unfortunately, Seat 6 and Seat 8 both check.

 Turn (630): I should not slow-play my hand any longer. If I hope to get any value out of it, I must lead out on the turn and start building a pot. I make a weak lead of 260 into a pot of 630. Seat 6 and Seat 8 both call.

 River (1,410): With 1,410 in the pot, I want to bet close to the pot to get value for my hand. I again lead out for 850. Seat 6 moves all-in for 2,455, and Seat 8 also goes all-in for 2,190! The action is back on me.

Wow! This hand has taken a completely unexpected turn! There is now 6,905 in the pot, and it is only 1,605 to call, but let me analyze the situation a bit before I make the call. I fired out a substantial bet on the river, and up to now, nobody appeared to have that strong of a hand. However, despite my large bet, not one but both of my opponents have moved all-in!

It is very unlikely that either of my opponents has two pair on this board. Seat 8, the pre-flop raiser, probably did not play AA in such a strange manner, although that hand remains a very slight possibility. His line would be very unusual for A-K as well. I would expect him to lay down either AA or certainly A-K given the action in front of him on the river. Therefore, it seems only logical that he has a set, most likely KK or perhaps 99.

Seat 6's move is just as surprising. However, along with the possibility of a higher set, he may have hit a straight on the river with 8-7. On such an uncoordinated board, it is hard to imagine that my opponents both have hands weaker than bottom set and yet are willing to move all-in. Of course, only one of them has to have me beaten to make this a good fold. Even though I am getting almost 4.5-to-1 on the call, given my read, I choose to lay my hand down.

Seat 6 shows 8♠ 7♣ for the nut straight, and Seat 8 shows 5♠ 5♦ for a set.

Note that Seat 8 chose to check his set in last position after raising pre-flop. By slow-playing his hand, he not only lost a chance to double up through me, as he probably would have by betting, but he also ended up losing the hand to a runner-runner straight. With position on his opponents and a hand with which he should want to build a large pot, he should almost always make a continuation bet on the flop, especially when the stacks are deep and he is up against more than one opponent.

Hand 12

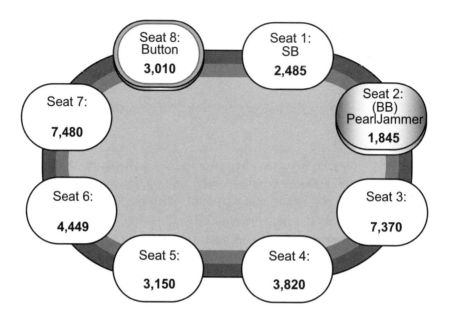

Setup: It is the early stages of a $150 buy-in, $55K guaranteed freezeout. The blinds are 30-60. I have lost a good portion of my starting stack and have fallen well below average in the very early going. I am not familiar with anyone at the table.

  Pre-flop (90): Seat 3 raises under-the-gun to 180. Seat 6 and Seat 1 call, and the action is on me. With a premium hand, and plenty of action in front, I have an excellent chance of doubling up. Clearly, I should reraise in lieu of taking a flop four-handed. I am definitely looking for action and want to play this hand for my entire stack. The question is how to achieve this.

There is currently 600 in the pot — 720 once I add my call — but because I will be out of position after the flop, I want to raise at least the size of the pot. A pot-size reraise would mean putting in almost half of my stack. One problem with a raise of this size is that it will probably appear to my opponents that I want action. If I put in this much of my stack, I might as well go all-in. An all-in reraise in this spot often looks very much like a squeeze play. In effect, my opponents are more likely to call a big all-in raise they consider weak than they are to call a smaller reraise. Since the raise came from under-the-gun and two players called, one of them is likely to have a hand strong enough to call a relatively short stack's all-in. Therefore, I choose to go all-in for 1,845. Seat 3 folds, Seat 6 calls, and Seat 1 folds.

Seat 6 shows T♦ T♥, making me more than an 80 percent favorite to double up! The board comes 9♦ 5♠ 3♠ Q♥ 8♦, and I double up.

This psychology can also be applied in reverse. Let's say you have a hand like A-Q or 88 in the same spot. Given the size of the pot, I would like to take the pot down immediately, if possible, accepting the risk that I might run into a premium hand. But while doing so, I want to discourage others from calling with semi-strong hands. Trying to represent strength, I might raise half of my stack, obviously committed but trying at the same time to send a message that I want action; in contrast, an all-in move might lead my opponents to sense that I want them to fold.

Hand 13

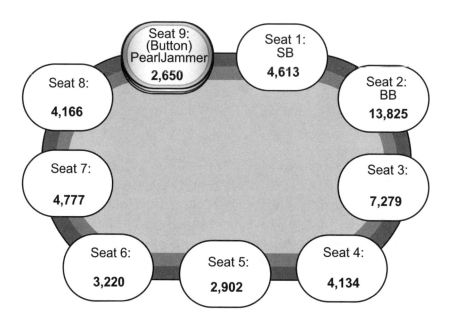

Setup: It is the early stages of a major $240 buy-in Sunday tournament with blinds at 40-80. Starting with 3,000 in chips, I have fallen well below the average chip stack but still have enough to work with given the slow structure. I am unfamiliar with most of my opponents, but the table seems to be playing tight, solid poker.

Pre-flop (120): The action folds to Seat 7 in the hijack, who raises the minimum to 160. The cutoff folds, and the action is on me. Generally, I do not give late-position minimum raises too much credit, though they can sometimes be traps. In this spot, A-Ks is certainly a reraising hand. With a short stack of about 1,500 or less, I usually want to shove all-in with A-Ks, hoping to get action from strong broadway hands but also willing to run a race against a pocket pair if necessary. However, my stack is a bit too big for a shove, so instead I reraise to approximately three to four times the original raise. I opt for the low side of this range, as I do not want to appear over-committed pre-flop, and thus reraise to 480. The blinds fold, and Seat 7 calls.

Flop (1,080): I have flopped a huge draw with two overcards, the nut flush draw, and the nut straight draw (not to mention a possible royal flush). If my opponents lead out, I would certainly shove all-in, even on a paired board. Besides, I would not expect my opponent to lead out with a J or TT in this spot, the only hands I truly fear. As expected, my opponent checks. With 1,080 in the pot, I want to make a standard continuation bet of about half the pot, willing of course to call an all-in. I bet 575, and my opponent calls.

 Turn (2,230): My opponent checks. With the turn card, my situation has changed dramatically from wanting to get all of my money in to being happy to take a free card. It is hard to imagine that my opponent does not have some sort of made hand on this board. With only 1,595 left and 2,230 in the pot, he will surely call my all-in bet. Therefore, I gladly take a free card in position and check.

 River (2,230): My opponent moves all-in, having me covered by more than 2,000. I hit the ace on the river, giving me a seemingly strong hand with aces, jacks, and a king kicker. So I should surely call the all-in, right? Not so fast! A-K is a relatively strong hand on this board, and I am getting over 2.5-to-1 on the call. However, I should consider my opponent's actions before acting myself. What hand range can I assign to my opponent that is consistent with his actions on each street, especially the all-in move on the river? Perhaps more important, with what range can he put me all-in given my actions throughout the hand, especially with the ace, a scare card, hitting the river?

I do not know much about my opponent, but given the way the table has been playing, I should assume that he is thinking somewhat rationally and is fairly tight. He should be able to put me on A-K or perhaps A-Q in this spot; I reraised a small raise in position, I made a continuation bet on the flop, and checked the turn where A-K and A-Q would not have improved. He would have no reason to put me on clubs; however, I certainly played the hand to this point like I had A-K or A-Q. Therefore, by moving in on the river once the ace hit, it appears my opponent wants me to call with A-K or A-Q. He probably believes that I am committed to the pot if I hit my ace, yet he does not want to give me the chance to check behind him on the river, a perfectly reasonable assumption.

If he should be able to put me on a big ace, and he wants me to call, then I should give him a range of A-J, K-Q, JJ, TT, or J-T. Any of these hands would be consistent with his actions on each street, as he would likely slow-play A-J, JJ, TT, and J-T on the flop by just calling; and he might just call with K-Q, looking to hit his draw, which he would have on the turn. I doubt he would bluff the river by pushing with anything less than A-K, as I appear pot-committed. Also, any hand with which he could call my reraise pre-flop, and my bet on the flop, should now beat A-K. Perhaps he could have A-Q or 9-8, but he probably would have mucked A-Q on the flop and 9-8 pre-flop. After such an analysis, even though I may appear committed to the pot, A-K becomes an easy fold.

I fold, and my opponent mucks his hand.[1]

---

[1] In chat after the hand was over, my opponent implied that he had TT, a very reasonable and believable holding considering his actions on each street. Although opponents lie all the time about their hands, I think he was telling the truth in this particular case.

Hand 14

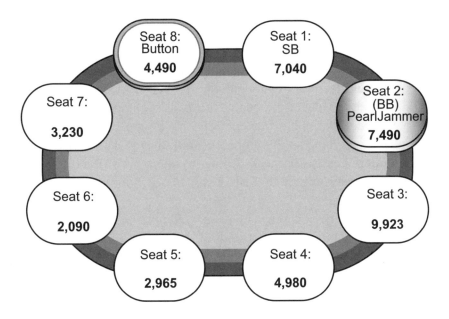

Setup: It is the early stages of a $150 buy-in, $55K guaranteed freezeout. The blinds are 50-100, and I am sitting comfortably with two-and-a-half times the starting stack. All of my opponents are unknown to me.

 **Pre-flop** (150): Seats 3 and 5 limp in, Seat 1 completes from the small blind, and I happily check my junk hand to see a free flop.

 **Flop** (400): I flop top pair with no kicker on a rather raggedy board. Seat 1 checks. At this stage in the tournament, I am not looking to play much of a pot with such a weak hand. I may choose to call a small bet on the flop if the last limper bets, as he might bet a very wide range if checked to. However, if the first limper bets, I will let my hand go, just as I would have if the small blind had led out. I check because I do not want to build a pot with such a weak, marginal holding when I am out of position. Both limpers check as well.

Turn (400): With all my opponents showing weakness on the flop, and an undercard to the Q hitting the turn, I now like my hand. Seat 1 checks. I should lead out for value and to protect my hand. With 400 in the pot, I bet 250, a little bit more than half the pot. Seat 3 and Seat 5 both call, and Seat 1 folds.

 River (1,150): With a complete brick hitting on the river, I should feel very confident that my pair of queens is the best hand. The deuce did complete a possible straight, but I do not expect that either player would have limped in with 5-4. If either player had done so, he probably would have taken a stab at the pot on the flop. I consider check-calling, trying to pick off a bluff from a missed broadway straight or flush draw.

However, both of my opponents have played passively throughout the hand, and it is likely that one or both of them have a jack. From their passive play, I doubt either opponent would bluff at the pot, and if either has a jack, they should not feel the need to bluff to win the pot. Therefore, I should not pass up the chance to bet my seemingly weak hand for value!

I want to bet small enough to be called by a jack or worse, perhaps even by two opponents, but not too small because I want as much value as I can get out of the hand. I bet 550 into a pot of 1,150. Seat 3 calls, and Seat 5 folds. Seat 3 mucks K♥ J♥. I win the pot with a pair of queens.

Note that although I do not advocate limping in with K♥ J♥ from early position, it is a reasonable hand to occasionally limp with when deep-stacked, in order to mix up your play. As the first limper, however, Seat 3 really should have led out for about 300 on the flop. If he had done so, I probably would have folded. Even if I had called, he could have taken a free card on the turn and perhaps won a nice pot if he hit his draw.

Hand 15

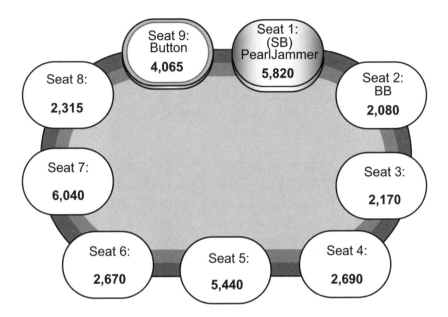

Setup: It is early in a $10, $100K guaranteed freezeout with close to 20,000 entrants, many of whom are satellite winners and/or inexperienced players. The blinds are 50-100.

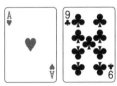 **Pre-flop** (150): Seat 7 limps in middle position. I am happy to complete from the small blind and see a flop. The big blind checks.

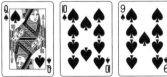 **Flop** (300): I flop bottom pair on an extremely coordinated board with three spades and three to a straight. I have no intention of continuing with this hand if either of my opponents bets. Yet both of my opponents check, giving me a free turn card.

Turn (300): My plans quickly change as I make trip nines with an ace kicker on the turn, a strong hand, but not too strong considering the nature of this board. I figure to have the best hand, so I can bet my hand for value, but I am also aware that if I am raised, my opponent might have been slow-playing a flush or straight on the flop. In such a low buy-in tournament with many inexperienced players, I should be more aware than ever of the possibility of opponents who choose to slow-play huge hands on the flop. They are often losing value by doing so, but many players at these stakes tend to make this mistake quite often.

Despite the risk, I must bet my hand for value as I probably have the best hand, but a hand that is vulnerable to several draws. I lead out for 200 into a 300 pot. The big blind folds, and the limper calls.

 River (700): This is a relatively safe river for my hand, as the only feasible way my opponent could have improved is if he chased the low end of a ***double belly-buster*** straight draw with 8-6. I am very happy not to see a spade, K, or 8 on the river as all of these would complete very reasonable draws.

I must choose whether to bet my hand for value or instead check, hoping to induce a bluff. I believe my opponent was probably on a draw, so there is no value in betting as he will not pay me off with a missed draw. I should therefore check and hope my opponent takes a shot at the pot with a bluff. However, if I believe that my opponent might have called with A-T, K-Q, or Q-J, then I should bet, hoping to sell a missed draw myself and get value for my hand. Given such a draw-heavy board, I decide it is most likely that my opponent missed a draw and has a hand with no showdown value, so I check.

My opponent bets 300 into a pot of 700. There is virtually no value in raising as it is very unlikely that he will call a check-raise with any worse hand than A-9. I must also bear in mind the slim chance that he might have slow-played a huge hand on the flop. I just call. My opponent shows 8♦ 4♦ for a missed gutshot, and I take down the pot with trip nines.

Note that my opponent limped in with a junk hand from middle position. This sort of play is often found in low-stakes tournaments such as this one, but rarely in higher buy-ins. When playing such low-stakes tournaments online (which can often offer incredible value due to huge, very weak fields), it is often best to play simple, ABC poker, especially in the early going, to clear what is commonly referred to as a "minefield" of weak players.

Hand 16

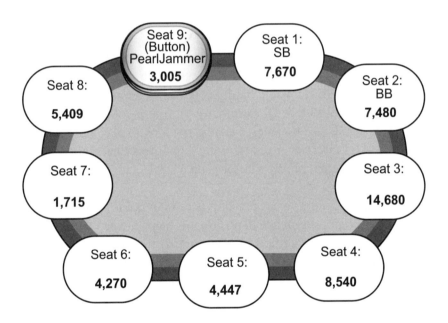

Setup: It is the early stages of a $150, $55K guaranteed freezeout with 50-100 blinds. I have barely more than the starting stack and have not played many hands.

Pre-flop (150): The action folds around to Seat 6, who raises two-and-a-half times the big blind to 250. I could make one of several plays with A-Q in this spot.

Folding would be fine as most players are raising with a relatively tight range at this stage of the tournament. I could be dominated by A-K or up against a big pocket pair. Even if I am dominating or racing with my opponent pre-flop, it can still be correct to fold A-Q if I think his range is very tight.

Reraising would also be acceptable as there are many hands against which I would be racing, such as low to middle pocket pairs, and reraising may induce my opponents to fold. However, some hands that I am dominating would also fold, such as A-J or K-Q. If I reraise and my opponent pushes all-in over the top, I would not want to call as he would probably only do this with A-K or a big pocket pair, a range which would mostly have me dominated. He would hardly ever call or reraise with any hand that I have beaten with A-Q, essentially turning my A-Q into a bluff! With 30 big blinds and no antes, I should not look to play a big pot pre-flop with A-Q. I rarely ever reraise with A-Q unless I have good reason to believe the original pre-flop raiser is on a steal.

Frequently cold-calling raises pre-flop is not advisable, but it can be a viable option, especially when in position. It helps to keep the pot small and avoids the risk of getting reraised out of the pot by the original raiser. If the raise in this hand had come from early position, I would have folded the A-Q, but since I am on the button and the raise was from middle position, I decide to call. The blinds fold, and I see the flop heads up against Seat 6.

 Flop (650): I flop top pair with a queen-high flush draw. My opponent leads out for 300 into a pot of 650. I should like this flop a lot, but I am wary of playing a big pot. If my opponent likes his hand enough on the flop to play against a raise, I could very easily be up against A-K with the king of spades, or perhaps even a flopped flush or set. I therefore choose to proceed with caution and keep the pot small by just calling.

Turn (1,250): This is a very bad card for me. I miss my flush draw, and another hand that has me beaten takes the lead. A-J is certainly within my opponent's range and would now be leading. My opponent checks. I could bet here for value with the aim of making a hand like KK (with the king of spades) pay to draw. However, there are very few hands that I beat that could conceivably call a bet on the turn. If I get any action from a bet on the turn, then it probably means I am behind. Also, if my opponent check-raises, I would face a very tough decision but would probably have to fold, as I would have to give him credit for A-K, A-J, or better. I check behind.

 River (1,250): My opponent checks to me once again. Here I should probably bet my hand for value, approximately half of the 1,250 pot. It is somewhat difficult, however, to get paid off by a worse hand on this board. My opponent would probably call a river bet with a weak ace, but A-T, A-9, and A-8 are the only hands in his range that I can beat. He might pay me off with a pocket pair, believing that I could be bluffing a missed flush draw, but this is probably more hopeful than likely. I choose not to go for value, hoping just to show down the winning hand. I check, and my opponent shows A♥ K♥ to win the pot.

He might have checked the river hoping to induce a bluff. He probably reasoned that he had the best hand, but that it would be hard to get value from it. Also, if he bet and I raised, he would have a hard time calling with A-K. He too took the conservative route by checking. Rather than push a small edge for value, he took a line to preserve his stack in case he was behind.

Hand 17

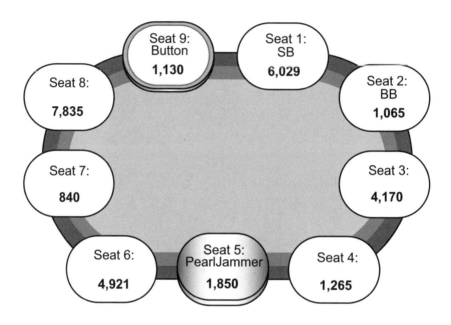

Setup: It is the early stages of a $50 buy-in, $15K guaranteed freezeout with a starting stack of only 1,500. The blinds are 60-120. I am unfamiliar with my opponents, but overall they seem to be predictable and somewhat passive as is usually the case in smaller buy-in tournaments.

  Pre-flop (180): Seat 4 limps in, and the action is on me. With no limpers in front, I would bring this hand in for a raise. However, with 15 big blinds, behind a limper I am in an awkward spot with 88. I could shove all-in, but I would prefer to be a little bit shorter-stacked to make that play profitable. I could raise, but then I would probably be in a tough spot on the flop if the limper or anyone else calls, as I would be committed to the pot and probably facing a couple of overcards. Either play is acceptable, but with 15 big blinds, my stack is just barely big enough to limp in behind a limper. I choose to limp in, hoping to have position against Seat 4 and the blinds in a small pot where I can bet most any flop or perhaps encourage more limpers, increasing my implied odds if I do hit a set.

Seat 6 limps in behind me, and the action folds to Seat 2 in the big blind. Seat 2 shoves all-in for 945 more. Seat 4 folds, and the action is on me. If Seat 4 had called or reraised all-in, I would have folded my middle pair and accepted a small loss on the hand. It would have been too likely that I would be up against at least one overpair to my 88. However, since Seat 4 has folded, with 1,485 in the pot and only 945 to call, my hand clearly becomes a call.

As short-stacked as Seat 2 is, he is likely to be pushing with a very wide range, virtually any two broadway cards, any pocket pair, or perhaps even a weak ace. Given that I have good equity against this range, and my opponent will only show up with a higher pocket pair a small percentage of the time, I should not pass up this opportunity for chips. The best play is to isolate by pushing all-in so as not to tempt the big-stacked limper behind me to call as well. I reraise all-in, and Seat 6 folds.

My opponent shows A♥ T♣ for two overcards, and I am off to the races. The board comes K♠ J♠ 4♥ 2♣ 6♥, and I win the race, increasing my stack to 3,215.

Hand 18

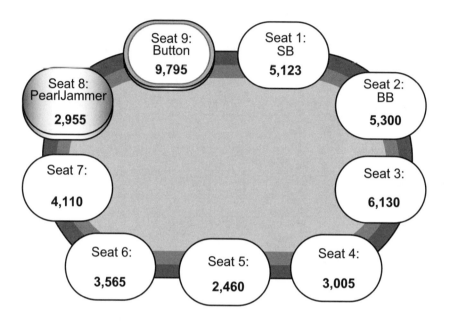

Setup: It is early in a $500 satellite to a major live event. I have approximately the starting stack and have not been involved in very many pots. The blinds are 60-120.

 **Pre-flop** (180): Seats 5 and 6 limp in middle position for 120 each. I choose to limp also, given the chance to get in a multiway pot cheaply with my strong position and disguised hand. The button folds, the small blind completes, and the big blind checks.

 **Flop** (600): The action is checked to me. Against a lone opponent, I will bet most of the time in this situation; however, betting into four opponents is just too risky. I would open myself up to a potential check-raise by betting and would have to fold. If any of my opponents even calls, I will have a hard time continuing with the hand unless I spike another 10 on the turn. Even a 7 is a dangerous card as an opponent holding 9-8 is a strong possibility

in this spot. Since my bet would also be very suspicious given my position, I would expect any player with a 10 (and certainly a better kicker) to either call or come over the top. I choose to check.

  Turn (600): This is an excellent card for me. It is highly unlikely that this card improved anyone's hand, so I probably still have the best hand and I have also picked up a ***backdoor***-flush draw.

The small blind leads out for 300 into a 600 pot. The big blind calls. Both limpers fold. I could argue for a raise here since the caller is very likely to be on a draw. Yet with these players having to act before three limpers on the flop, I believe that the small blind may have checked a jack on the flop, or even two pair. I could easily be reraised off my pair and flush draw, a very strong hand with which to peel off a cheap river card. Just calling also helps me to control the size of the pot and not risk getting raised out of it. I thus choose to call.

 River (1,500): Bingo! This is probably the best river card for me. My opponents check. Clearly I must now bet the river for value; it is only a matter of how much to bet. I could easily have been on a draw given that I checked the flop and only called the turn, so my opponents could easily expect that I am bluffing.

My goal is to try to induce a weak call from one of my opponents. Sometimes a smallish bet will achieve this aim by keeping the price reasonable, given my opponents' stack sizes. On the other hand, sometimes players will fold to a smallish bet because they think you are looking for a call. A larger bet can look suspicious since your opponent thinks you are dissuading a call. I lean toward betting the larger amount because I get paid off better when my opponent takes the bait. I bet 1,150, approximately three-quarters of the 1,500 pot. Unfortunately, both opponents fold.

Hand 19

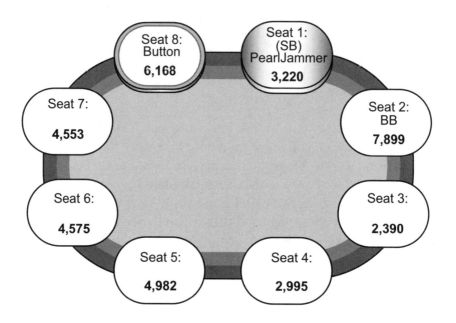

Setup: It is early in a $100 freezeout, the blinds are 75-150, and I have approximately the starting stack. I have created a tight image as I have not played many hands so far.

 Pre-flop (225): The action folds to seat 6, who raises to 500 from the hijack seat. The cutoff and button fold, and the action is on me. I quickly dismiss flat-calling the raise as I do not want to try to trap out of position with a hand vulnerable to two overcards. A reraise is certainly in order, so I just need to decide the amount.

I would normally raise to about 1,500, three times the original bet. However, this would be almost half of my stack. I would not fold on the flop after putting in this much of my stack, even if the flop came ace high. Therefore, the best option would be to go all-in now.

An all-in bet of 3,220 may seem like an overbet, but just taking down the pot pre-flop would increase my stack by over 20 percent. Of course, what I would most like in this spot is to be called by a hand that I am dominating. Some opponents will look at a big all-in bet and sense weakness, so I think an all-in bet actually has a better chance of being called by a lower pocket pair than merely a reraise to 1,500. I shove all-in for 3,220. The big blind and Seat 6 quickly fold.

Hand 20

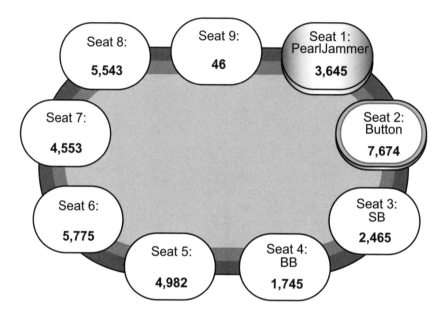

Setup: This is the same $100 freezeout as the previous hand, about one orbit later. The blinds remain 75-150.

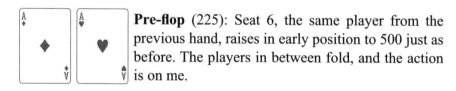

Pre-flop (225): Seat 6, the same player from the previous hand, raises in early position to 500 just as before. The players in between fold, and the action is on me.

It is important to maximize the profits of your premium hands, especially aces. As a general rule of thumb, against a raiser I will usually push all-in with a pair of aces if my stack is less than 12 big blinds. I want to get the raiser to commit his chips now so that I don't give him a chance to give up if he doesn't like the flop.

If the stacks are deep, I will also almost always reraise to clear the field and better define my hand to see the flop. Merely cold-calling raises with deep stacks is quite risky, as playing "only" one pair after the flop can be very dangerous.

The middle range of stack sizes (of either myself or my opponent), somewhere between 12 and 20 big blinds, is where I will consider slow-playing my aces before the flop. Cold-calling in this spot can sometimes induce a player behind me to reraise, commonly referred to as a squeeze play. If not, I have position against an opponent who is likely to make a continuation bet. Given the right stack size, this gives me an opportunity to increase my stack significantly simply by getting my opponent to bet the flop. If he decides to call a raise on the flop, I will take my chances with a premium pair given my stack size. Whether or not I slow-play with a stack of this size is generally dependent on the likelihood of my opponent calling a reraise or not before the flop.

In this particular hand, given Seat 6's quick fold in the previous hand and the unlikelihood of my opponents in between waking up with a hand strong enough with which to play behind two raises, I choose to flat-call. The button and the big blind also call behind me.

Flop (2,075): I am not excited to take the flop four-handed; however, this is an excellent flop for me! The only hand I need to worry about is 66, as it is very unlikely that any of my opponents has a deuce. Most important, if anyone has a pocket pair, I am very likely to be paid off. Seat 4 checks, and Seat 6 bets 1,450 into the pot of 2,075. I could flat-call this bet, but with only an additional 1,595 behind, I choose to go all-in. I can be very confident that Seat 6 has a pocket pair given the size of his bet and that he will call my all-in, and it is possible that I could get action from a player behind me with a pair as well. I go all-in for 3,145.

Seats 2 and 4 fold, and Seat 6 calls my all-in, showing T♥ T♣. The T♦ comes on the turn and the 8♥ on the river. My opponent hits his two outer and wins the pot with tens full of twos.

Hand 21

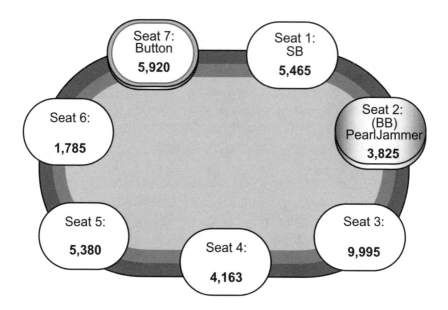

Setup: About two hours into a satellite for a major live event, I face a blind-versus-blind situation against a very aggressive opponent. In a blind-versus-blind confrontation in the previous orbit, this opponent check-raised me on the flop when I tried to steal the pot. The blinds are 100-200.

Pre-flop (300): The table folds around to the small blind, who limps in for 100 more. I check my option as I am more than happy to take a free flop with a junk hand.

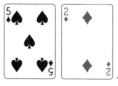

Flop (400): My opponent bets 250 into a 400 pot. I have flopped an open-ended straight draw on a rainbow board. Having position on my opponent, holding a good draw, and facing a relatively small bet, I am certainly continuing with the hand. Based on previous blind-versus-blind play with this opponent, I know that he is probably going to make this bet with any two cards, whether he hit the flop hard or completely missed. I could raise, but if my opponent has a strong hand like two pair or top pair, or even a hand as weak as middle pair, he may choose to reraise, pricing me out of the hand. I do not want to risk being priced out of my draw.

Also, I know my aggressive opponent is likely to have air in this spot, and most opponents who bet with complete air on the flop will shut down on the turn. Therefore, just calling may allow me to steal the pot on the turn if my opponent checks in front of me. Of course, if I am up against a made hand, l welcome the opportunity to draw cheaply to my open-ended straight in position. I call the 250 bet.

 Turn (900): Yahtzee! I have turned the second nut straight! Unfortunately, my opponent checks to me. I could check behind and hope to get value out of my hand on the river, but with a hand this strong, I very rarely want to slow-play. If I were to check, and a 7, 5, or 2 were to hit the river, I could get very little value out of my hand, even if he has a very strong second-best hand. Because my opponent has proven himself to be very aggressive, betting here may induce him to check-raise me with any sort of made hand or perhaps even on a bluff or semibluff. Of course, I also want to get value for my hand.

Since I know I should bet my monster, I must decide the right amount to bet. A less than half-pot bet may induce a check-raise, but if my opponent is drawing, I would be allowing him to draw to beat me too cheaply. Worse yet, too big of a bet may kill my action! I aim for a balance that does not give any information away or scare my opponent away. I choose to bet slightly over half the pot, 550 into 900.

To my delight, my opponent check-raises to 2,550, practically putting me all-in! I reraise an additional 825 all-in, as the pot is now big enough that I am not worried about losing my opponent. Although it is possible that he holds 7-5 for the nut straight, this would be an unavoidable cooler, just unfortunate circumstance. My opponent calls and shows J♣ 5♣ for an open-ended straight draw, which would only chop the pot if made. The T♣ falls on the river, and my straight holds to double me up.

Note that my opponent led with complete air on the flop, a very common move in blind-versus-blind situations. When he picked up a draw on the turn, he tried to see the river cheaply but then got greedy when I bet my hand. He made a big mistake to put in so many chips on a draw with one card to come. Inducing opponents to make mistakes like this can be crucial in building big chip stacks in tournaments.

Hand 22

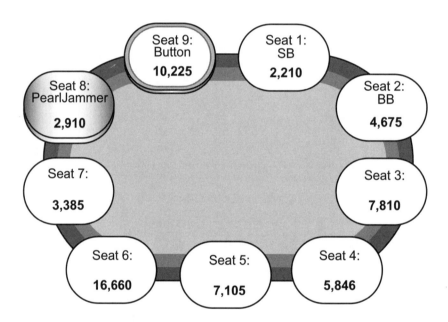

Setup: It is early in a $50 freezeout, and I have played very few pots. I have close to the starting stack of 3,000. The blinds are 100-200.

Pre-flop (300): The under-the-gun player in Seat 3, who has been fairly active, limps. The remainder of the table folds around to me. I could raise to try to take the pot down pre-flop or perhaps to isolate the limper. However, this is quite risky, especially given the size of my stack. To effectively isolate, I would need to raise about one-third of my stack. If I get any action, it will almost surely be against a better hand, and I might find myself pot-committed against a dominating hand.

The under-the-gun limper presents an interesting situation. If this player had been playing very few pots, I would throw my A-J into the muck as I would be too worried about him limping in with a big pocket pair or a bigger ace. However, because he has been active, I want to take a flop with him in position. I choose to limp in behind. The button also limps, the small blind completes, and the big blind checks. Five players see the flop.

   Flop (1,000): I flop top pair with top kicker, a strong but somewhat dangerous hand given two broadway cards on the flop. The small blind, Seat 1, leads out for 800 into a pot of 1,000. The big blind and the under-the-gun limper fold. Seat 1 has only 1,210 left after betting 800, so he is clearly pot-committed. He could have flopped two pair from the small blind or perhaps even a set of threes. However, most players first to act would try to trap with hands stronger than A-J on this flop, hoping to check-raise with so many limpers in the pot. His most likely holdings here would be a jack with a weaker kicker than mine or a semibluff with an open-ended straight draw, K-Q, Q-9, or 9-8. I am confident that I am ahead, so I reraise enough to put Seat 1 all-in. I raise to 2,400.

The button folds, and Seat 1 calls, showing Q♣ J♠. The 2♥ hits the turn and the 7♦ on the river, and my hands hold up.

Hand 23

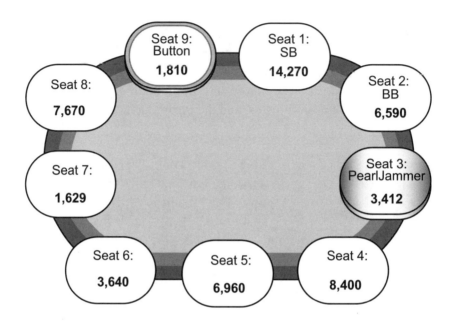

Setup: I am in a $100 freezeout in the last level before the antes kick in. The blinds are 100-200, and I am well below average with just above the starting stack. Seat 8 is a very smart, aggressive player whom I respect a lot.

  Pre-flop (300): With only 17 big blinds, I am definitely willing to get all of my money in the pot pre-flop. I open for my standard raise of two-and-a-half times the big blind to 500. Seat 5, with about 7,000 in chips, reraises to 2,000. Seat 8 then reraises all-in from the cutoff for 7,670! The action is back to me.

When I open-raised with QQ, leaving me with less than 3,000 in chips, I was hoping to get action. However, with all the action behind me, it is time to reanalyze the situation. My opening raise was from under-the-gun, and having a short stack, I should assume that my opponents give me credit for a real hand. They should probably give me a range of 88+, A-Q+, and perhaps A-J or K-Q. Therefore, for Seat 5 to reraise, most likely assuming I am committed, I should give him a range of about TT+ and A-K, perhaps as weak as 99 or A-Q.

Because I know that Seat 8 is a very intelligent player and is not going to make a big mistake for his entire stack at this stage of the tournament, I should give him credit for knowing what I know about both my range and Seat 5's range. I should also assume that he would err on the side of caution and not shove in his stack with a hand as weak as JJ and perhaps not even A-K, having no money invested in the pot. Therefore, I should be able to narrow his range down to AA, KK, QQ (although there is only one combination remaining for QQ), and perhaps A-K.

Normally in this situation, A-K is more likely than AA or KK because there are 16 combinations of A-K versus 12 combinations of AA or KK. However, in this spot, it is reasonable to assume that Seat 8 may have chosen to fold A-K, so AA and KK become much more likely possibilities. Since I am in a coin flip against A-K and dominated by the over-pairs (I also must consider the possibility that Seat 5 has reraised with AA or KK), I choose to fold my QQ. Seat 5 also folds, and Seat 8 mucks his hand.

Hand 24

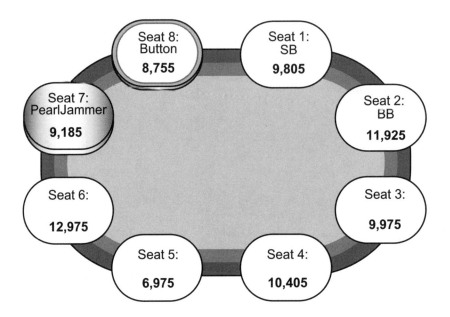

Setup: It is the middle stages of a $200 freezeout, and most of the table is relatively deep-stacked at 100-200 blinds.

  Pre-flop (300): The action is folded to me, and I put in my standard two-and-a-half times the big blind raise of 500. This is a very questionable play as K-T is a very weak, trouble hand. Even if I flop either pair as top pair, I could be in very bad shape against many reasonable hands. However, at a tight table, I will often steal with this hand in late position. The button and the small blind call, and the big blind folds.

   Flop (1,700): I flop top pair with the second-best kicker. Without hitting two pair or trips, I could not ask for a much safer-looking flop for my hand. Seat 1 leads out for 500, less than one-third of the 1,700 pot. I could certainly raise in this spot as I figure to have the best hand. It would be a ***probe*** raise, though, since I would have to fold if either player played back at me. Even if I were just called by either player, I would be very leery that

I did not have the best hand. I opt to keep the pot small and just call the bet, seeing what develops on the turn. Seat 8 also makes the call, and I see the turn three-handed.

 Turn (3,200): This is a very safe card for my hand. The only way this card could have helped another player is if the original bettor or button had a hand with a gutshot draw like A-5 or 6-5. However, both of these hands would be very unlikely in this spot. Again, Seat 1 leads out for 500. This bet is extremely small, as the pot is 3,200. I do not believe that I can give up on the hand at this point, although I am still very worried about my opponent's holdings. This is precisely why a hand like K-T is such a trouble hand to begin with!

I decide to raise to find out for sure where I stand. My opponent's small bet allows me to raise without committing myself to the pot. I hope to either take the pot down or at least chase out Seat 8, giving me position on the river. If either player plays back at me, I know I will give up the pot. A raise should at least chase out the button unless he is slow-playing a monster as he will be facing a bet and raise, an always difficult spot. If Seat 1 calls and we see the river heads up, I should be able to check behind on the river. A small raise thus enables me to "buy a cheap showdown" by taking control of the hand with no intention of betting again unless I improve. However, I am not trying to risk a lot of chips in hopes of bluffing out a better hand as my hand has plenty of showdown value. I raise to 1,450, approximately three times my opponent's bet. Seat 8 folds, but Seat 1 makes the call.

 River (6,100): Yet again, this is a safe card for my hand. Nonetheless, I am not confident that I have the best hand. Seat 1 checks. By raising on the turn, I have put Seat 1 on the defensive. He now gives me the option of whether or not to bet my hand. If I bet, I might get called by a hand such as Q-T or J-T, but these hands are unlikely to have called me pre-flop from the small blind. I think my opponent may have a pair beaten. He may have nines or fives, but he is unlikely to call me on the river with one of these hands. I check behind, choosing not to attempt a very risky value bet.

My opponent shows J♦ J♠ and wins the pot.

Hand 25

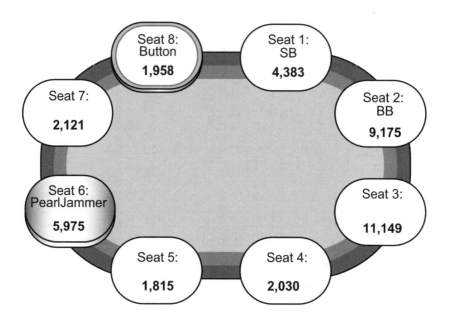

Setup: It is the early-middle stages of a $200 buy-in, major Sunday tournament. The blinds are 100-200, and my stack, which is a little under double the starting stack of 3,000, is about average for this stage of the tournament. I am unfamiliar with my opponents.

 Pre-flop (300): Seat 3 opens for 700 under-the-gun. Seats 4 and 5 fold. My opponent opened the pot for three-and-a-half times the big blind from first position. Both the size and position of his raise are unequivocal signs of strength. I can expect my opponent to have a high pocket pair or A-K most of the time. Flat-calling the raise and then looking to raise all-in on most any flop is an option. However, I prefer to reraise pre-flop, attempting to get all of my money in now.

If I flat-call and my opponent misses the flop with A-K, I may not get any more action. Also, if my opponent has a pocket pair such as JJ or TT, and a couple of overcards flop, I will probably lose my opportunity to double up. If either my stack or my opponent's stack were in the

12-20 big blind range, the flat-call would be much more profitable. In that case, my opponent would be committed or all-in with almost any continuation bet, so I should get paid off in full. When you flat-call when stacks are deep, you risk allowing your opponent or subsequent callers the chance to catch up too easily on the flop. Post-flop play can then become dangerous when it does not need to be.

Unfortunately any reraise will clearly commit me to the pot, and if my opponent analyzes the situation well, he should be able to put me on a very narrow range of AA, KK, QQ, and A-K. After all, I am coming over the top of a large under-the-gun raise and committing a stack of 30 big blinds to the pot. Against an unknown opponent who is representing a lot of strength, I can expect to get action most of the time. I do not want to reraise the minimum, thus telegraphing my hand. I also do not want to shove all-in, because that may help my opponent lay down middle pairs or A-K or A-Q. Note the difference between this hand and hand #19 where I pushed with QQ. In that hand, I started with only 15 big blinds and in this hand I have 30 big blinds. Pushing with a stack of 30 big blinds isn't nearly as likely to generate action as a push with 15 big blinds.

I reraise to 2,350, approximately three times my opponent's bet. Seats 7, 8, 1, and 2 fold. Seat 3 reraises all-in. I call, and my opponent shows T♠ T♣. The board comes 8♣ 7♠ 6♦ A♣ 2♦, and I win with a set of aces, doubling up to 12,250.

Note that a strong opponent should be able to lay down TT in this spot but will almost certainly go broke with KK, QQ, A-K, and maybe JJ. I was fortunate that even though my opponent had a hand on the weak end of what I believed to be his range, he still stacked off to me.

Hand 26

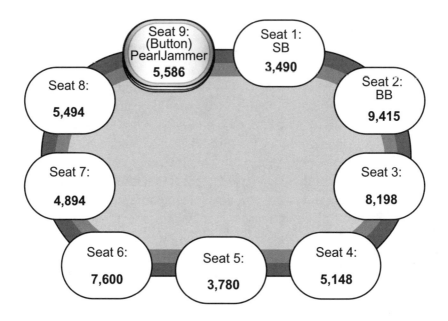

Setup: It is the middle stages of a $50, $50K guaranteed freezeout with blinds of 100-200. I have no information on the players in the blinds.

  Pre-flop (300): The action is folded to me. My hand is not very strong, yet it is strong enough to attempt a button steal. I raise two-and-a-half times the big blind, my standard raise, to 500. The small blind folds, but the big blind makes the call, defending with his rather large stack.

   Flop (1,100): I have flopped second pair but with a very weak kicker. My opponent checks. He probably knows that my range is very wide on the button and could include almost any two cards. He also wields a very big stack, and I am not sure if he tends to play back at players he perceives as weak. If I bet and he raises, I would be inclined to throw my hand away. Although I have a piece of the flop, my hand is not strong enough to play a big pot.

I would rather take a free card, hopefully improving my hand, and then re-evaluate the situation on the turn. I check.

 Turn (1,100): An absolute brick hits, and my opponent checks to me again. With two checks from my deep-stacked opponent, I now believe that I am leading with my pair of kings. Although it is possible that he has checked an ace twice, or a king with a better kicker, it is more likely that he has a weak hand such as suited connectors (perhaps with an eight), or perhaps lower broadway cards like J-T. I could bet now to take down the pot and not give a free card to a potential gutshot-straight draw, or I could give my opponent one more chance to catch up.

Conventional wisdom argues for a bet, not giving a free card; however, I prefer a check in this spot. Since I checked the flop in part to feign weakness, my opponent might expect me to try and steal the pot on the turn and attempt an ambitious check-raise bluff if I bet the turn. It would be very difficult to call such a raise and play a big pot with my stack at this stage. I prefer to check again, denying him this opportunity and keeping the pot small. Checking also tempts my opponent to use his big stack and bluff into me on the river. If he has no chance to win at a showdown, he may take a shot at the pot. If he checks to me a third time on the river, I will be even more confident that my king is good and that I am certainly able to value-bet it. My opponent may pay me off with some very weak holdings on the river, thinking that I am stealing the pot. I check again.

 River (1,100): My opponent again checks. Clearly, it is time to value-bet. My bet should be on the small side as I must convince my opponent to call with a weak hand. However, it should not be so small that it is obvious I am going for a value bet. I bet just over half the pot, 650. My opponent calls and mucks Q♠ T♣, and I take down the pot.

Hand 27

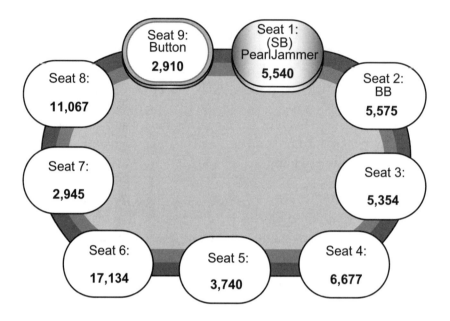

Setup: I am in the early-to-middle stages of a $300 freezeout. The blinds are 100-200 with a 10 ante.

  **Pre-flop** (390): The action folds to me. I am familiar with my opponent in the big blind, a strong and somewhat aggressive player. If I were to raise with my weak ace, I would have to fold to a reraise. I prefer not to raise with weak aces in deep-stacked blind-versus-blind situations in order to disguise my hand and control pot size. I therefore limp, and my opponent checks.

 Flop (490): I flop top pair with a weak kicker on a board that offers many potential draws. I could check to my opponent, hoping to get him to bluff at the pot. My opponent might bet with a 9, 7, straight draw, or flush draw, but he might also choose to take a free card, which could be very dangerous to me. If I were to lead out, I would not be giving away my hand as I could make this bet with a very wide range of hands. Additionally, I would ensure that my opponent does not get a free card while also getting value for my hand. I bet 300 into a 490 pot.

My opponent raises to 1,050. He may have made this raise with anything from complete air to a hand as strong as two pair. However, the fact that I have an ace makes it less likely that he has one. Also, he is somewhat unlikely to have checked an ace after limping, and he may perceive my bet as a steal or a weak hand such as middle or bottom pair. Given my opponent's wide range, so many possible drawing hands and so few likely made hands, I make up my mind at this point that I probably have the best hand. The decision now is whether to call or reraise, and if the latter, how much?

Calling in this spot and then checking the turn would be too weak a play and a potential disaster. If my opponent has a draw or weak pair, he is unlikely to put another chip in the pot unless he makes his hand. By calling the flop and then checking the turn, I am giving my opponent two chances to improve his hand without charging him to do so. Another option would be to call and then lead out on the turn. If a blank hits the turn, I may be able to convince him that I have a draw with this line of action and get him to make a second, more ambitious play at the pot. However, the downside of this play is that I would let him get to the river facing only a single bet on the turn. If he makes a big hand on the turn or river, it would be very difficult to get away from my hand as the pot would be rather large and his hand would be hard to pinpoint. Therefore, I much prefer to reraise now on the flop.

A reraise to approximately 2,800 would be reasonable, but I prefer an all-in reraise in this spot. By shoving, I charge my opponent the maximum for a draw. If he has a double draw, like J-T, T-8, or 8-6 of diamonds, I am at least forcing him to call off all his chips if he so chooses. By making such a large overbet, my opponent might also convince himself that I am weak and on a draw, and he could call me with a hand as weak as a pair of nines. It may seem unlikely, but stranger calls have been made. I shove all-in for 5,330, and my opponent folds.

This sort of hand is tough to play; I am basically risking my entire stack, fully trusting that I have made the correct read. In essence, I am risking

5,000 in chips to win the 1,700 in the pot, not the best risk-reward ratio. If I am called, I will be behind in most cases. However, you must learn to trust your reads to be successful in tournament poker. In this particular hand, the key piece of information is that my opponent didn't raise pre-flop, which most opponents would do with A-7 or higher. I won't always be correct, but I am willing to take the risk to increase my stack by 1,700, with the possibility of increasing it by even more if called.

Hand 28

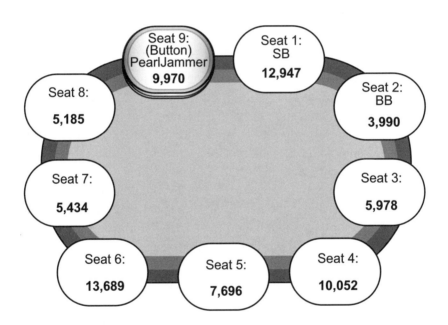

Setup: The blinds are 120-240, and antes of 25 have just been introduced in a $150, $55K guaranteed tournament. I have a very good stack and have been opening many pots, especially in position.

 Pre-flop (585): The action is folded to me and I put in my standard raise, just under two-and-a-half times the big blind to 575. The small blind defends and calls my raise, and the big blind folds. I have not played many pots with this player but believe him to be somewhat active and understandably suspicious of my button raise.

 Flop (1,615): My opponent checks. I have flopped top pair top kicker, but with three hearts on the board, my hand is vulnerable. I do not have to worry about any possible two-pair combinations on this flop, though. Given my opponent's chip stack, it isn't unreasonable for him to call pre-flop with 55 or 22, so a set is a small possibility. With a strong piece of this flop, and having raised from such a suspicious position, I should be confident to put out a continuation bet for value. This bet also protects my hand, as I should charge my opponent for a fourth heart given the dangerous board.

I bet 765, approximately half the 1,615 pot. My opponent check-raises to 2,300.

In deciding whether to re-shove all-in (or reraise an amount that commits me to the hand), call, or even fold to this bet, I must quickly analyze the decisions I will face on future streets.

I decide against shoving in or reraising at this point because it is very unlikely that I will get called by a worse hand. My opponent would probably need a flush or set to call, or perhaps K-J, Q-J, or J-T, where his kicker is a heart. With these weaker jacks and the flush draw, my opponent would be approximately 50/50 to win, and with the money he has already invested, I would expect him to call. I may also be up against A-x with the ace of hearts. If my opponent check-raised me with this hand, he would probably feel pot-committed and call my all-in, thinking he has 12 outs when he actually has only nine. This is a hand from which I would welcome a call. However, I am willing to take the risk of allowing a fourth heart to hit for the sake of pot control at this relatively early stage of the tournament.

Folding in this spot would be too weak of a play since I took the flop heads up, and my opponent could easily be assuming that I simply made a continuation bet with a weak hand given my position. Thus, his range for check-raising is much wider than if I had opened in early position.

Calling is arguably a weak play as well because if my opponent has one heart (a very likely holding), I am allowing him to set his own price. However, I have position on him and would much prefer to commit my money to this pot after a safe turn hits. If I call and see a fourth heart hit the board, I can safely assume I am beaten if my opponent bets, because I believe he must have at least one heart or a set to make this check-raise.

If he doesn't have a heart, then a fourth heart on the turn would probably cause him to shut down and check. Most turn cards would appear safe for me, though, and I could then feel confident enough to put my opponent all-in or put out a strong bet if he checks. With any turn card, jack or below (or an ace), I would feel very confident getting my money in. By just calling now, I am representing a flush draw to my opponent. I expect him to bet at least 3,000 on an unthreatening turn, at which point I will raise all-in. The only turn cards that I am unsure how to handle are a non-heart king or queen. If one of these cards hits, I will have to make my decision based on the size of my opponent's bet.

I choose to call based on my assumption that I am ahead but knowing that the turn card will better define my hand's strength. I have planned ahead, knowing that I will get the majority of my money in with only one card to come if a safe turn card hits, but fold to a bet if a fourth heart hits instead.

 Turn (6,215): This is an excellent turn for my hand. I now feel extremely confident that I am well ahead. The worst-case scenario is that in the unlikely event that my opponent flopped a flush or a low set, I now have outs on the river to make a full house.

My opponent goes all-in, and he has me covered as I have 7,070. Since I knew when I called on the flop that if a safe turn card hit I was committing my stack, I can make this call without any further analysis.

My opponent shows 9♠ 9♥ for a flush draw. I must dodge a 9 or heart on the river (aside from the A♥) to win. Sigh. The K♥ falls on the river, and my opponent wins with a flush! Although I lost the hand, my analysis helped me get my money in well ahead with only one card to come.

Hand 29

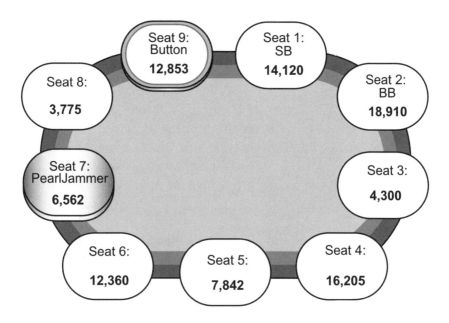

Setup: I am well below average but not short-stacked in a $100 *rebuy tournament* a few levels after the rebuy period has ended. The blinds are 150-300 with a 25 ante.

  Pre-flop (675): The action is folded to me, and I raise my standard two-and-a-half times the big blind to 750. Seat 9 on the button and Seat 2 in the big blind both make the call.

   Flop (2,625): I flop top pair, top kicker on a very safe board. Seat 2 checks, and the action is on me. I should bet approximately one-third to one-half of the pot, my standard continuation bet. Because my opponents expect me to make this bet now with any two cards, it will not give away the strength of my hand. I bet 1,150 into the 2,625 pot. Seat 9 calls, and Seat 2 folds.

Turn (4,925): I am very confident that I have the best hand. If my opponent has me beaten, my stack size and the pot size dictate that I am willing to go broke. The only concern now is how to get my opponent's money in the pot on the next two streets.

If I were certain that my opponent was as strong as A-Q or A-J, I would bet out now and easily get his money in. However, I cannot give him credit for a hand that strong. In position, he merely called my bet on the flop. He might have perceived this bet as weak since I will probably make a continuation bet with any two cards. Thus he might have called with anything from a weak ace to an unimproved pocket pair. He might have even *floated* with air, hoping to take the pot away on the turn if I show weakness with a check.

If I bet the turn, my opponent will in all likelihood give up on his unimproved pocket pairs or weaker hands, as my bet clearly commits me to the pot. However, if I check the turn, he will likely try to take the pot away no matter what he holds. If he has an ace, I will get his money in either way. The only risk in checking is that my opponent takes a free card and improves to the best hand on the river, but my analysis makes me almost certain that my opponent will bet the turn.

I check, and my opponent moves all-in. This is precisely what I wanted him to do. I make the call, and my opponent shows 9♦ 9♥. The 2♦ hits the river, and I win the pot with aces and a king kicker.

Hand 30

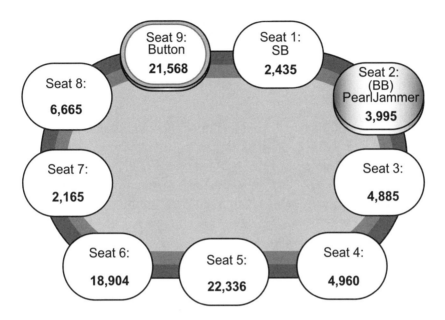

Setup: It is the middle stages of a $50 freezeout, and I am new to the table with no information on any of my opponents. The blinds are 150-300 with a 25 ante.

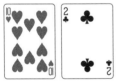 **Pre-flop** (675): Seat 6 limps, the button limps, and the small blind completes. I check my option, happy to see a free flop.

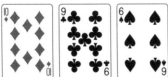 **Flop** (1,425): I flop top pair with a horrible kicker on a somewhat dangerous board. There is no flush draw, but a straight is possible. The small blind checks. I could bet out, but if called or raised, I would have a hard time continuing with the hand. Both limpers are sitting on large stacks, so I choose to check, figuring one of them will bet, giving me more information.

Seat 6 bets 675 into a pot of 1,425. Seats 9 and 1 fold. I now find myself heads up against a single opponent who did not show any strength pre-flop. If I were to call and see the turn, only a T or 2 would improve my hand, while plenty of cards would scare me. Since my top pair figures to be the best hand against a single opponent with a wide range, and I am relatively short-stacked with the size of the pot now being more than half my stack, I should raise. With only 3,670 chips left, looking at a pot of 2,100, my raise should be all-in.

Given the size of the pot, I would like my opponent to fold hands such as K-Q, K-J, or 9-8, which all have nine or 10 outs. However, I am still the favorite to double up if my opponent calls. I may even get action from hands like A-9, 88, or 77, with which my deep-stacked opponent may talk himself into calling with, believing I am trying to steal the pot on some type of draw. Of course, if I am beaten on the flop, I will certainly be called and almost certainly will be out of the tournament. This is a risk I must be willing to take given my stack size and my opponent's range.

I raise all-in for 2,995 more, and my opponent folds.

Hand 31

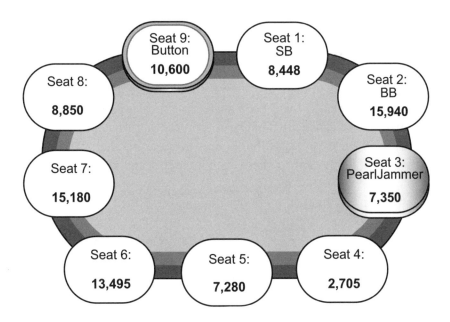

Setup: It is the middle stages of a $100 rebuy tournament. The rebuy period is over, and the blinds are 150-300 with a 25 ante. My table is stacked with many very aggressive players.

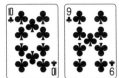 **Pre-flop** (675): In order to remain unpredictable to my opponents, I elect to raise with this suited connector from early position. Often when called by one or two opponents, my continuation bet will be more credible due to my early position raise. Also, whenever I connect with the flop with a suited connector from this position, I have a high likelihood of getting paid off and winning a big pot because my hand is so well disguised. I raise two-and-a-half times the big blind to 750. Seat 8 calls from the cutoff, and the button and blinds fold.

Flop (2,175): With a flush draw, I will often lead out, especially given my early-position raise pre-flop. However, appropriate table dynamics and stack sizes suggest taking a different approach to this flop. There is 2,175 in the pot, so if I lead out for approximately 1,200 and my opponent raises, he would be committed to the pot due to our stack sizes. I would not want to move all-in with only nine outs when I expect my opponent is committed. If my opponent just calls, I will be in a similarly tough spot on the turn if I miss my draw. Because my table has been very aggressive, I expect my opponent will bet if I check. If he chooses to check behind, I will at least get a free shot at my draw. I check, and my opponent bets 1,200.

Since my opponent called an under-the-gun raise for almost one-tenth of his stack, I can assign him a fairly specific range. Pocket pairs are very likely along with A-Q, A-J, or perhaps a weaker suited ace. Suited connectors are also a possibility, as are K-Q and K-J. It is also possible that my opponent is slow-playing a big hand like AA, KK, or A-K. Let me assume that my opponent is betting in this spot when checked to, regardless of his hand. With the majority of the hands in his range, he will fold to a check-raise. He can only continue if he is slow-playing, hit a set, or has K-Q or K-J. Facing a check-raise, he would likely fold hands as strong as QQ or perhaps even K-Q or K-J, fearing that he is beaten. If he does have a big hand, such as A-K or a set, at least I would have outs with my flush draw. The only hands where I would be in terrible shape would be higher flush draws. Yet even in this unlikely case, I would have six outs twice[2] so long as the flush does not hit on the turn.

I check-raise to 3,300, knowing that I am committed to calling my opponent's all-in if he pushes. I could check-raise all-in, but a smaller raise usually looks stronger and should clearly tell my opponent that I am pot-committed. Often an all-in check-raise appears too much like a draw, precisely the information I do not want to give away. My opponent folds.

---

[2] This refers to the two cards coming on the turn and river.

Hand 32

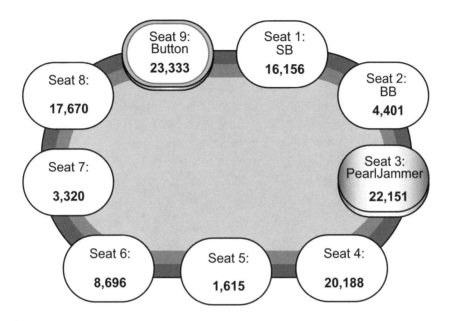

Setup: It is the middle stages of a $150 freezeout. The blinds are 150-300 with a 25 ante.

 **Pre-flop** (675): I put in my standard raise of just under two-and-a-half times the big blind to 725. The action folds around to Seat 8, who calls. The button and blinds fold, too. I see the flop heads up against another deep-stacked opponent.

   Flop (2,125): I flop top pair, top kicker, which is a good flop for me but has some potential flush and straight draws. I should make the same continuation bet that I would make on virtually any flop, continuing my representation of strength begun with the under-the-gun raise. I lead out for 950, approximately half of the 2,125 pot, and my opponent calls.

Turn (4,025): If I lead out again and get action in the form of a call or a raise, I will be involved in a very big pot, perhaps playing for my whole stack. So before I follow through with another bet on the turn, I should analyze my opponent's hand range to see what hands make sense given his play thus far.

He may have a queen with a weaker kicker; however, he would probably not call my under-the-gun raise with many of these hands. I expect K-Q would fall within his range, but probably no other queens. He might have flopped an open-ended straight draw with K-J or J-9, but again, these are unlikely to be in his pre-flop calling range. He could have called on the flop with a flush draw, but I have the ace of hearts. A flush draw is still a possibility but less likely, given that the ace of hearts is out of play. He might have called pre-flop with a strong ace, such as A-K, A-Q, or A-J, but he probably would have reraised pre-flop with A-K or raised on the flop with A-Q.

It would also make sense for my opponent to have a pocket pair. Middle to low pocket pairs are very likely holdings for people flat-calling pre-flop raises with deep stacks. My bet of less than half the pot on the flop may have enticed him to call in position with an unimproved pocket pair, still believing it to be good. If I lead at the pot a second time on the turn, these hands will likely fold, but they may pay me off on the river if I can convince my opponent that his pair is good. My opponent could also be slow-playing a hand that beats me. TT and 33 are possibilities, and if I lead out and get raised by one of these hands, I will be drawing dead and may have a hard time getting away from my hand.

I decide to check to manage the size of the pot in a vulnerable situation. I protect myself if I am against a set, while at the same time, if my opponent checks behind, I may be able to get a value bet paid off by a weak hand on the river. My opponent checks, too.

 River (4,025): This is a complete rag, an excellent card for me. It is time to take my opponent to value town! If he has missed a draw, then the optimal play is to check and induce a bluff. However, I am losing value if he has any hand worse than A-Q with which he might pay me off. My check on the turn helps me sell a bluff on the river and thus get paid off by much weaker hands. With

4,025 in the pot, I want to bet the maximum that I believe my opponent will call. I bet 2,450, a little more than half the pot. My opponent calls and mucks JJ at the showdown.

If I had checked the river, perhaps he would have tried to value-bet his JJ, sensing it to be good. However, most of the time, he would probably check behind, hoping to win at the showdown without risking any more chips or being check-raised. Thus, a check on the river more often than not would have lost me a lot of value.

Hand 33

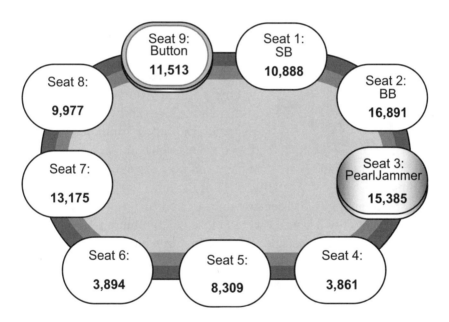

Setup: It is the middle stages of a $1,000 buy-in satellite to a major live event. There are 70 players left, and seven packages will be awarded. The blinds are 200-400 with a 25 ante. I am above average with about 15,000 chips, and I should have a tight image as I have not played many pots. I am familiar with several very strong, experienced players at my table, including Seat 2.

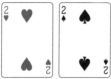 **Pre-flop** (825): I could easily justify folding small pocket pairs in early position at this stage of the tournament. However, I often choose to open-raise with them, as my early-position raises garner respect. My continuation bets are also more respected from this position, and when I do flop a set, my hand will be very well disguised.

In a satellite tournament such as this one, my opponents are likely to give my raise even more respect than usual and will usually fold their low or medium pocket pairs because they are focusing more on surviving than on building a big stack. This is precisely why I should exploit this tendency and open up my game a bit more, especially in early position where opponents are more likely to give me credit for a big hand and not re-steal. I make my standard raise of two-and-a-half times the big blind to 1,000. The action folds to the big blind in Seat 2, a strong opponent, who defends.

 Flop (2,425): Of course, no flop will excite me unless I hit my miracle set. However, given my position and the fact that my opponent has called from the big blind where he may choose to defend with a wide range, this is a spot where I truly must forget about my own hand and play my opponent's. I should continuation-bet here virtually 100% of the time, continuing my representation of strength that began with my under-the-gun raise. I want to bet small, not only because I want to lose the minimum if my opponent check-raises, but also because this is a spot in which I may want to fire two or maybe even three shells on upcoming streets. The smaller my bet on the flop, the smaller my second shell on the turn needs to be. I bet 1,250, approximately half of the 2,425 pot. My opponent calls.

 Turn (4,925): This card puts four to a straight on the board as well as a second, though unlikely, flush draw. My opponent again checks. This is an excellent spot to fire a second shell, especially given two important factors. First off, I am in a satellite tournament where conserving chips is more important than going for the win. Secondly, my opponent understands this, so he should be capable of laying down a hand. Even if my opponent has a hand as strong as A-T or Q-J for two pair, what can he reasonably expect to beat?

Virtually any two broadway cards beat even a hand as strong as A-T and leave him drawing extremely thin. He would most likely not expect me to fire a second shell on such a board if had a pocket pair below TT. I should not expect my opponent to have a set, as he most likely would have check-raised the flop. I would not expect my opponent to hold A-K here either, as he would have reraised with such a strong hand pre-flop. The only hands I fear are K-Q, K-J, or K-T. If my opponent has one of these, he will let me know now, but he will probably fold anything else.

I once again make a relatively small bet of 2,150, less than half of the 4,925 pot. My small bet here may help convince my opponent that I want action, and of course it risks less of my stack if I find out that my opponent still likes his hand. My opponent folds.

Hand 34

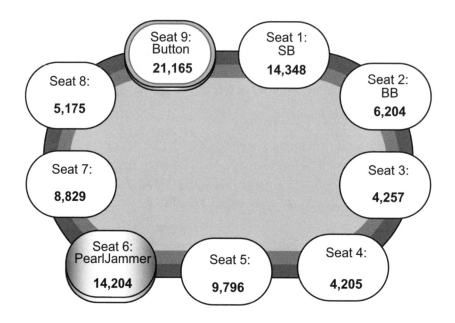

Setup: I am near the bubble of a $50, $50K guaranteed freezeout. The blinds are 200-400 with a 25 ante. There are 174 players left, and the tournament pays 153. The average stack is 10,000.

  Pre-flop (825): Near the bubble, I am opening up my raising range from middle position, and K-J easily falls in this new range. The action folds to me, and I raise two-and-a-half times the big blind to 1,000. Seat 7 and Seat 1 both call.

   Flop (3,625): I have flopped top pair on a relatively safe board, yet I must be concerned about my kicker. A-K and K-Q are legitimate hands with which my opponents may have called my raise. Although one should reraise with A-K in either of their positions given their stack sizes, I encounter plenty of players online who just call raises with A-K in similar situations, especially on the bubble. Seat 1 checks.

If I bet and get raised by either opponent, it will create a very complex decision. I could *three-bet* all-in, hoping my opponent is making a move; however, I would only get called by a stronger hand or perhaps a flush draw. Against most opponents, I should fold if I get raised, essentially turning my bet into a bluff. If I check, I disguise the strength of my hand and may be able to get value out of it from weaker hands on later streets. I may also induce a weaker hand to try to steal the pot. I check, and Seat 7 checks as well.

 Turn (3,625): This is an absolutely beautiful card! Although I still risk being dominated by A-K or K-Q, it is now highly unlikely, as both of my opponents showed weakness on the flop and I can now account for three of the kings. More important, it will be very difficult for my opponents to put me on such a strong hand, so the value I can get from my hand is greatly increased.

Seat 1 leads out for 2,000 into a 3,625 pot. Given the action behind him on the flop, Seat 1 may lead here with a wide range. If he has a pocket pair or an 8, he probably believes it to be the best hand. He may also be betting a flush draw, but most opponents who check flush draws on the flop continue with this action on the turn. It is also possible that I am beat by a K with a better kicker or a slow-played set; however, at this point, I am willing to go broke with my hand.

I could raise now, as I might get action from an opponent putting me on a steal, but I would risk scaring away my other opponents, especially due to their stack sizes and the bubble. Seat 1 has about 11,000 left after his bet, so if he faces a raise now, he would feel like he will be put to the test for all of his chips on the river. I do not want to give him that impression as it would probably scare him out of the pot, convincing him to fold on the turn. Therefore, the best option is just to call, feigning weakness, and wait until the river to get value from my hand. Calling might also induce Seat 7 into trying some tricky play or even calling with a middle pair. I call the 2,000 bet. Seat 7 folds.

 River (7,625): The flush draw hits, which is definitely not what I want to see. My opponent checks. I did not put him on the flush draw before, and his check on the river further convinces me that he has a middle pair. With 7,625 in the pot,

I must attempt to extract some value from my hand. My opponent has about 11,000, and my bet should be designed so as not to hurt my opponent too much. I want him to be able to make the call but not feel like his stack is crippled by it. A bet of approximately half the pot seems to be the most I could reasonably hope he would call with a middle pair. I bet 4,250. My opponent calls and mucks 8♥ 7♥.

Hand 35

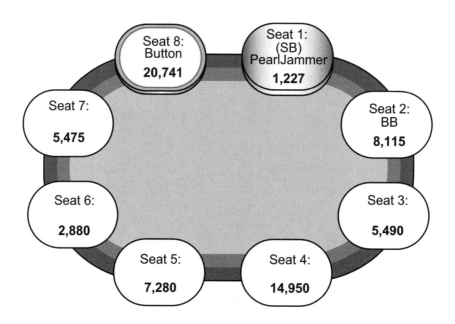

Setup: I am in the middle stages of a $100 freezeout, and I am extremely short-stacked with only 1,227 chips. The blinds are 200-400 with a 25 ante.

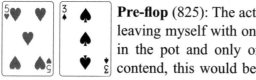 **Pre-flop** (825): The action folds to me. I could fold, leaving myself with only 1,002 chips, but with 825 in the pot and only one opponent with which to contend, this would be a very weak play. Winning the 825 in the pot would make such a difference to my stack that many players would argue that I should push all-in with any two cards. If I

were to push, my opponent would have to call only 802 more to win 1,827. He would be looking at 2.28-to-1 pot odds, and given my enormous range from the small blind, he should call every time. So let me assume that my opponent will call 100 percent of the time in this spot. I can also safely assume to be well behind this random hand the vast majority of the time.

There is a third option to employ to give myself one additional way to win this pot. I could limp and then shove on the flop regardless of the board! Since I know I am getting called if I shove all-in pre-flop, and I expect to be well behind a random hand, why not give myself my only shot at winning without a showdown by limping in? If I limp and my opponent shoves, I will get the same odds as he would get if I had shoved, so I would naturally make the call with the 5-3. However, if my opponent checks, I will get the chance to shove all-in on the flop for 802 into a 1,025 pot. If he whiffs the flop, he might fold! Note that there is a pretty good chance he will fold whenever he whiffs since he most likely would have pushed pre-flop with A-x or K-x. I complete from the small blind for 200, and my opponent checks.

   Flop (1,025): Although I whiffed the flop, I will stick with my pre-flop plan. I shove all-in for 802 chips. My opponent folds!

I like to call this play the "limp and go," which is a variation of the "stop and go." The "stop and go" is where you call a pre-flop raise, knowing you will be the first to act post-flop. Then, on the flop, you move all-in, regardless of the flop, hoping your opponent missed and will fold. This play is most often used when you would have little chance of your opponent folding pre-flop if you were to reraise him all-in, because he would be pot-committed. The "limp and go" is basically the same concept, except that you are limping into the pot pre-flop rather than calling a raise.

Hand 36

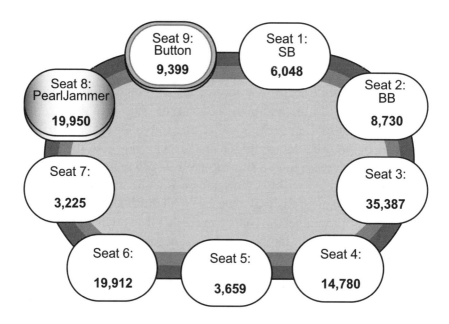

Setup: It is the middle stages of a $10 rebuy, $15K guaranteed tournament. The blinds are 200-400 with a 50 ante. I am unfamiliar with my opponents but expect much of the play to be weak and somewhat predictable in a very low buy-in tournament.

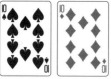 **Pre-flop** (1,050): Seat 4 raises three times the big blind from early position to 1,200. Seat 7 then moves all-in for 3,175. The action is on me in the cutoff.

With a hand as strong as TT, I am certainly willing to gamble against Seat 7's short stack of only 3,175. After all, his M[3] is only 3, so he should be very desperate to get his money into the pot with any reasonable holding. However, I have to reassess the situation because his all-in move is over the top of an early-position raise. Seat 7 should still be moving in with

---

[3] M is the ratio of your stack to the current total of blinds and antes, representing the cost of playing one full orbit. M and its implications were popularized in the book *Harrington on Hold'em Volume II*, by Dan Harrington and Bill Robertie.

any pair, probably 77 or above, or any two strong broadway cards, A-J, K-Q, or better. I should be willing to gamble against this range. Seat 4's potential holding is of more concern.

I have no information on Seat 4 except that his hand is strong enough to raise from early position. He is equally likely to have a higher or lower pair than mine. He also could be raising with a very wide range of broadway hands. I am probably ahead of him more often than I am behind. However, if I move all-in or reraise to approximately 7,000, isolating Seat 7, I would essentially be risking three-quarters of my stack against Seat 4. I would not expect Seat 4 to call (or move all-in over the top of my reraise) unless he had a higher pocket pair or perhaps A-K, but if he does wake up with one of those premium pairs, I would be crippled. If I do force him to fold, my reward will be a coin flip against Seat 7 with a little bit of dead money in the pot. There is not enough potential upside to risk endangering my stack.

I have determined that it is not worth moving all-in or reraising, but is cold-calling Seat 7's all-in an option? If I call, Seat 4 will probably only move all-in with pairs that have me beaten or with A-K. However, if he has one of these hands and pushes, I will be forced to fold. Even if he chooses to just call the all-in as well, I will probably have to hold up against three or four overcards between both Seat 4 and Seat 7. I have position, but it would be difficult to continue with the hand post-flop if any overcards hit the board. Cold-calling Seat 7's all-in is essentially a spew. Therefore, I choose to take the safe route and fold.

Seat 4 calls and shows A♠ J♠. Seat 7 shows A♣ Q♦. The board comes K♠ Q♣ 9♥ 6♠ 7♣, and Seat 7 wins with a pair of queens.

This is a marginal situation where I see a lot of players shove their stack in with TT. At times, this can help them build a large stack if the original raiser calls off with A-K and they win a coin flip. However, it will also unnecessarily bust them from many tournaments at an early stage. When faced with an early position raiser with a similar large stack, I will usually choose to err on the side of caution and not risk my entire stack to isolate a short stack. Note that if I had a stack of about 8,000 or less in this same spot, I would be much more inclined to gamble!

Hand 37

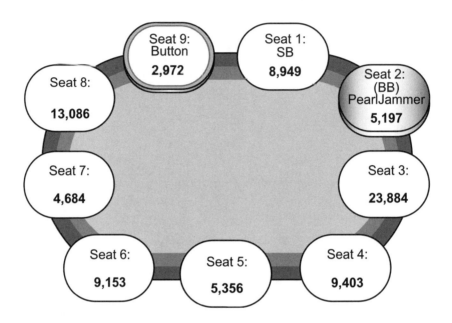

Setup: I am in the middle stages of a $150, $55K guaranteed freezeout, and I have a fairly short stack. The blinds are 200-400 with a 50 ante.

 **Pre-flop** (1,050): Facing an early-position raise, I would fold this hand with no second thought. However, the action is folded around to the button, a very strong, aggressive player with whom I have a lot of experience. This player also knows me to have a relatively tight range at calling off my chips. He is very short-stacked with just under 3,000, and shoves all-in from the button. The small blind folds.

I must assess the pot odds I would be getting to call his all-in and compare this to how often my hand would win against the range of hands that he would shove from the button. With the blinds, antes, and my opponent's bet, there is 3,972 in the pot, and it would cost me 2,522 to call, giving mc pot odds of 1.57-to-1. I would need to be getting at least 2-to-1 odds here to make this a call with virtually any two cards. Even if I were getting 2-to-1, I would usually fold offsuit hands like 9-2, 8-3, etc.

Although the pot odds would indicate calling against a very wide range with virtually any two cards, losing approximately half of my already short stack would cost me almost all of my *fold equity* for future hands. This would greatly decrease my chances of coming back without picking up very strong hands. Therefore, I must be confident that my opponent's range is wide enough to call with my K-7 suited and approximately 1.6-to-1 pot odds.

Based on previous experience with this opponent, I know that he is well aware of tournament dynamics. As a strong, aggressive player, he understands that with each round costing 1,050 and his stack under 3,000, he must look for any chance he can get to pick up chips without a showdown. With the action folded to him on the button, he would most likely raise with virtually any two cards. In order to accumulate chips, I should be willing to gamble and make this call, knowing that even if I am wrong in this instance, in the long run, my K-7 suited will be getting the proper pot odds.

I call his all-in, and he shows T♥ 4♦. The board comes 9♣ 6♣ 4♠ A♣ 3♠, and I make the nut flush, busting a strong opponent.

Hand 38

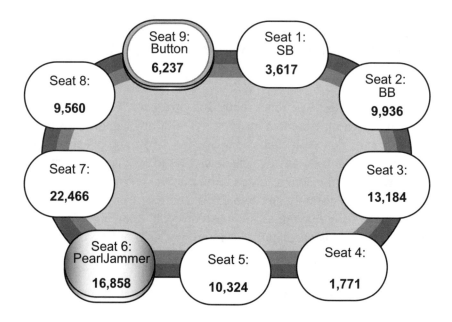

Setup: I am on the bubble of a $69 freezeout, and I have been opening a lot of pots, creating a very loose image. The blinds are 200-400 with a 50 ante.

 **Pre-flop** (1,050). The action folds to me, and I make my standard raise of slightly less than two-and-a-half times the big blind to 950. Seat 7 reraises to 3,333. The remaining players fold.

Seat 7 is the chip leader at the table and is probably aware that I have been opening plenty of pots and that we are on the bubble. I can safely assume that he is reraising me with a fairly wide range. Therefore, folding A-K in this spot is out of the question. I must decide whether to call and play a flop, reraise, or shove all-in.

If I call, I will miss the flop about two-thirds of the time. The pot would be almost 8,000, but with over 13,000 left, I would not be committed to it. However, because I know my opponent's range is wide, I risk getting bet off the best hand too often when I miss the flop.

The better play is to reraise. I am out of position, so my reraise should be to at least three times my opponent's bet. With less than 17,000 in my stack, if I reraise, I should just go ahead and move all-in since I am pot-committed. This bet will usually get my opponent to fold medium pocket pairs, TT through 77, as he would have to risk the majority of his stack in a spot where he might be dominated. It will likely move him off hands like A-Q, A-J, and K-Q as well, but given the bubble situation and my loose image, I may be fortunate enough to get a call from one of these hands, which may well double me up. I shove all-in, and my opponent folds.

Note that A-K is a good hand with which to go all-in when the stack sizes are right. The only hand against which I am in major trouble is AA, and it's less likely that my opponents hold AA given that I have one ace in my hand. If my opponent calls with a pair QQ or lower, I am just a very slight underdog. Even against KK, A-K will win about 30% of the time. In other words, you rarely go wrong by pushing A-K when the stack sizes are relatively small.

I did not manage to get the most ideal result from my play, a call from a dominated hand. However, I did pick up 4,383 chips without having to see a flop, increasing my stack by over 25 percent!

Hand 39

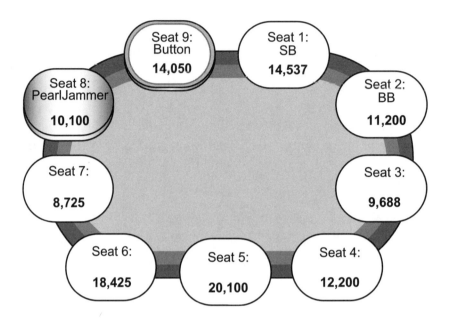

Setup: It is the early stages of a major $500, $1 million guaranteed Sunday tournament where I began with 10,000 in chips. The blinds are 300-600. Seats 3 and 7 are very strong players. Seat 6 has become my target, as he is playing too many hands and I have excellent position on him. He has called me down with very marginal hands twice, once picking off my bluff and once helping me build my stack back up.

 Pre-flop (900): The action folds to Seat 6, who open-raises to 1,450, just under two-and-a-half times the big blind, a rather typical raise in this tournament. Seat 7 folds, and the action is on me.

I rarely slow-play my big hands, as I risk letting opponents catch up too cheaply and can sometimes lose value when scare cards hit. However, this appears to be a good situation for me to get tricky and cold-call a raise pre-flop for several reasons. My history and experience with Seat 6 tells me that he is likely to pay me off if he hits any piece of the flop. Also, because of my stack size, any reraise will clearly commit me to the pot. Seat 6 is most likely raising with a marginal hand, looking to pick up the blinds, so any reraise should scare him out of the pot. Finally, by cold-calling, there is always a chance that I will induce a squeeze play from the button or one of the blinds. With 3,800 in the pot, if one of them picks up a medium to strong pocket pair or an A-Q or better (or perhaps worse, if they mistakenly sense an opportunity to pick up dead money), they may move all-in. However, if I reraise, I may scare them off unless they hold a premium pair or possibly A-K.

Since I will only have 8,650 chips left with which to play post-flop, I should have no problem getting all of the money in on the flop if my opponent hits any piece of it. If I had 20,000 in chips instead of my current stack, I would be putting myself in a much riskier situation with AA by not protecting my hand pre-flop. I call Seat 6's raise, and the remaining players fold.

   Flop (3,800): My opponent checks. On such an uncoordinated flop, I could check my aces behind my opponent. However, because he has called me down lightly before and rarely passes up an opportunity for a continuation bet, I sense that he will not give up on the pot if I bet. If he has nothing, he may be ready to make a move at the pot, hoping that I am weak. Of course, if he has a real hand, such as an unimproved pocket pair or top pair, I would like to get the money in now as a high turn card might scare him off.

I bet 1,850, approximately half the pot. This bet should create the impression of fold equity if my opponent wants to make a move, as it does not commit me to the pot. My opponent check-raises to 5,400, essentially putting me all-in. I move all-in for an additional 3,250, and he quickly calls with T♦ 9♦, drawing to five outs twice. My opponent hits trips on the turn and takes down the pot.

My slow-play essentially knocks me out of the tournament, as my opponent would certainly have folded if I had reraised pre-flop. However, I got the money in with the best hand on the flop, and should not be dejected at my misfortune. I should not let the final result of the hand discourage me from reasoning through similar situations in the future and making similar plays.

Hand 40

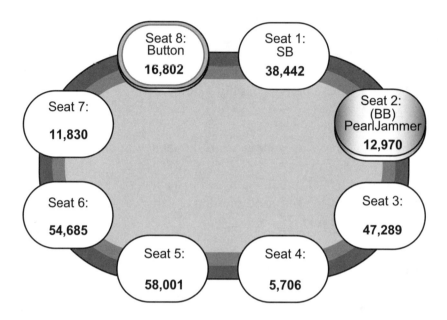

Setup: I am in the middle stages of a $100 rebuy tournament. The rebuy period is long over, and the blinds are 300-600 with a 50 ante. My stack is below average, yet I still have room to maneuver with an M of almost 13. Seat 3 is a very strong, tricky player who usually plays a loose-aggressive style but has the ability to switch gears. The rest of the players are relatively unknown.

  Pre-flop (1,300): Seat 3, under-the-gun, raises to 1,600. Seat 1 calls from the small blind, and the action is on me. There is 4,200 in the pot, and it would cost me only 1,000 to see a flop with my suited one-gapper. I do not often call raises with speculative hands this deep into tournaments; however, my knowledge of Seat 3's range and the improved pot odds from Seat 1's call entice me to see the flop. I make the call and see the flop three-handed.

Flop (5,200): I flop middle pair on a draw-heavy board. Seat 1 checks. I could lead out into the pre-flop raiser; however, since I know him to be aggressive, he may come over the top with a very wide range, putting me to the test. I would rather check to him, allowing him to take the lead, as he is almost certain to make a continuation bet regardless of his hand. I check, and Seat 3 bets 2,985, approximately half the pot. Seat 1 calls.

My first instinct should be to fold, as I expect one or both of my opponents have at least top pair. However, there are several factors at play that all point toward a different conclusion and persuade me to make a play at this pot. First of all, Seat 3 is a strong, aggressive player whose range for raising under-the-gun is very wide. I can assume he is raising with any pocket pair, strong broadway hands, many suited connectors, and many suited aces. He could have a strong hand on this flop, but it is very likely that he is making a standard continuation bet. My estimate is that I beat at least 50 percent of his range. Even if he has me outkicked with A-J, K-J, or J-T, it would be very difficult for him to call a check-raise with Seat 1 still left to act.

Seat 1's hand is a bit of an enigma. His call on the flop may represent a draw on such a draw-heavy board, yet it is certainly possible that he has a made hand. Also, both of my opponents are deep-stacked, a factor that increases each of their ranges.

The pot of roughly 11,000 would make an enormous difference to my stack, increasing it by over 100 percent. I am not certain that I have the best hand, and I would be risking my tournament life by moving all-in, but given my analysis of my opponents' potential holdings, this seems like a gamble worth taking. If I run into a big hand, I will probably still have five outs twice.

I check-raise all-in for an additional 8,335. Seat 3 folds, and Seat 1 calls, showing T♠ 9♠ for an open-ended straight draw and a backdoor-flush draw. The 6♦ and 4♣ fall on the board and I almost triple my stack!

Hand 41

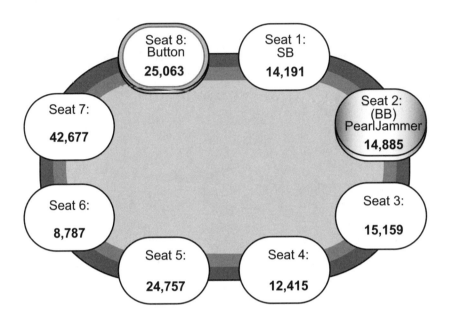

Setup: I am nearing the bubble in a $200 major Sunday tournament. The blinds are 300-600 with a 75 ante. There are 161 players left, 90 spots pay, and the average stack is 16,000. I know none of the players at my table.

 **Pre-flop** (1,500): Seat 3 limps in under-the-gun. The action folds to the small blind, who completes. I must now decide whether to raise with my middle pair or just check it and take a flop with a relatively strong, disguised hand. I am not worried about the small blind completing, but the under-the-gun limper poses a threat. I have not seen this player limp before, and have no way of knowing if he is relatively weak or limping in with a monster looking to trap.

If I raise from the big blind, I should raise approximately four times the big blind to about 2,400. However, if I raise and the limper moves all-in, I will probably fold my hand. I would have to assume he is very strong and with no further information, my hand becomes a clear fold. I would put him on a range of AA through JJ and A-K with only a small chance that he limped in with a lower pocket pair and got out of line, hoping to push me off a big hand. If my opponent does not move all-in, he is likely to fold lower pocket pairs but probably call with overcards. Thus I would push out the hands that I dominate and be forced to play a big pot post-flop, out of position against unknown overcards. It is therefore likely that I would only get action post-flop from hands that beat me, unless I am fortunate enough to flop a 10 and have him hit one of his overcards or pick up a big draw.

Another option is to move all-in pre-flop, which would increase my stack by 17% if successful or perhaps double me up if the limper calls me with overcards and I win a race. However, he would probably only call with higher pocket pairs and A-K, a range against which TT is in bad shape. I choose to check and take a flop.

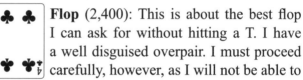 **Flop** (2,400): This is about the best flop I can ask for without hitting a T. I have a well disguised overpair. I must proceed carefully, however, as I will not be able to get all of my chips in on this flop and get action from a worse hand. Seat 1 checks, and the action is on me. Leading out seems reasonable as I may get action from a 9 or a straight draw if Seat 1 has checked such a hand. It is unlikely, however, that Seat 3 has a 9 or a draw on this board given his early-position limp. If he raises on the flop, I would be put in a very tough spot and would probably be forced to fold, as I could only beat a bluff. Yet Seat 3 will probably bet this flop, representing strength, whether he is strong or not. Therefore, I check. Seat 3 bets 1,800, and Seat 1 folds.

Before I get too excited that the limper has bet just as I expected, and check-raise him, I should consider what this will accomplish. There is currently 4,200 in the pot, so if I were to take the pot down now, it would substantially increase my stack. However, if I check-raise, I will only get action if Seat 3 has me beaten! His range is most likely any pocket pair, AA through 22 and several broadway hands. If I check-raise, he will give me action with higher pocket pairs and sets but most likely fold unimproved broadway hands and low pocket pairs. Therefore, the only value in check-raising is in trying to win the pot right now without letting my opponent improve.

If I had about 8,000 or less, moving all-in now would probably be the preferred play given my stack's potential increase. However, with 14,000, I should not risk my tournament life at this point in the hopes that I might have the best hand. Yet my hand is certainly too strong to fold. I am better off calling my opponent's bet and re-evaluating based on his action on the turn. I call.

 Turn (6,000): Even though this card would improve my opponent's hand if he had a 9, I am not concerned as it is very unlikely that he limped in with a 9. At this stage of the tournament, few opponents will ever open-limp with hands such as A-9 or T-9s, especially from under-the-gun. If my opponent has me dominated with an overpair, this card may actually stop him from betting and save me money in a pot in which I otherwise would have lost my stack. For the same reasons that I did not check-raise on the flop, I should check to my opponent now. I check, and my opponent checks.

 River (6,000): With my opponent's check on the turn and a rag hitting on the river, I should now bet for value. The turn card may have scared my opponent into checking an overpair. However, if I bet now on the river, he would probably just call with such a hand, as he would be scared to raise. If my opponent is sitting on an overpair, by betting only half the pot I might save some chips, *blocking* my opponent from making a bigger bet that I would probably have to call.

What is more likely is that my opponent has an unimproved broadway hand or a lower pocket pair rather than an overpair. He might pay me off with either of these hands as he could easily put me on a missed straight draw on this board. T-8 and 8-6 are both reasonable hands for my opponent to put me on. On the other hand, he should be wary of 6-5 or any 9, also reasonable calling hands on the flop, which would have improved to very strong hands by the river. Nonetheless, I should bet my hand for value, with the additional benefit that it serves as a blocking bet if my opponent does indeed have a higher pocket pair.

I bet 3,250, about half of the 6,000 pot. My opponent calls and mucks 5♦ 5♥.

Hand 42

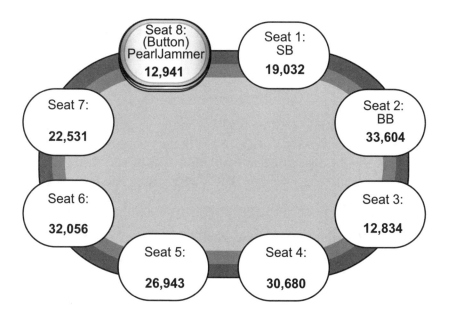

Setup: I am on the bubble in a $200 Sunday tournament with well below the average stack, which is 26,000. 94 players remain with 81 paid, and the blinds are 500-1,000 with a 125 ante. Seat 1 and Seat 4 are both extremely strong, aggressive opponents, and I have had trouble finding spots to pick up chips at this table. I have open-raised twice in the last few orbits with marginal hands, only to be forced to fold to reraises. Although I am playing to win, not to cash, I am very much aware that I need to double up very soon or risk blinding out before making the money.

Pre-flop (2,500): The action folds to me. With 2,500 in the pot and such a strong hand on the button, I am certainly willing to risk my tournament life with this hand given my small stack size. With an M of about five, moving all-in would be a very reasonable move, not an overbet. However, before I shove in my stack, I should consider my table image and how I can best induce action with my hand.

If I had moved all-in once or twice at recent opportunities, then I should continue with the trend and move all-in here. After all, raising a different, somewhat small amount should announce to my opponents that I want action! However, because I have twice raised my standard two-and-a-half times the big blind and then folded to reraises in recent orbits, I should continue with this trend and open for the same amount. My opponents may view this raise as just another steal attempt and apply pressure as they have before.

Because I am in prime stealing position on the button rather than early position, the relative value of my A-Qs is improved dramatically. My opponents should expect me to open-raise with a very wide range in this spot. I wish to induce action with such a strong hand, not scare my opponents away.

I raise to 2,500, and Seat 1 in the small blind moves all-in for 18,907. The big blind folds, and I call. Seat 1 shows K♥ Q♥. The board comes J♥ 7♠ 6♣ 5♠ 8♥. My ace high holds up to win, doubling me up at a crucial time!

Note that if I had moved all-in with my A-Q, the small blind likely would have folded his hand. Because he had seen me raise and fold recently with a similar stack, he thought that it was worth the risk to try to move me off my hand with a relatively strong hand himself. However, if I had moved all-in, his only options would have been to fold or call off two-thirds of his stack on the bubble with K high. As he is a strong, experienced player, I could reasonably assume that he would lay down K-Q to an all-in shove in this spot.

Hand 43

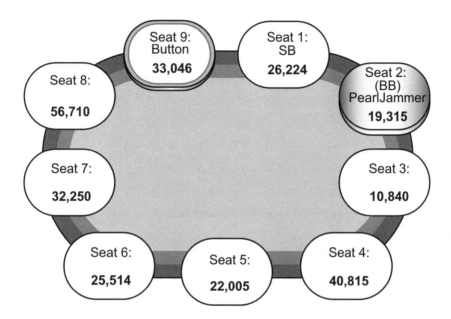

Setup: It is the middle stages of a $10 rebuy, $55K guaranteed tournament. The blinds are 500-1,000 with a 100 ante. There are 611 players left and 270 spots pay. The average stack is 26,000. I am not familiar with anyone at my table, but I can assume most players are weak in such a low buy-in tournament with a large field.

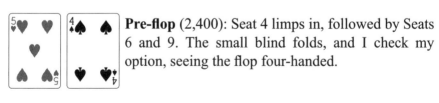

Pre-flop (2,400): Seat 4 limps in, followed by Seats 6 and 9. The small blind folds, and I check my option, seeing the flop four-handed.

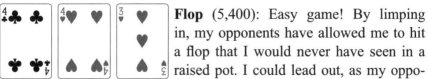

Flop (5,400): Easy game! By limping in, my opponents have allowed me to hit a flop that I would never have seen in a raised pot. I could lead out, as my opponents would probably not expect me to lead out with trip fours on the flop. However, this would certainly kill any potential action if my opponents have all limped in with unpaired broadway cards or high suited connectors. If at least one opponent has an overpair, I will probably get action by leading out; however, an opponent with an overpair will likely bet anyway if I check. I much prefer to lead out on a K-4-4 or A-4-4 flop than on this flop, as my opponents would be much more likely to have connected on those flops. I check, not minding that I may be given a free card but hoping that I will induce a bet.

Seat 4 leads out for 5,000 into a pot of 5,400. Seats 6 and 9 fold, and the action is back to me. With his bet of almost the full pot after limping in early position, I am very confident that Seat 4 has an overpair. His only other plausible hand would be a flush draw; however, his early-position limp and his bet size both seem to indicate that he limped with a pocket pair that he is now trying to protect.

My options now are to reraise or flat-call. If I reraise based on my stack and the size of the pot, then my raise would be all-in. This bet may allow my opponent to get away from his hand. Flat-calling my opponent's bet would probably give away my hand against a strong opponent, but based on his early-position limp and the size of his bet, I can assume that my opponent is a weak player. By flat-calling, I will try to convince my opponent that I have a flush draw, or perhaps if he is a really weak player, he may put me on a 3. I call.

 Turn (15,400): Normally when I call a bet out of position, I will check to the bettor on the next card. This, however, is an excellent spot to lead into the bettor! If I check, I risk my opponent checking behind. I have 13,215 left, and if no money goes in on the turn, my opponent may be able to fold for a 13,000 bet on the river, especially if a heart hits. I want to ensure that money goes into the pot on the turn. By leading out with a very small bet, my opponent will probably be incapable of folding any pair. This will allow my all-in bet on the river to be a smaller bet into a larger pot than it would be if we had both checked the turn. Also, my lead may induce my opponent to raise, putting me on a flush draw or a 3. I bet 3,650.

My opponent raises to 17,300, enough to put me all-in. I call, and my opponent shows 8♦ 8♣. The 3♣ hits the river, and I win with a full house.

Hand 44

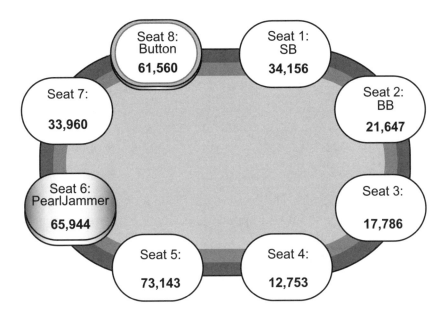

Setup: It is near the bubble of a $10 rebuy, $55K guaranteed tournament. I have been opening a lot of pots, but have only shown down big hands. The blinds are 500-1,000 with a 100 ante.

  Pre-flop (2,300): It is folded around to me, and I raise to just under two-and-a-half times the big blind to 2,400, my standard raise. The cutoff folds, the button calls, and both blinds fold.

 **Flop** (7,100): I could make a continuation bet with this flop, but being out of position, I decide to try to keep the pot small by checking and letting my opponent take the lead. I would be happy to see my opponent check behind, after which I would lead out for about half the pot on any turn, given his show of weakness. However, if he bets small, I will happily call and see a turn card, as I have a very well disguised double belly-buster draw. We are both deep-stacked, so if I hit, I could win a very big pot. Mixing up my

play by passing on an opportunity to lead with a continuation bet might also help lend more credibility to my continuation bets in future hands.

My opponent bets 3,000 into a 7,100 pot. His bet is small, leaving his hand range very wide. He could be betting any pair, even low pocket pairs, trying to take the pot away cheaply. He might also have a draw, perhaps as weak as a gutshot. Although it is much less likely than one pair, he might even have a set and be trying to induce a check-raise with a weak bet. I figure A-K, K-Q, and K-J are all unlikely as he would probably protect those with a bigger bet; and in the case of A-K, he would probably have reraised pre-flop. I call, welcoming the opportunity to chase a disguised draw cheaply.

 Turn (13,100): The 2♠ isn't what I am looking for. I check, as I rarely lead into an opponent to whom I have given control of the hand.

My opponent bets 4,000 into a 13,100 pot. I could just call here and chase my draw as I certainly have proper implied odds to do so. However, I would have virtually no chance of winning the pot if I were to call and miss my draw. My opponent's bet seems to scream weakness. First, he made a rather small bet on the flop and then bet less than one-third of the pot on a draw-heavy board; two flush draws and several straight draws are all present. Players with strong hands on boards where there are lots of draws will generally try to protect their hands by betting an amount closer to the pot size.

If I were to check-raise here, I could represent having slow-played a very big hand. My opponent could put me on a set or A-K, as these hands would certainly make sense from the line I have taken. More important, if my opponent does not have at least a strong king himself, he is very likely to give up on the pot. With my deep stack and the threat of a large bet on the river, I may also scare my opponent off a hand as strong as K-J or A-9.

I check-raise to 11,500. My opponent thinks long enough that he times out and then folds. His long thought leads me to believe that he folded a middle pocket pair or perhaps a 9 or a weak king. It is very likely that he would have called my small check-raise with any draw, and if he had complete air, he probably would have folded fairly quickly. Note the small size of my check-raise.   I was able to win a 17,100 pot while risking only 11,500.

Hand 45

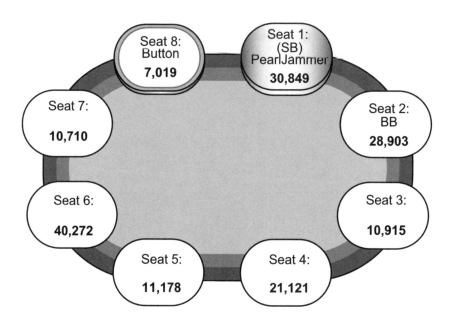

Setup: I am near the bubble of a $50, $50K guaranteed freezeout with blinds of 500-1,000 and a 100 ante. There are 172 players left with 153 spots paid. The average stack is 20,000. I am new to the table and have no information on any players.

  Pre-flop (2,300): Seat 6 opens for 2,680, a fairly standard opening raise at this stage in the tournament. The cutoff and the button fold, and the action is on me. I have 30 big blinds in my stack, and my opponent has more chips.

I must reraise as I should not look to trap a fellow deep-stacked opponent this late into the tournament, especially when I would be forced to play the rest of the hand out of position. Ideally, I would like to get all of my money into the pot pre-flop with such a strong hand. However, shoving all-in here as a reraise would not be practical as most opponents would fold all but AA, QQ, A-K, and perhaps JJ to such a bet.

Instead of shoving, I should reraise to approximately three times my opponent's bet. My goal is to induce my opponent to make a mistake, either by calling my reraise or by reraising again himself. If my opponent simply calls, I am ready to commit myself to the pot unless an ace flops. I reraise to 6,950, leaving almost 24,000 behind.

The big blind folds, and Seat 6 reraises all-in for 40,172. I call, and he shows 6♥ 6♠. The board comes K♣ Q♦ T♠ A♦ Q♠. I win the pot with a full house, doubling my stack!

Note that my opponent would have certainly folded his hand if I had reraised by moving all-in pre-flop. It is likely that he would have also folded if I had reraised much larger, thereby appearing to commit myself to the pot. The key to inducing my opponent to shove all-in in this spot is to appear to leave myself with plenty of room to get away from my hand. My opponent may try to bully me with his big stack if he believes that he has fold equity. This is especially true since we are near the bubble and I will not call off my chips pre-flop without a premium hand.

Hand 46

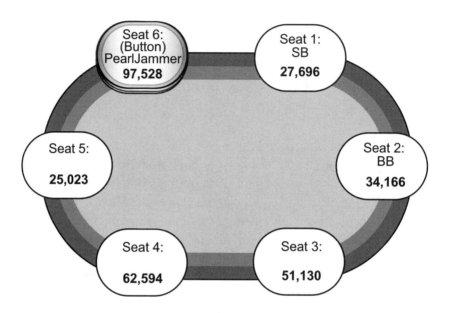

Setup: I am on the bubble of a $30 rebuy, $16K guaranteed tournament. The blinds are 800-1,600 with a 200 ante. There are 20 players left and 18 spots are paid. The average stack is 47,000, and I am second in chips. I have been at the table only a couple of orbits during which I have open-raised a few times but not yet reraised anyone pre-flop. I know Seat 1 and Seat 3 to be strong players, but I am not familiar with the other players.

 **Pre-flop** (3,600): Seat 4 open-raises to 3,825, a little less than two-and-a-half times the big blind but a very standard raise at this point of the tournament. The cutoff folds, and the action is on me. In most tournament situations, I would toss A-6 offsuit into the muck without thinking twice; however, this spot is almost tailor-made for a re-steal! Let's look at the factors that lead me toward taking a shot at this pot.

Given that we are right on the bubble, most players will not want to take any unnecessary risks with their chips. This is precisely why I should be looking for opportunities to attack and accumulate! Also, the table is playing short-handed because of the number of players left in the tournament. Many players are not accustomed to short-handed play; however, most are aware that they need to loosen up their opening range. In this case, Seat 4 is relatively deep-stacked, so at a six-handed table, I can assume that he is opening with a very wide range. However, he should not want to play a pot against an opponent who has him covered when he is out of position without an extremely strong hand.

Also note that my opponents have not seen me reraise pre-flop a single time at this table. Once I have done this a few times, I can expect more alert opponents to play back at me with a rather wide range. But for now, my image should give me plenty of credibility. There is no reason for my opponents to doubt the strength of my hand. Finally, with the blinds, antes, and my opponent's raise, there is 7,425 already in the pot, and a relatively small reraise to approximately 10,000 should be enough to get the fold I want.

I only have to be successful 57% of the time to break even on the steal. Given my opponent's wide opening range and his narrow calling range (or reraising range), I can expect him to fold at least 80 percent of the time here. Of the times that he calls, I will have position and be able to gauge whether or not a continuation bet should work from the texture of the flop. Of course, once in a while, I will actually hit the flop hard as well!

The biggest risk in making this re-steal is that one of the blinds could wake up with a big hand and move all-in. However, given the action in front of them, they should assume that either I, or Seat 4, or perhaps both of us have a very strong hand! They would need an absolute monster to play, probably JJ or better or A-K, especially since we are on the bubble.

Having an ace in my hand adds a bit of value as it makes it slightly less likely that any of my opponents have an ace with a strong kicker. On the other hand, I would prefer to have some sort of suited connector or perhaps a low pocket pair when making this play. In this case, if I am called, I will at least have the chance to make a very strong, completely disguised hand on the flop. Observe that in this particular spot, though, my cards hardly matter. A re-steal should be profitable with virtually any two cards!

I raise to 9,750, and everyone folds.

Hand 47

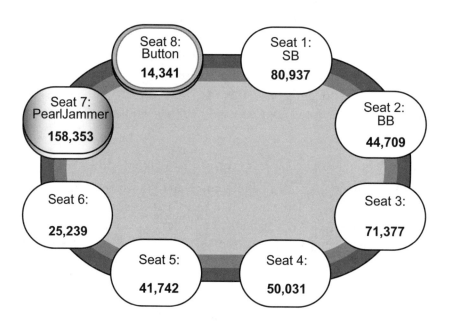

Setup: I am on the bubble of a $100 rebuy tournament. The blinds are 1,000-2,000 with a 200 ante. There are 40 players left, 36 spots pay, and the average stack is 58,000. Even though I am among the chip leaders, I believe that I have a relatively tight image based on things said in the chat box and on not having been involved in many pots lately. I am familiar with Seats 1 and 2 and know that they are strong, loose-aggressive players, capable of moves and thinking on a high level, especially on the bubble of a relatively high buy-in tournament.

Pre-flop (4,600): It is folded to me. I am aware that Seats 1 and 2 in the blinds are capable of playing back at me, and therefore I am not raising with as wide a range as my stack and the bubble may suggest. However, in this position, both players will be forced to play out of position if they choose to play. My hand is certainly strong enough to steal from this position, and my relatively tight image should garner a bit of respect.

I see that Seat 8 on the button is very short-stacked. If he moves all-in over the top of my raise, I do not mind calling such a low percentage of my stack with a reasonable hand. I raise to 4,850, just under two-and-a-half times the big blind, my standard raise at this point. Seats 8 and 1 fold, but Seat 2 defends from the big blind.

 Flop (12,300): I have completely missed this flop. Despite this, I should not give up on the hand, especially because we are on the bubble and I can apply pressure to a player who is just below the average stack. My opponent checks. My first instinct should be to make a continuation bet, using the bubble as extra leverage to get my opponent to fold. However, my opponent is a high-level player, certainly not a pushover, and he expects me to throw out a continuation bet almost 100 percent of the time. He may choose to check-raise or move all-in with any pair or perhaps the naked A or K of diamonds. Any check-raise of a continuation bet would commit him to the pot. Basically, if he gives me any action on the flop, I will be done with the hand. Therefore, I decide to throw him a curveball by checking the flop.

 Turn (12,300): My opponent bets 8,000. There are now four diamonds on the board, and my hand is complete trash. However, my opponent is very capable of making moves and knows that if I do not have a diamond, I cannot call his bet. Also, by checking the flop, I could easily represent having taken a free card with a big diamond! If I call or raise and my opponent does not have the A or K of diamonds, he will certainly suspect that I have one of them. Moreover, I expect my opponent is bluffing in this spot more often than not, because he has to have one specific card (or perhaps one of two) to be content with his hand.

If I raise, I will lose a lot of chips if I am in fact running into a monster. However, by just calling, I risk fewer chips and can use my position on the river to take the pot away if my opponent shows weakness! Just calling (i.e., floating the turn) also may be more convincing in this spot than raising, as my opponent is much more likely to view a raise as a potential bluff than a call.

Also note that the only potentially scary river would be one that pairs the board. In the unlikely event that my opponent has a set, he will obviously feel very confident in his hand on the river if the board pairs. He would almost certainly lead out with a full house on the river because he would want, and expect, to get action from a big flush. If he leads out on an unpaired river, I plan to fold anyway, as he would likely only do this with the A or maybe K of diamonds. Even if he has top pair now, he could not possibly think it is good once I call on the turn. Therefore, unless he has a big diamond in his hand now, my call should lead him to believe that his hand is worthless. I call 8,000.

 River (28,300): This river does not change anything, and my opponent checks. I called on the turn just to take the pot away on the river, so I will do just that. I want to make my bet appear like a value bet. However, I should not make it so small that my opponent is tempted to make a cheap Hero call. I should also not make it too big so that I don't risk too much of my stack in the rare case that my opponent is trapping me on the river. I bet 16,500 into a pot of 28,300, and my opponent folds.

Hand 48

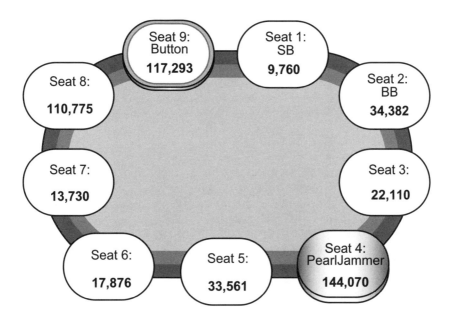

Setup: I am on the bubble of a major Sunday $200 freezeout. There are 902 players remaining, and 900 spots are paid. The blinds are 1,500-3,000 with a 300 ante. I am not familiar with any players at my table, and I have the chip lead at the table.

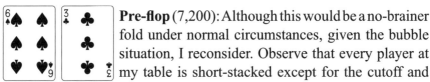 **Pre-flop** (7,200): Although this would be a no-brainer fold under normal circumstances, given the bubble situation, I reconsider. Observe that every player at my table is short-stacked except for the cutoff and the button. If I were opening in late position, I would have to worry about those players playing back at me, but when I raise from early position, they will most likely fold anything but premium hands such as TT+, A-K, and A-Q. Just like the short stacks, they do not want to make a big mistake on the bubble against the one player at the table who has them covered.

If there were less than 900 players left in the tournament, I would not consider raising in this spot, as there are many short stacks that could take a stand with a very wide range of hands. However, since I am right on the bubble, these short stacks are most likely content to survive until the bubble is burst. With 7,200 in the pot, and my standard raise of two-and-a-half times the big blind to 7,500 sufficient to take down the pot pre-flop, I am getting such a good return on my steal investment that I should be open-raising at every instance where I reasonably expect to win the pot. I raise to 7,500 and everyone folds.

Hand 49

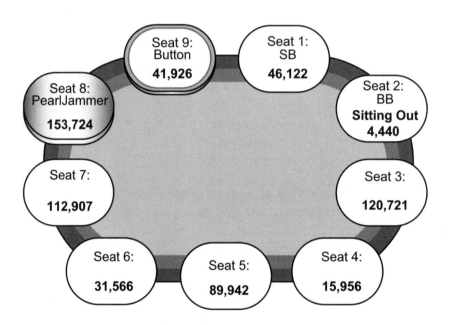

Setup: I am near the bubble of a $10 rebuy tournament with a $55K guarantee. The blinds are 2,000-4,000 with a 400 ante. There are 257 players left, and 225 places are paid. The average stack is 60,000. I have just been moved to a new table, and I am not familiar with any of my opponents.

Pre-flop (9,600): The action folds to Seat 7, who raises three times the big blind to 12,000. Before I muck my hand as I normally would with such a trash hand, I should evaluate the situation.

Like me, Seat 7 is deep-stacked with about 100,000 left after his opening raise. Given his position and his stack, I can expect him to open with a very wide range. I also note that Seat 2, the big blind, is sitting out! If Seat 2 were present, I would not consider a re-steal with such a weak hand, as he would clearly be committed to the pot. However, unforeseen circumstances can arise when playing online, and he may have been drawn away from the computer by an emergency or simply because he is having Internet connection issues. Nonetheless, his absence makes his big blind a prime target from which to steal. Seat 7 is certainly aware that Seat 2 is sitting out, and therefore I can assume that he has widened his range even more than usual.

Unless he has a premium hand with which he feels he should re-push all-in, I can assume that Seat 7 will probably not want to play a pot for a reraise out of position. I can also assume that Seats 9 and 1 will not want to play for their entire stacks unless they have extremely strong hands. They must be concerned about both Seat 7 and me having very strong hands in front of them, and it is clear that I will be committed to the pot against either of them if they were to push all-in.

A reraise to approximately two-and-a-half times Seat 7's bet is enough to give the appearance of strength but not commit myself if Seat 7 were to re-shove. I will risk approximately 30,000 to increase my stack by 21,600, an excellent risk-reward ratio given the circumstance. I reraise to 29,500 and everyone folds.

Hand 50

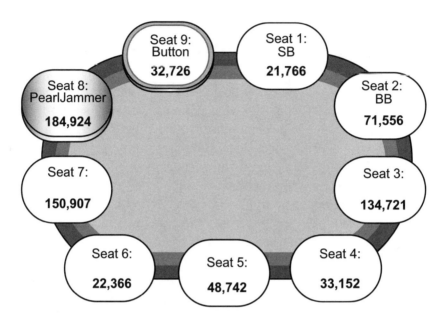

Setup: This is the same tournament as in the previous hand. The blinds are still 2,000-4,000 with a 400 ante. There are now only 235 players left, and 225 places are paid. The average stack is 65,000. I am not familiar with any of my opponents, but the table is playing very tight overall as most players seem content to survive until the money.

 Pre-flop (9,600): The action is folded to me. With a dominating big stack on the bubble, I do not need much of a hand to open-raise in this position; J-8s is certainly good enough to take a shot at the blinds. With 9,600 in the pot, my standard raise of 9,500 gives me an incredible risk-reward ratio, allowing me to profitably open up with a very wide range. I raise to 9,500. The button and the small blind fold, but the big blind calls. My raise of less than two-and-a-half times the big blind encourages more people to protect from the big blind than a larger opening raise would; however, this allows me to use my post-flop skills and position to my advantage as well.

Flop (24,600): I have flopped a flush draw. My opponent checks. There is almost 25,000 in the pot, and my opponent has approximately 62,000 remaining. If I put in a standard continuation bet of about 13,000 to 15,000, I would be allowing my opponent to check-raise all-in with an ace or even a queen, as he might put me on a steal.

If I shove all-in instead, I will put my opponent to the test. He would have a nearly impossible call with a queen and a rather difficult one with just an ace. I do not expect him to have a hand as strong as A-K or A-Q, as most likely he would have shoved all-in pre-flop over the top of my raise with either of these. If he makes the call, I have about a 36 percent chance of winning the hand with my flush draw. However, most of the time, I expect my opponent will fold. I move all-in, forcing my opponent to risk his entire stack on the bubble to make the call. He folds.

Eric "Rizen" Lynch

Hand 51

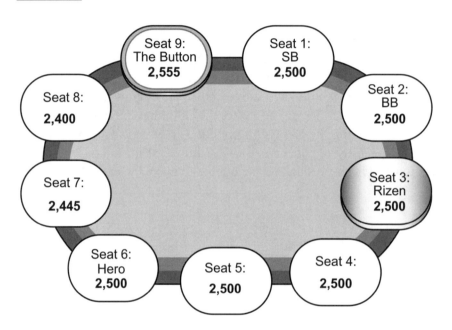

Setup: It is very early in one of the major Sunday $200 tournaments filled with satellite players. The blinds are only 5-10. The big blind at this particular table is a very good, very tight player. He's capable of making some moves post-flop, but is fairly tight and conventional pre-flop.

 **Pre-flop** (15): Tens can be very tricky to play deep-stacked and out of position post-flop in a nine-handed game, but it is still a premium hand worthy of raising. However, it's best to proceed with caution post-flop if you encounter much resistance. I raise to 35, and it is folded to the small blind, who calls. The big blind makes it 160. Given my read on the big blind, it is very likely he has a big hand. With stacks this deep, though, I can easily call the 125 into the 230 pot and try to hit my set. It is also likely that if I call, the small blind will come along as well,

creating an even better situation if I spike the set. I call the 125, and so does the small blind.

 Flop (480): This is one of the worst possible flops I could hit a set on. First off, I put the big blind on a big hand. Since he's a tight pre-flop player, I doubt he's raising JJ here, but AA is definitely part of his range as well as A-K, KK, and QQ. It's tough to put the small blind on a hand as well. The small blind checks, and so does the big blind. If I were heads up with the big blind, I would bet every time here, fully expecting him to have KK or QQ most of the time. On this board, if he had AA or A-K, I really doubt he would slow-play his hand given all the draws out there.

The small blind is a bit of a wild card, though, and if the big blind does have KK or QQ, he's drawing to six outs. In these Sunday tournaments, I tend to play a bit more conservatively early on these draw-heavy boards, and I would rather keep the pot under control on the flop than play a huge pot against a draw early. I also believe I have a really good handle on where the big blind is at, given our history. I check behind.

 Turn (480): If someone did have the spade draw, it just came in. The small blind leads for 70, an extremely small bet for this pot. The big blind flat-calls the 70, which now makes me feel quite confident he has either KK or QQ, as it makes almost no sense to raise to 160 pre-flop, check the flop, and call 70 on the flop with any other hands.

In my experience, a really small turn bet on this type of board is either a complete bluff, a made king-high flush (the nuts), or a dry K♠. Occasionally, it's scared money who tried to slow-play K-Q offsuit deciding to bet, now that he's scared of the flush. Either way, there are too many river cards I don't want to see to let my opponents get there cheaply. I don't want to see a spade (except the J♠), a king, or a queen. I raise to 525 to protect my hand.

If the small blind goes all-in, I am going to hate it, but I simply can't let my opponents have a cheap shot at outdrawing me here. Given the action so far, it's very unlikely the big blind is beating me, but the small blind probably doesn't know that and will feel "squeezed" by my raise since he has the big blind to act behind. This should prevent him from making any sort of crazy bluff all-in moves with a dry K♠ or something. The small blind folds, and the big blind folds, showing Q♣ Q♦ and confirming my read.

Hand 52

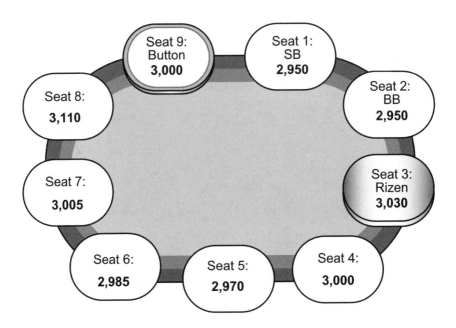

Setup: It is very early in a $300 weekly freezeout. The blinds are 10-20. This tournament has many satellite players but a lot of regulars, too. I haven't been at the table long enough to have gained any real reads on the other players. Some players at the table may recognize my name and reputation, though, and that may factor into their decisions.

 **Pre-flop** (30): Pocket nines is a solid hand, and with the blinds this low in relation to the stacks, both limping and raising are good options. Many players prefer to limp, but I prefer to raise because it gives my hand a lot of deceptive value when I hit. It also allows me to make continuation bets into many types of flops, as my raise implies

strength. I raise to 60, Seat 5 calls, and so does Seat 8 in the cutoff. The rest fold, and the flop is three-handed.

 **Flop** (210): For pocket nines, this is one of the better flops that doesn't have a nine in it. It definitely makes sense to go ahead and value-bet here. I bet 140, Seat 5 raises to 360, and the cutoff folds.

There are several dynamics to account for here: First, I raised from under-the-gun, which shows a lot of strength. Players typically pay a lot more respect to someone who raises from early position than someone who raises from a later position. This makes it much less likely that my opponents think I'm bluffing. Second, my opponent reraised with another player to act between him and me. This is another sign of strength from him, as he still has to worry about the cutoff having a hand. Finally, it is unlikely he called from early position with a hand like aces, kings, or queens; he isn't going to want to have to play those big pairs in a four- or five-player pot. Calling at these limits simply encourages action behind him, so it is unlikely he is sitting on a premium pair.

This narrows his likely range to a lot of pairs and suited connectors that play fairly well in multiway pots. This flop hits a lot of those hands very hard. If he has something like 7♣ 6♣ or 4♣ 3♣, I'm not very far ahead of him at all. If he has something like A♣ 4♣ or J♣ T♣, then I'm actually behind in terms of equity in the pot even if I am ahead at the moment with a made hand. I'm also WAY behind 88, 55, and 22. While it's possible he has something like A-8s, these types of hands do not make up a very big part of his range.

It's possible that I'm ahead; however, when I'm ahead, I am not very far ahead, and when I'm behind in this situation, I'm absolutely crushed. Additionally, I face the possibility of two progressively larger bets on the turn and river when I'm out of position. With the exception of a nine, there aren't many turn and river cards I'll be happy seeing. Having a seat this early in the tournament is worth a lot more than fighting over this small pot. I'd rather make a small mistake here by folding when I'm ahead than make a big mistake on those occasions when I am absolutely dominated and losing a very big pot. I decide to make the prudent fold.

Hand 53

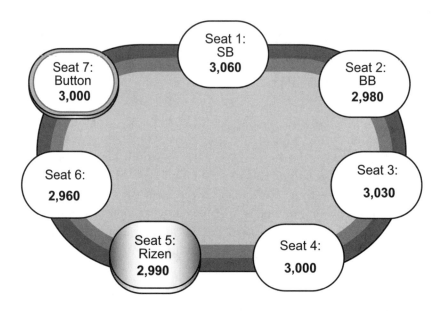

Setup: I have seen the first few hands of a $1,000 buy-in tournament with blinds of 10-20. The button in this hand is someone I've played with frequently. He is a pretty tight player and has lots of respect for my play, having made some big laydowns against me in the past.

  Pre-flop (30): This is not a great hand, but it's one worth playing if it's folded around and I can open the betting. It is folded to me, and I raise to 60, the button calls, and everyone else folds.

   Flop (150): This is a decent flop for top pair with the second-best kicker. Because I act first, betting here seems reasonable. I can't afford to give a free card with a board having two suited cards and a J-T for possible straight draws. I bet 100, and my opponent goes into the tank actually calling for his time bank before finally making a minimum raise to 200.

A minimum raise with this type of board is a very weird play. My initial thought is that he has some sort of flush or straight draw and he's trying to buy himself a cheap free card, hoping that I might just call the minimum raise and then check to him on the turn. This would be much cheaper for him than having to call a (probably) bigger bet on the turn if he just calls my flop bet. If that's the case, the standard line with these stacks against an opponent who has position is to go ahead and call and lead on the turn with any card that doesn't complete the draw. The problem on this board is that I don't know if he has a flush draw, a straight draw, or some combination thereof. Also, as a thinking player who respects my play, he could have a monster hand, knowing that I'll spot the weakness in his raise and potentially attack it. There are too many turn cards I don't like, and the pot is still relatively small in relation to our stacks.

In addition, even if I am ahead, it's not by much and I am out of position. I make the prudent play by folding what might be the best hand, rather than play a big pot out of position with absolutely no clue where I am.

Hand 54

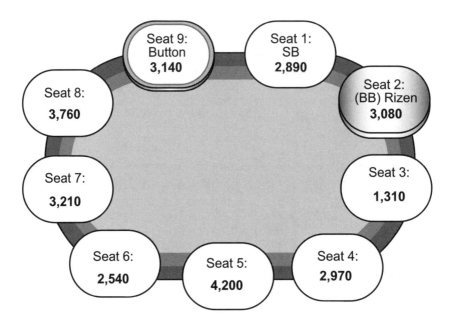

Setup: It is very early in a nightly $150 buy-in $100K guaranteed tournament and blinds of 10-20. I haven't had enough time to establish any significant reads or image. This tournament is filled with lots of satellite players who are not accustomed to playing a high buy-in tournament like this. They are also not accustomed to playing against high-quality opposition.

Pre-flop (30): Seat 4 raises to 70. Seat 9 on the button cold-calls, and it is folded to me. I call the additional 50 chips, and we go to the flop three-handed.

Flop (220): This is a great flop for me in many ways. It's very unlikely someone has 5-4, although 5-4 suited is a hand the button might call with. Another hand the button might call with is 22, which would be ideal.

The question I have to ask myself is, how can I extract as much value as possible from the hand? I could check to the preflop raiser and give him a chance to make a continuation bet and then raise. The problem with that line is that it shows a lot of strength and is likely to slow down my opposition unless he has flopped two pair or better. I could also slow-play until the turn, but without position there is no guarantee the original bettor will bet again on the turn, and it is quite unlikely he'll bet again without an ace.

If someone does have an ace, the best way to disguise my hand and rake a big pot is by leading out. By making what looks like a probe bet to figure out where I am in the hand, I can trick my opponents into thinking my holding is much weaker than it actually is, and hopefully they will attack that weakness by raising to build a bigger pot. With any luck, by the time I reveal the strength of my hand (with a big bet), there will already be plenty of chips in the pot and my opponents will feel pot-committed. The best-case scenario is that one of my opponents holds an ace with a strong kicker, overplays his hand, and loses his entire stack. I bet 140, the early-position player folds, and the button calls.

 Turn (500): The flop result is a little unexpected. I thought the original raiser had a big hand and would raise me on the flop. Instead, the original raiser folded and the button caller called. Most of the time A-K and A-Q reraise preflop, but this early in a tournament you sometimes see players cold-call with those hands. Lots of players like to call preflop with suited aces, too, so it's possible the button has something like A-5s or A-4s, or even better A-3s or A-2s for two pair. A-J and A-T are also possibilities, as is pocket deuces, 5-4s or 6-5s. There's also a chance he's on something like 44 or 55 and decided to peel a card with the pair plus a gutshot-straight draw. Looking at the possible range my opponent is on, most of the non-made hands probably aren't going to put many more chips into the pot now that the turn has missed them, and I'd rather not give him a free card to draw out on me, or allow him to see a river cheaply. Instead, I want to make a bet that extracts the maximum value possible from all the made hands that I am ahead of and that are strong enough to continue with. Here it makes sense to make a good-size bet in relation to the pot, so I bet 400, and the button calls.

River (1,300): Given the range I put my opponent on, this card doesn't change the situation a lot. If he has A-T, he might think he just made his hand, but every other one of his holdings has the same hand strength now as it did on the turn. He has called a flop probe bet and a decent-size turn bet, so he's likely to call any reasonably sized river bet as well. I don't want to put him all-in as that may scare away a lot of hands I want to call. Something just under a pot-size bet should get a call, and if he does have A-T or has been slow-playing 22, it will give him a chance to come over the top for the rest of his chips. I bet 1,100, and the button calls, showing A-K.

Hand 55

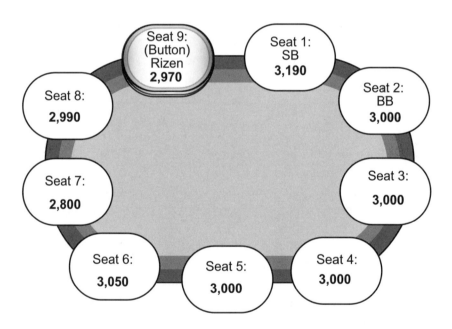

Setup: It is the third hand of the nightly $55K guaranteed $150 buy-in tournament with blinds of 10-20. I have no significant reads on the table and no image at this point.

Pre-flop (30): A-K is a very strong hand but also a very difficult hand to play when the stacks are really deep. When you have this hand, you're going to miss the flop a fair amount of the time; and even when you hit, most of the time you just have one pair, which usually isn't worth getting all your chips in the middle with when you have more than 100 big blinds in your stack. Often, if there is an early-position raiser this early in a tournament, I will just call with A-K, and with significant action in front of me I'll even toss it into the muck. In this instance, though, it's folded to a player in middle position, who raises to 60. A-K is way ahead of a middle-position opener's range, so I reraise to 250, and it is folded back to the middle position player, who calls 190. The pot is heads-up.

Flop (530): This is a bad flop for my hand. It's very coordinated with lots of potential draws on board, and my opponent could easily have a made hand here. To compound the problem, the middle-position player leads into us for 320. Often when a player calls a raise preflop and then suddenly leads out on the flop, he has either some sort of weak made hand or a draw. If my read on the opponent discerned he was capable of laying down a hand like A-T, 88, or a flush draw here, I would probably come over the top with a raise. I have no such read here, and it's super-early in the tournament. A raise would risk one-third of my stack. Until I get a better grasp on the table, it's smart to just cut my losses and find better spots to accumulate chips. I fold.

Hand 56

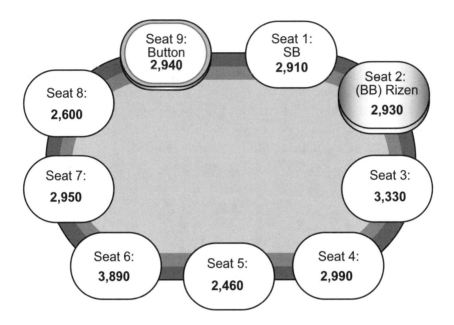

Setup: It is very early in a Sunday $216 buy-in tournament. The blinds are 10-20. It's a tough field with no satellite players, leaving mostly high buy-in regulars and Sunday tournament regulars. We're less than three orbits into the tournament, so we have no significant reads or image at this point. Surprisingly for this tournament, I know very few players at the table from previous play.

  Pre-flop (30): Pocket jacks is a very strong hand from any position. I'll play it strongly unless the action ahead is very strong. The action is folded to a middle-position player, who raises to 70; the cutoff calls 70, and it is folded to me. I have a strong hand against a single middle-position raiser and a cold caller in the cutoff, so a raise makes sense here. I could play it more passively since I'll be out of position post-flop, but it's very likely that I have the best hand here, so I'll raise a little more than the pot to 310. To my surprise, both the middle-position player and the cutoff call.

Flop (940): This is a pretty dry flop. I made a good-size raise preflop, so without reads I have to assume that my opponents are only calling with solid hands—at least decent-size pocket pairs for the most part, although I would say that A-T and even J-Ts could be in some people's ranges here. There are other hands players would call with preflop, but those are the only ones that would be able to continue on this flop. Since I probably had the best hand preflop and I have an overpair to the flop, a continuation bet makes sense here. I bet 700, the middle-position player goes all-in for 2,640, and the cutoff calls all-in for 2,290.

Oops! Given the fact that this flop is really dry (has no reasonable draws that people might push with), it appears that both players should have made hands here. While it's conceivable that the middle-position player has something like A-T and I could be ahead of him, after the cutoff cold-calls, I am almost certainly behind. Most likely I am up against at least A-T and a set (perhaps 66), and it's even possible I am against two sets here. There is just no way I can call with this action on this particular flop. I fold, the middle-position player shows QQ for an overpair, and the cutoff shows TT for a flopped top set and wins a 6,220 pot.

This is a spot that gets a lot of players into trouble when they have overpairs and there is significant action in front of them. The dry flop makes these kinds of decisions much easier since there are no reasonable draws in my opponents' range of hands. I put one third of my stack in and lost, but at least I lived to fight another day rather than making a bad call and drawing to two outs.

Hand 57

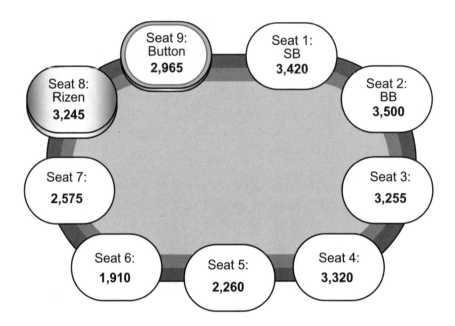

Setup: It is somewhat early in a $1K event with blinds of 15-30.

 **Pre-flop** (45): I don't really like playing aces with bad kickers too often, but early in deep structured events I will open with them in late position if I have an ace and a wheel card, because I hit more disguised two pairs and straights that way. It's folded to me, I raise to 90, and both the button and the small blind call.

   Flop (300): This isn't a great flop for me, but it probably didn't help my opponents either. The small blind checks, and I make a continuation bet of 210. The button calls, and the small blind folds. At this point, I would expect the button to raise most of the time with a Q, slow-play a 6, and call with most pairs better than sixes but worse than queens. There are potentially other hands in his range, but those are the ones that make the most sense from the action so far.

Turn (720): The turn card likely misses both of us. Given the range I have my opponent on, a lot of players have a hard time calling a second bet here with a pair less than queens. I can make a bet of 60 to 65 percent of the pot and safely fold if raised. If he only calls, I should have a very good handle on what my opponent is holding. I bet 475, and my opponent calls.

River (1,670): Normally, I'm reluctant to fire again on the river on a paired board. Fortunately, the river card is probably the best "bluff card" in the deck. An ace would be better, but I have an ace and believe there is a very good chance my opponent is holding a middle pair, so an ace would give me a made hand and not a bluff. This card is just too perfect to not bluff at given my read on my opponent, so I fire the third *barrel* and bet 1,000. My opponent types "sigh" in the chat box and folds.

Hand 58

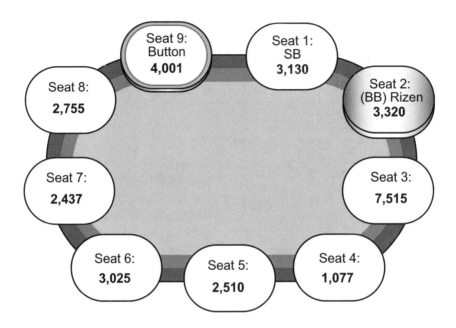

Setup: It is early in a $200 second-chance tournament on a Sunday, and the blinds are 15-30. These tournaments don't have satellites, so the fields tend to be much tougher than the main events on Sundays.

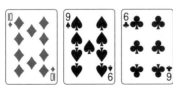 **Pre-flop** (45): 9-6 is just a terrible hand, but in this instance seat 4 calls, and it is folded to me, so I get to play heads up for free.

 **Flop** (75): I hit bottom two pair for a "big blind special." The bad news is the board is pretty coordinated with lots of possible straight draws. Bottom two pair is a much more vulnerable hand than most people think, and as such, it needs to be played fast on the flop in these situations. It's not really a good candidate for slow-playing given the texture of the board and the vulnerability of the hand. I lead for 60 into the 70 pot, and the early-position player calls.

Turn (195): The ace is a bad card in the sense that it kills a lot of action a fair amount of the time. Because this player called from early position and didn't raise, it's tough to put him on a big ace. At this point, his most likely hands are things like K-Qs, Q-Js, J-Ts, K-Qo, 88, and 77. All those hands are reasonable limping hands that could call on that board given the strength of the hand and the strength of the draw. It is also remotely possible that my opponent has a set, but as I have one of the sixes and one of the nines, it's very tough for him to have 99 or 66. This leaves only TT as a likely set hand, and most players would raise with TT. My hand is still strong enough to bet, though, and still vulnerable enough that I can't afford to allow a free card. I bet 150, and my opponent calls.

 River (495): My worst fears are realized on the river when the ten pairs, *counterfeiting* my pair. Betting now is essentially a bluff. Of all the possible hands I listed on the turn, the only ones I beat that may call me are 88 and 77. Both of those hands are very hard-pressed to call a third bet on the board, though, with what amounts to third pair. If I check, I can turn my hand into a bluff catcher and get K-Q, Q-J, and maybe even 88 or 77 to bluff at the pot if they feel that's the only way they can win. If I check and my opponent makes a huge bet, I'll probably be forced to fold, but if he makes a reasonable bet, I can turn my hand into a bluff catcher and hopefully snap him off.

I check, and my opponent bets a small 180 into the 495 pot. These types of small river bets into large pots are often either very strong or very weak hands. Given the odds I am getting, it makes sense to try to pick him off if he's trying to buy the pot with a missed straight draw. I call 180, my opponent tables K♣ Q♦ for a busted straight draw, and I rake in an 855 pot.

Hand 59

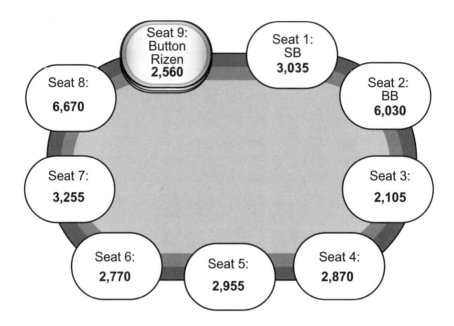

Setup: This is a big $200 second-chance Sunday tournament, and the blinds are 15-30. It's still very early in the tournament, but the table has been surprisingly active with a few double-ups already. No one has shown down unreasonable hands, though.

 Pre-flop (45): A-K is a big hand, especially in late position, but you have to be careful with stacks this deep not to commit too much of your stack when you miss the flop or just have a single pair. It is folded to me on the button, and I make a standard raise to 90. The small blind folds, and the big blind calls 60.

 Flop (195): This could be a dangerous flop. It's very coordinated with lots of straight and flush draws out there, and lots of hands with a Q or a T in them are calling me out of the big blind preflop. On the plus side, I do have a gutshot-straight draw, a backdoor-flush draw, and two overcards. Both checking behind on this flop and making a standard continuation bet are reasonable. By making a continuation bet with this type of hand, you will often get the option of a free card on the turn when he calls, plus you can always win when he folds the flop. The downside is that if you are check-raised, you'll probably have to let your hand go and miss the opportunity to improve. Here, the big blind checks, and I opt to make a continuation bet of 120. The big blind calls.

 Turn (435): This is an interesting turn card. I may now have the best hand, but the K♦ also completes the flush draw, and it's always possible my opponent has something like K-Q here. I now have top pair with top kicker along with a broadway-straight draw and the nut-flush draw. The hand is simultaneously powerful and vulnerable here. The best line to take is to check behind on the turn and reevaluate on the river. If I bet and my opponent raises, it would be disastrous, as I would lose an opportunity to draw to a big hand and my opponent might force me to fold the best hand. If I check and I don't hit the flush draw, I'll probably call a river bet or bet when checked to, because it's very unlikely I'll get checked to twice with a hand that beats me. I also create some deceptive value by checking the turn, as my opponent may think his Q-J or J-T is good here and value-bet the river when he might fold on the turn. If I bet here, I really can't stand to be raised. The big blind checks, and I check behind.

 River (435): This river card is very unlikely to change anything. It pairs the board, and I just pulled ahead of a hand like Q-T that may have been trying to slow-play. The big blind bets 210. I stick with my plan from the turn and just call his bet, knowing he is unlikely to call a raise with a hand I beat. The big blind turns over 3♦ 2♦ for a flush and wins a pot of 855. I did a good job of keeping the pot under control and minimizing my losses here, while at the same time not allowing my opponent to take me off my draw. I'll note that the big blind defends frequently and very lightly, as 3♦ 2♦ is a very poor hand to be defending your big blind with.

Hand 60

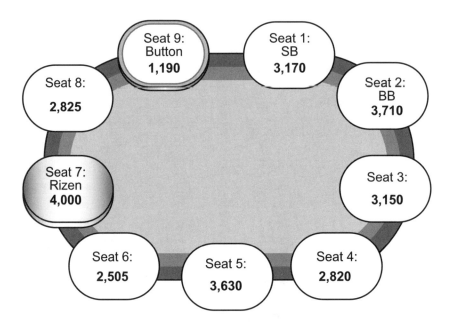

Setup: It is very early in a second-chance $200 tournament on a Sunday with blinds of 15-30. These tournaments often have very tough fields since they run very few satellites and the buy-in is fairly large for an online tournament. I haven't been at the table long, but the player in Seat 3 has been playing recklessly, aggressively betting and calling with some really weak hands.

  Pre-flop (45): K-Q suited is a solid hand and plays well from many positions against both a single opponent and in a multiway pot. The reckless player in Seat 3 raises to 90, another early-position player calls, and it is folded to me. I call. The button calls too, but everyone else folds. The pot is four-handed.

   Flop (405): Top pair can be a very tough hand to play in multiway pots. You have to be careful not to aggressively build a big pot when players could easily hold hands like A-Q, a club draw, 7-6s, or even a set, given a board like this.

The initial raiser checks, as does Seat 4. I make a value/probe bet of 275. I really don't want to give three other players a free card on this board, but I don't want to bet so much that if I run into a bigger hand, I lose a lot of chips. The button folds, and the initial raiser calls. Seat 4 folds, and I'm heads up with the aggressive player.

 Turn (955): This is a pretty innocuous card, and my opponent checks. I would bet here against most opponents. Betting prevents your opponent from drawing a free card, and if check-raised, you can safely fold against the typical player. This player has been so wildly aggressive and unpredictable, though, that checking behind has a lot of merit. First, this prevents me from having to make a difficult decision against a maniacal opponent if he check-raises. Second, I can induce him to bluff on the river with many worse hands, given his aggressive and unpredictable nature. So I check behind.

 River (955): The river is not the greatest card, as it makes the club draw, but I checked behind on the turn at least partially to induce a bluff from my opponent. He quickly obliges, betting the size of the pot (955). While this is not one of the cards I wanted to see, I know how aggressive this player has been and reluctantly call 955. My opponent shows A♦ K♦ for a complete bluff, and I win a 2,865 pot.

Hand 61

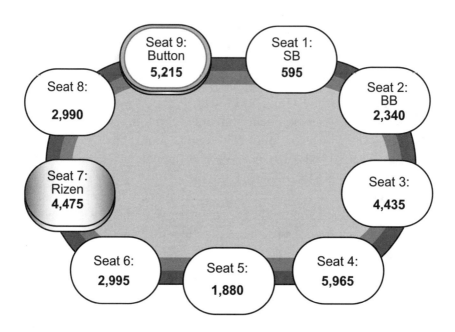

Setup: It's early in a nightly $150 tournament with blinds of 20-40. The big blind is a solid player I have played against many times. He is typically pretty tight but very capable of making some strange moves.

 **Pre-flop** (60): This is a borderline hand to play from the hijack this early in the tournament; A-9 offsuit is easily dominated. If it is folded to me, I will raise, especially since I know the big blind is tight. It is folded to me, and I make a standard raise to 120. It is folded to the big blind, who calls.

 **Flop** (260): A good flop for me. The only hands I really have to worry about my opponent having are A-T, A-J, 55, and 44. He would have reraised me with A-K or A-Q. He could be getting tricky with AA, but since I have an ace in my hand and there's one on the board, it's extremely unlikely he has the other two and decided not to reraise with them. Surprisingly, my

opponent leads into me for 175. Against most players, this lead into the pre-flop raiser out of the blinds is often a weak hand, often some sort of drawing hand semibluff. Given there are no flush draws on the flop, he could easily have something like 33 or 22 and hope that the ace scares me enough into folding. It's possible he has 7-6 suited or something, but from a player this tight, it would be out of character. If he's not semi-bluffing, the other most-likely scenario is that he has something like 88 or 77 and believes he may have the best hand. Early in a tournament, when I am this deeply stacked, I often like to call in situations like this and let my opponent bluff off more chips when he's behind. If a scare card comes on the turn, I haven't invested a whole lot at this point. I call the 175.

 Turn (610): This is a pretty safe turn card. Given the range and read on my opponent, this shouldn't have helped him. TT could be in his range, but I'll let the betting clue me in. The big blind checks. This almost certainly indicates a weak holding. I could bet here, but there aren't that many river cards I don't want to see. If I bet, my opponent will almost always fold a non-ace hand, but if I check, he may think I have something like 7-6 or 77 and may try to bluff on the river, allowing me to extract more value out of my hand. I check behind.

 River (610): The backdoor flush got there, but my opponent likely would have fired again on the turn if he picked up the flush draw. 88 also just got there. If my opponent bets, I will be calling most bets. If I raise, the only hands likely to call will be ones that beat me. If he checks, I'll make a value-bet and hope something like 77 gives me a *crying call*. The big blind does check, I bet 400, and the big blind folds.

Hand 62

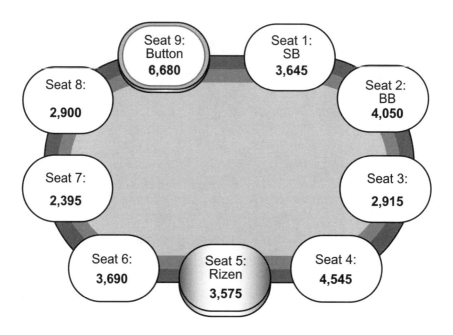

Setup: It is very early in a nightly $150 tournament. The blinds are 20-40. I have just been moved to this table, so I have no reads on any of the players and they have no reads on me.

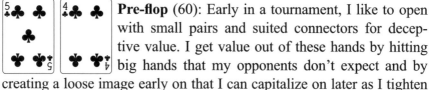 **Pre-flop** (60): Early in a tournament, I like to open with small pairs and suited connectors for deceptive value. I get value out of these hands by hitting big hands that my opponents don't expect and by creating a loose image early on that I can capitalize on later as I tighten up my range of hands to more premium ones. It's folded to me, and I raise to 120. Seat 7 calls, and everyone else folds.

Flop (300): I have flopped an inside straight draw and a backdoor-flush draw. The flop texture is OK because either a big part of my opponent's range missed here or he can't feel too good about his hand (something like 77, for example). It's worth taking a stab at the pot, and if I make the straight on the turn, my opponent will never be able to put me on that hand. I bet 200, and my opponent calls.

 Turn (700): The turn is great for two reasons. First, I have picked up the flush draw, so now any club or any seven fills in my hand. Second, the ace is a great bluff card. My opponent is going to assume big aces are a big part of my early-position raising range, and suddenly his queen or pocket tens don't look so good. I can apply a lot of pressure by betting again here, and even if he decides to call, I still have a lot of outs. I bet 500. My opponent thinks a while before folding and I win a 700 pot.

Hand 63

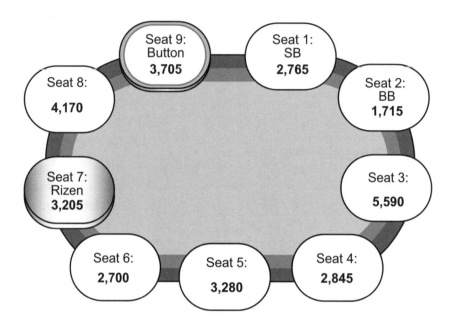

Seat 9:
Button
3,705

Seat 1:
SB
2,765

Seat 8:
4,170

Seat 2:
BB
1,715

Seat 7:
Rizen
3,205

Seat 3:
5,590

Seat 6:
2,700

Seat 5:
3,280

Seat 4:
2,845

Setup: It is early with 20-40 blinds in one of the $200 second-chance tournaments on a Sunday. The fields in these are typically fairly strong players, but play at this table has been pretty loose, and some weak hands have been shown down.

 Pre-flop (60): K-Q offsuit is a fairly strong hand, and I will always open with it in middle position. With these blinds and no antes, if one of the early-position players opens the pot, I will fold most of the time unless I have a significant read on the player. It is folded to me, I raise to 120, and only the big blind calls.

 Flop (260): This is an excellent flop. I have top pair with the second-best kicker and am probably ahead unless he defended with K-J or 33. I could be up against better hands such as KK, JJ, or A-K, but I would expect most players to reraise those hands against an opponent in the hijack. My opponent might also be sitting on a draw, with a hand like Q-T.

The big blind leads into me with a pot-size bet. These sorts of lead bets into preflop raisers are often weak made hands or draws. In this instance, the board offers very few draws, so it's very likely he's on a hand like K-9 or Q-J.

Given my read, if I raise here, I let him off the hook with his weaker hands. If he is ahead, it would be tough for me to fold if he comes back over the top for the rest of his chips, since he only has 1,335 in chips remaining. I think it's best to flat-call here and give him some more rope to make a bigger mistake later rather than raising now so that he plays his hand correctly by folding. Even if he improves to a better hand, it won't be disastrous, given that his chip stack can't eliminate me. I call 260.

 Turn (780): The turn makes the board a rainbow. It's very unlikely he defended with K-5 or J-5 in the big blind. A remote possibility is 55, but most players wouldn't take a stab at the pot on the flop with 55 here. My opponent goes all-in for 1,335, or a little under twice the size of the pot. Since the board doesn't really contain any obvious draws here, it's very unlikely that he's making this huge bet with a strong hand to prevent me from drawing out on him. This bet just screams, "I have a weak hand, please fold now!" If he's willing to make this sort of play with K-J, then I guess he deserves my chips. I call 1,335, and he shows K-9 for top pair with a weak kicker. The river is a little too close for comfort when the 8♣ comes off, but in the end, my K-Q holds up and I win a 3,450 pot.

Hand 64

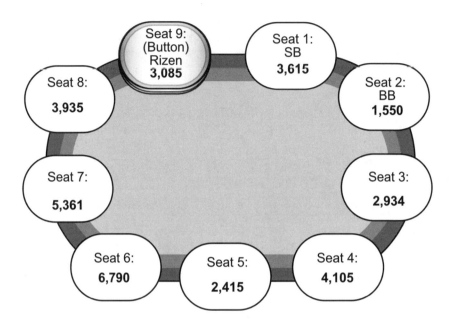

Setup: It's the second level of a $55K guaranteed nightly tournament with blinds of 20-40. I've played with the cutoff several times before and know his opening-hand range from late position is very wide. True to form, he has already won several pots without showdowns with late-position raises and then continuation bets on the flop when called.

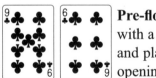 **Pre-flop** (60): It is folded to the cutoff, who opens with a raise to 120. I know, given my previous read and play so far, that early on in this tournament his opening range is super wide. When the stacks are still relatively deep compared to the blinds, I like to occasionally bluff-raise aggressive opponents preflop, especially when I'm on the button. This often slows down aggressive players when you act behind them and gives you the advantage later on in the tournament of getting to open more pots in late position.

In deeper-stacked poker, you want to bluff-raise with the best hands you wouldn't normally play, but you also want to bluff-raise with hands that won't get you into kicker trouble if you do happen to hit a flop. I prefer to bluff-raise with suited two-gappers and unsuited connectors. These hands are still capable of hitting big concealed hands if I get called preflop, but they're weak enough hands that I can fold if my opponent four-bets and not feel too bad about missing the chance to the see the flop. Compare this to hands like suited connectors or one-gappers where there is a lot of value in seeing the flop. With those hands, I don't want to risk being four-bet, so I would just cold-call for value.

I make a pot-size reraise to 420, and the cutoff calls.

 **Flop** (900): I would have preferred to just end this hand preflop, but this isn't a bad result. By re-raising preflop, I represented a big hand, such as a big ace or a big pair. This flop is going to be very difficult for the cutoff to continue playing without an ace. If the cutoff leads out and bets, it will be very difficult for me to continue with my hand; but if he checks to me, I should be able to make a fairly standard continuation bet of about two-thirds of the pot and take it down fairly frequently. The cutoff does indeed check, I bet 600, and the cutoff folds. I take down a 900 pot.

Not only do I win a nice-size pot in this hand, but I have also sent a message to Seat 8 that he can expect to get reraised if he continues to raise loosely from late position. Hopefully this will slow him down and allow me to play more pots from position in the future. If he continues to make loose raises from late position undeterred, I can continue to reraise more liberally until he either gets back in line or makes a big mistake when I pick up a big hand.

Hand 65

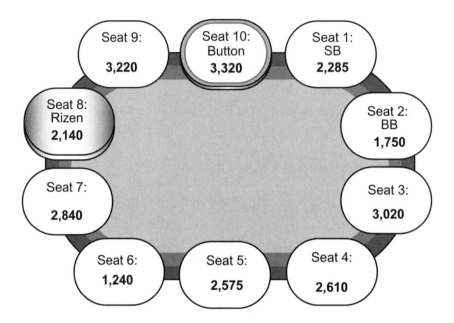

Setup: It's very early in a nightly $20K *bounty* tournament with the blinds at 20-40. I don't have any significant reads on the table yet. I've been somewhat active, opening a few pots and then having to make laydowns when I missed the flop and my opponents didn't fold to my continuation bets.

 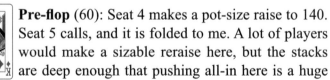 **Pre-flop** (60): Seat 4 makes a pot-size raise to 140. Seat 5 calls, and it is folded to me. A lot of players would make a sizable reraise here, but the stacks are deep enough that pushing all-in here is a huge overbet and making a standard reraise will commit about a third of my stack preflop. Thus far, I've also had a lot of my raises called, and with an early-position raiser in this hand, it is likely I will be called again. With stacks of these sizes and an early-position raiser, I often like to smooth-call here preflop. That gives my hand some deceptive value in that it's hard to put me on A-K when I just call preflop, and it allows me to get away cheaply when I miss. I call, and everyone else at the table folds.

Flop (480): This is one of the better flops for my hand. The only real negatives are that there are two spades on the flop and that any broadway card can complete a straight. Conversely, my opponents might put me on one of these draws, allowing me to get good action on the hand.

Seat 4 most likely has a strong hand, as he opened from early position. A-K, A-Q, and A-J are all in his range, and possibly K-Q as well. Many players will open with a variety of pocket pairs from early position as well, so TT through 66 are also possibilities. AA is a remote possibility, but since I can already account for two of the aces, it's very unlikely. He can also have a lot of pairs that missed here, and without significant reads, he could be opening with hands such as suited connectors or even random hands that I would usually not put him on.

The middle-position caller to his left probably has a strong hand as well. His range is pretty close to the same, although I would say that if he had AA, KK, or QQ, he probably would have reraised preflop to discourage multiway action.

Seat 4 bets 225, or slightly less than half the pot. That's a very weak bet size, but the fact that he is betting into two opponents makes it a little stronger. This makes me think that he has some sort of made hand that he feels the need to bet with, but not one that's super strong. Some trickier players are capable of doing this with their monsters to try to induce a raise from their opponents. The player in middle position folds.

I could raise right here, but I have position, and there aren't many cards I'm afraid to see on the turn. I don't want to see a J, which improves A-J, K-Q, and perhaps even JJ; or a Q that improves A-Q and QQ. I wouldn't be happy to see a spade on the turn, but it's hard to put the early-position player on a flush draw here. I decide to smooth-call the 225 and reevaluate the situation on the turn.

 Turn (930): This is one of the better turn cards for me. Unless he was playing something really odd like 9-8s, it's very doubtful the turn improved his hand. The early-position player leads for 350, which is another really small bet in relation to the pot. A lot of tricky players are capable of betting weak to induce a raise once on the flop, but rarely will they do it twice, especially with a flush draw out there. This leads me to believe that his hand is probably exactly what it appears to be—some sort of made hand that's not very strong—and that he's trying to control the size of the pot by leading with small bets. He probably holds a hand like A-J or KK.

There is 1,280 in the pot, and I have 1,775 behind. There doesn't seem to be any point in allowing my opponent to get another cheap card. With the pot being sufficiently large, it makes sense to get the rest of the chips in now and hope he can't get away from his hand. I raise all-in to 1,775, and the early-position player calls. He shows A-J, and the river is the T♦. I win a pot of 4,480.

Hand 66

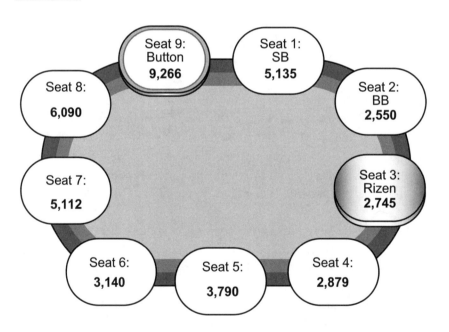

Setup: This is a nightly $150 tournament with the blinds at 25-50. Thus far, my table has been aggressively reraising, with Seat 5 in particular having reraised me twice in the last couple of orbits.

Pre-flop (75): Pocket jacks is a strong hand from any position and are worthy of a raise. I raise to 150, and Seat 5 raises to 400. It is folded back around to me. This player has aggressively reraised me several times so far. However, I've also raised under-the-gun this time, which represents a lot of strength. He's also probably aware of the fact that he's been reraising me a lot, so he may be a little less likely to do it as a steal the third time in such short fashion. I take all of this into account, but at the end of the day, his raise is pretty small and I only have to call 250 more into a 625 pot. I'll have 2,345 more behind to potentially win if I hit a big hand. I call 250.

   Flop (875): This isn't the greatest flop for me. It's very coordinated with two diamonds and two broadway cards, one of which is an overcard to my pair. Also, I am out of position, which will make controlling the size of the pot very difficult. In this situation, it is often best to just check and fold rather than play a big pot out of position with second pair and tons of potentially scary cards to fall on the turn and river. I check, and my opponent bets 400.

This is an oddly small bet for this particular board and pot size. It's less than half the pot and exactly the size of his preflop bet. In my experience, these bets are almost always either something like a completely missed A-K that feels obligated to continuation bet, or a very big hand—in this case I would say pretty much exclusively QQ, TT, or A♦ K♦ (since I have the J♦). A quick way to find out which this is would be to make a very small check-raise, perhaps even a minimum raise to 800; however, I like a raise to 1,000 better. It will have committed half my stack to this pot, but it will immediately reveal if I am ahead.

Alternatively, I could just call and then check and fold on the turn. Most players aren't capable of firing two barrels on a board like this with nothing. The downside to that line is I could be allowing my opponent to make the best hand by giving him a free card. He could also check behind with a better, made hand on the turn, and I'll lose another bet on the river. Finally, he may check behind on the turn, and then a scare card (an ace, king, or diamond) may come on the river, giving me a very difficult decision. Also, my original plan of folding isn't a bad one. My opponent gave me odds to draw to a set preflop, and now that I've missed, I can just give up rather than trying to play this hand for value. After some deliberation, I decide to call 400 and reevaluate on the turn.

 Turn (1,675): OK, so the turn is a blank and shouldn't have improved my opponent's hand. Given my preflop and flop reads, I should safely be able to check and fold here. If he checks behind, I probably have the best hand and will have to reevaluate the situation based on the river card. I check, and my opponent bets 600, which again is less than half the pot by quite a large margin. At this point, even though his bet is very suspicious, I should just cut my losses and move on. This just isn't the kind of line a player on a bluff takes, and if I call here, the pot will be big enough that any reasonable river bet is going to be for most, if not all, of my stack. Note that there is virtually no card in the deck that will make me confident that I have the best hand. Unfortunately, the emotions from being constantly reraised get the best of all of us, and these middle pairs are especially tricky. Rather than taking the prudent route, I call 600 more!

 River (2,875): This completes the diamond flush. One line would be to try and represent a flush here since I've checked and called every street, but the pot is so big at this point that my opponent is unlikely to fold a big hand. I could also check here, and the flush card may scare my opponent enough to give me a free showdown. I decide to check, and my opponent bets 1,200, which is not quite the rest of the chips I have left. It's almost impossible that he would bet all three streets here as a bluff, but I inexplicably call 1,200 anyway, and he shows me Q♥ Q♠ for the flopped nuts. I lose a 5,275 pot.

I've included this hand because middle pocket pairs are especially tricky to play. I see players all the time make the same 250 "investment" I did in trying to hit a set, and then overplay their pair post-flop in a marginal situation. Early in the hand, I should have seen the warning signs that would have allowed me to get away from my hand and preserve my stack for better opportunities later in the tournament. Unfortunately, I let emotion and frustration get the best of me in a tricky situation.

Hand 67

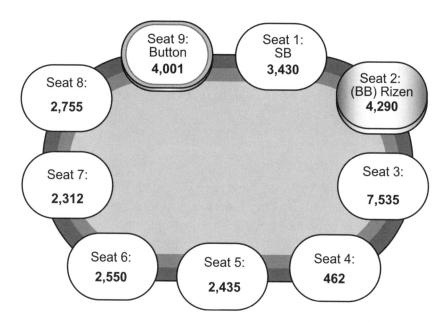

Setup: I am playing a Sunday $200 second-chance tournament with blinds of 25-50. These tournaments don't get any satellite players like the major Sunday tournaments, so the fields are generally filled with tougher players.

 **Pre-flop** (75): It is folded around to the small blind, who calls, and I get to see a flop.

 **Flop** (100): This is a monster flop for me when playing blind against blind. I have a pair plus the second nut-flush draw. The small blind makes a pot-size bet of 100.
A lot of players just call here, not realizing the strength of their hand. In addition to the fact that you have a very strong hand, raising the flop makes it look like you hit a queen or a 10. This adds a lot of deceptive value to the hand, as you can hit a flush, king, or deuce, and your

opponent may still believe you have just a queen. With that in mind, I raise to 300, and my opponent calls.

 Turn (700): Presto! I complete the flush draw and have the second-best hand possible at the moment. My opponent checks. Now it's time to see how much value I can get out of the hand. If I bet too much, I am likely to scare away my opponent, but I need to bet enough to build a pot so that I can make a reasonable-looking bet on the river and still get paid. I decide to bet 425, and my opponent calls.

 River (1,550): My hand strength is still the same, but the jack on the board actually hurts me a little since it's a scary card for my opponent. He may not be as willing to pay me off on the river if he thinks I might have been playing K-9, J-T, or 9-8 here. Therefore, rather than punishing my opponent with a 1,200 or so bet on the river, I bet a modest 900. My opponent calls and mucks Q-T.

In hindsight, I realize I was lucky that my opponent didn't play his hand a lot faster on the flop. He probably would have called a bigger bet on the river, but against my opponent's *range* of hands, I will extract a greater overall value with this line of play.

Hand 68

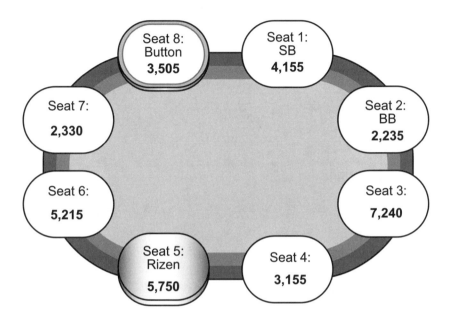

Setup: It's early in a major $150 buy-in nightly tournament with 40-80 blinds. I've already been very active and increased my stack to 5,750 without showing down many hands.

Pre-flop (120): It is folded to me, and I make a standard raise to 240. It is folded to the big blind, who makes it 480. Now, most players think this is the "minimum raise," but it's actually not. Since I raised 160 to 240, the minimum raise would be 400, not 480. This is significant because in an online tournament, players occasionally misclick "minimum raise," but the fact that it was to 480 means the player actually put thought into the raise and chose that amount.

This kind of raise often indicates a very big hand, especially when the player making it just put in almost a quarter of his chips. While A-K is a very strong hand, I am just about certain this player has a big hand and will almost never fold. Since a big part of A-K's value comes from being able to make players fold, it makes more sense here to call and see a flop than to go ahead and push all-in. I call the 240 raise.

 Flop (1,000): This is a bad flop for me. Since I have A-K, a big part of my opponent's range is QQ and JJ. I'd like a free card here to try to hit a T on the turn. If the big blind bets, I'm done with the hand. Fortunately, the big blind checks, and I check behind.

 Turn (1,000): This is a dangerous card. I made a hand, but my opponent could have easily checked to me with AA, QQ, JJ, and possibly even A-Q or A-J as an attempt to trap. I am still going to proceed, but with caution. The big blind bets 500, giving me 2-to-1 pot odds. This is a tricky situation: If I call the 500, I am getting really good odds to call on the river if he pushes, and it's going to be tough to lay down top pair here. In addition, the bigger question right now is whether or not I am getting the correct odds to call in this situation. Let's look at the mathematics of this in more detail.

Let's assume that his range is AA, KK, QQ, JJ, A-K, and A-Q. All of these hands make some sense given the action so far. Given this range, I can figure out the total number of hands he could be holding and look at what percentage of these are beating me. There are three combinations each of KK, QQ, and JJ (e.g., K♣ K♠, K♣ K♦, and K♠ K♦). There is only one possible combination of A♣ A♠ given the A♥ on the board and the A♦ in my hand. There are six combinations of A-K and six of A-Q. This is a total of 22 hands. Some percentage should always be assigned as a complete bluff, so I'll add two more hands that are bluffing hands, for a total of 24 hands.

Of these 24 hands, I beat five of these: the two bluffs and the three KK combinations. I am behind 13 combinations, and I am tied with six combinations (A-K). When behind, I have some outs. In summary, I am ahead or tied about 45 percent of the time and am getting 2-to-1 pot odds to call.

Running this scenario in a poker-odds calculator shows that I'll win about 25 percent of the time, lose about 50 percent of the time, and tie about 25 percent of the time. This gives me approximately 38 percent pot equity.

Given the fact that I also have implied pot odds if I catch the straight on the river and have position on my opponent, I'll call the 500 to re-evaluate on the river. This is borderline play. You must be confident of your decision-making abilities on the river and be willing to let your hand go in the face of strength from your opponent; otherwise, folding is the better option.

River (2,000): This card brings in the flush draw, but a flush draw is unlikely in this situation. A pre-flop raiser would generally play a draw a lot more strongly than this, so I am not super concerned with it, although it remains a remote possibility. Again, I am going to be in a tough spot if my opponent pushes, but luckily for me, he checks. Given the range I put him on, it is very unlikely he would check with a better hand than mine. He may make a crying call with K-K or fold A-K, allowing me to pick up additional chips. I push all-in, making him play for his remaining chips, and he types KK into the chat and folds.

Hand 69

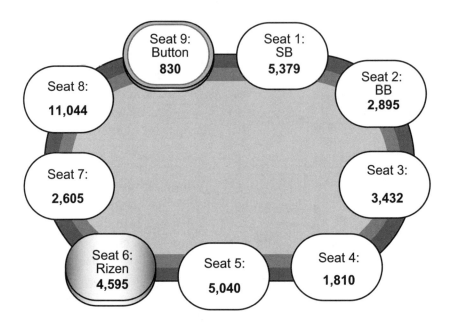

Setup: This is a nightly $55K guaranteed tournament with a $150 buy-in. The blinds are 40-80. There are daily satellites for this tournament, so there is a mix of very tough players and much softer satellite players. I have just been moved to this table and have no significant history with any of the players and no current image.

  Pre-flop (120): K-Js is a reasonable hand in middle position. I will often open the betting with K-Js, and if the effective stacks are deep enough, I will some-times call raises with this hand. The player under-the-gun calls. The action is folded to me. Because this is the type of hand I like to see a cheap flop with, I call. The cutoff calls, and it's folded around to the big blind, who checks.

Flop (360): This is a good flop for my top pair with a king kicker. I am concerned about the potential flush draw (diamonds) while Q-T, T-9, and 9-7 have straight draws. Despite this, I still feel pretty good about my hand.

The big blind checks, and Seat 3 bets 240. I know nothing about the under-the-gun player, so I'll have to make some assumptions about his play. Most players call under-the-gun with pocket pairs, and the trickier ones will call with their monster hands, hoping another player will raise pre-flop. I could smooth-call this bet, but that gives the two players to act behind me exceptionally good odds to draw to a straight or a flush if they have it, or even to peel a card off with something like A-8. I don't want to allow a cheap draw. I only have one pair with moderately deep stacks and so I don't really want to build a big pot, especially when my opponent could be holding an overpair or even a set.

I make a minimum raise to 480. That should look strong enough to force most of the draws out and get me heads up with Seat 3. Minimum raises can be very scary for your opponents. Here, for example, my opponent not only has to call the 240, but faces the possibility of having to call increasingly large bets on the turn and river as the pot grows. I am offering him the pot odds to call if he flopped a draw, but it will be very tough for him to continue with his medium-strength hands if he's a reasonably good player, which he may or may not be. As yet, I have no read on his play.

Seat 3 reraises to 1,250. Now I am probably in huge trouble. There are players capable of interpreting my minimum raise as weak and making a move here, but most of the time this betting indicates I'm going up against either a slow-played big pair or a flopped set. Something like A♦ 8♦ is a remote possibility, too, as sometimes players like to call with suited aces pre-flop. If I call here, I must assume that I'll be playing for my entire stack, as he will probably move in on the turn. My hand isn't strong enough to continue and I fold.

.Hand 70

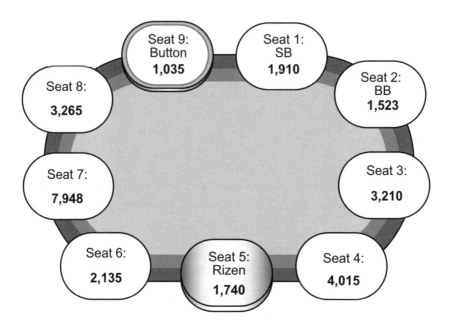

Setup: This is the $150 buy-in $55K guarantee nightly tournament. The blinds are 40-80. It's late in the first hour, and the table has been pretty tough, playing back at me a lot with reraises and calling my continuation bets down lightly. Unfortunately, they've been right so far, and I've been caught holding very little, so my image is pretty loose.

 **Pre-flop** (120): I like to open-raise pocket pairs from all positions as long as I'm not short-stacked. It adds deceptive value to those hands, while at the same time I can pick up the pot on later streets by representing strength. Consistently raising smaller pairs will also allow me to get paid off more on premium hands such as AA or KK since my opponents can't automatically assume that I have a huge hand later on. Ultimately, it's a good way to keep your opponents guessing and add variety to your preflop strategy. It is folded to me in middle position, and I raise to 240. Only the small blind calls, which is good because I have position on my sole opponent.

Flop (560): This is actually a really good flop for a pair of threes. I would make a continuation bet here 100 percent of the time if I had a normal image. However, my opponents have been playing back at me quite frequently, and I don't have enough chips to withstand a check-raise here. I really want to see a showdown without giving my opponent a chance to take me off my hand. The plan here is to check behind on the flop and then either fire out on most turn cards or even raise on a reasonable turn card if the small blind leads into me. The small blind checks, and I check behind.

 Turn (560): This is not the best card in the world for my hand. Lots of hands that hit this board would call from the small blind. I am behind to K-Q, K-J, Q-J, Q-T, or J-T. If the small blind bets, I'll probably just fold. If he checks, I can either check behind and hope for a cheap river showdown, or take one stab at the pot and then hope my turn aggression will induce a river check so that I can show it down. The small blind checks, I fire 325, and the small blind calls.

 River (1,210): And some people call me a luck box! You can't rely on hitting two outers, but every now and then they can be a pleasant surprise.

There is no possible way my opponent can think that a 3 helped me. I have played the hand rather weakly thus far, so it would be difficult for my opponent to put me on anything better than one pair. The pot is just a little bigger than the rest of my stack, so no matter what happens, I am just going to jam it all-in and hope he caught a big enough piece of the board to call. The small blind checks, I push all-in for 1,175, and the small blind calls. The small blind shows A-Q, and I win with a set of threes. Very lucky!

In hindsight, not betting the flop could have easily cost me this pot. The flop was so dry that even with my image, I probably should have bet, knowing that I probably had the best hand and that it would be tough for the small blind to have hit any piece of the flop. The small blind did me a favor by not raising the turn, though, and I got lucky and made him pay.

Hand 71

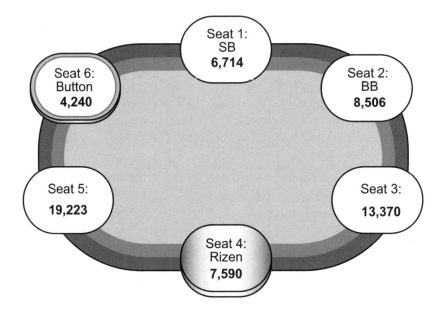

Setup: It is early after the rebuy hour in a $100 rebuy 6-max tournament with blinds of 40-80. This particular tournament attracts many of the top players and Seats 1, 2, 3, and 5 are all well-known Internet pros. I have been playing very loosely and aggressively since the rebuy is over, and I've had a couple of players play back at me, particularly on ace-high flops, where I have been folding to resistance so far.

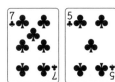 **Pre-flop** (120): With the blinds low in relation to the stacks, the high implied odds increase the value of a hand like this. Pairs and suited connectors become much more valuable when the stacks are deep. In this case, I have a low-suited one-gapper, which I will often open with in these deeper 6-max tournaments. The early-position player folds, I raise to 240, and Seat 5 calls in the cutoff. Everyone else folds.

Flop (600): I flop a flush draw and a weak running straight draw. While this flop does hit a lot of his calling range with pairs or draws, my hand has a lot of deceptive value if we hit. By maintaining control of the pot, I can win if he folds, or maybe win a big pot if I hit and he has an ace. I make a continuation bet of 425. My opponent thinks for a bit and then raises to 1,100.

This raise seems weak if he really has an ace, as it is gives me a good price to call with draws. This often means that either it's a complete bluff or my opponent is making a semi-bluff himself with something like K-Q, K-J, Q-J, 8-7, or even another club draw. A real made hand would have made a larger raise to price me out, especially as my opponent is a well-known Internet pro who is aware of all this. It's possible he's leveling me by inducing a third bet with this suspicious raise, but given that I've been very aggressive so far and folding to lots of flop raises, it's more likely he's just trying to pick up a cheap pot. If I'm wrong, I should at least have some outs to the flush. I make a pot-size raise to 3,900, which should make it very clear to my opponent that I'm not going anywhere in this hand, and my opponent folds.

Hand 72

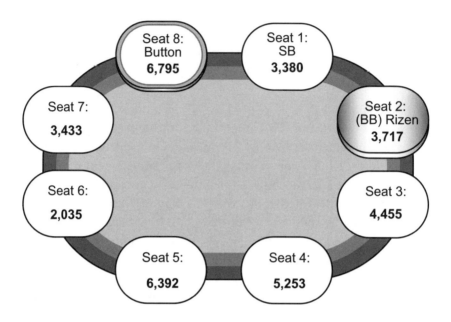

Setup: It is the beginning of the second hour of a nightly $55K guaranteed $150 buy-in tournament. The blinds are 40-80, and the table has been active, but players have had good cards at the showdowns.

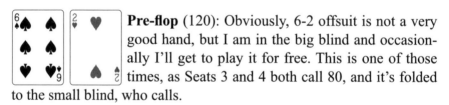

Pre-flop (120): Obviously, 6-2 offsuit is not a very good hand, but I am in the big blind and occasionally I'll get to play it for free. This is one of those times, as Seats 3 and 4 both call 80, and it's folded to the small blind, who calls.

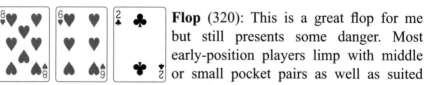

Flop (320): This is a great flop for me but still presents some danger. Most early-position players limp with middle or small pocket pairs as well as suited connectors. Something like T♥ 9♥, 88, 66, and 22 are all well within their range. I like to play bottom two pair very fast against multiple opponents, which helps me define my hand as quickly as possible. For example, by betting out, if there is a raise and a call or a raise and a reraise, I would have no problem mucking my hand. If I tried to slow-play and check, it would be much more difficult to know where I stand if there is a bet and raise when it gets back to me. Betting out also adds some deceptive value because your opponents expect you to slow-play when you hit the flop this hard.

The small blind checks, and I bet 240. Seat 3 folds, and Seat 4 makes a minimum raise to 480. The small blind folds.

A minimum raise on the flop is a very strange play. Sometimes it signals a monster, and other times it's either a drawing hand or a weaker made hand (maybe A-8 or something) trying to buy a free card or find out where they are. If I raise here, I'll likely chase out all the hands I am way ahead of. If my opponent has a big draw, he may even four-bet all-in, giving me a very difficult decision. I believe it's best to play it somewhat conservatively this early in the tournament, so I just call with the intention of re-evaluating based on the turn action. I call 240.

 Turn (1,280): This card seems benign. It completes a straight if anyone is holding 5-4, but that is unlikely given that the limpers are in early position. There are several reasonable lines here. I could lead out to prevent my opponent from taking a free card when he's drawing. Checking is reasonable as well, because he will probably define his hand for me, by either taking the free card or making a move at the pot. If I check, though, I think I have to plan on calling because my line will make my opponent think hands like A-8 or even 9-8 are good. I can't really check-raise here because then I'll only get action from hands that beat mine. I take the conservative route and check, and my opponent checks behind.

 River (1,280): This card doesn't complete any draws, but my bottom two pair has just been counterfeited by any 8 and any 6. Even a hand like 77 is ahead of me now. I can't really bet and expect any worse hand to call, so I check. My opponent checking behind on the flop indicates that his most likely hand is a draw, so checking the river may induce a bluff. I check; my opponent checks behind and shows A♥ 2♠ for flopped bottom pair with a backdoor-flush draw. He played this hand very strangely, so I'll make note in the future that his minimum raises on the flop often indicate weak made hands, and I'll adjust my play accordingly.

Hand 73

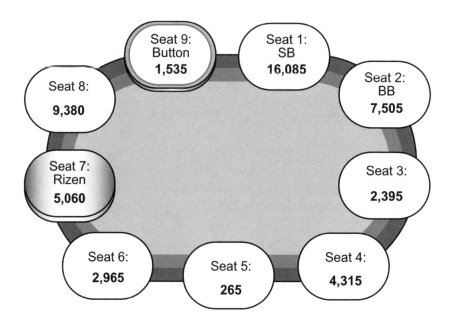

Setup: This is a nightly $120 bounty tournament. The blinds are 50-100. Play has been fairly tight so far, although I've been very active at the table and have picked up many pots uncontested both preflop and with continuation bets on the flop.

  Pre-flop (150): K-Qs is a strong hand, and I will often raise from many positions. It is exceptionally strong in the hijack when folded to me. Depending on the effective stacks, the position of my opponent, and the size of the preflop raise, I may even call a raise with it. If an aggressive enough player raises with it from later position, I'll reraise with it as well, although no one at this table fits that description very well. In this particular hand, it is folded to me, and I raise to 300. The big blind calls.

Flop (650): This is a good flop for me to represent an ace. There are flush draws and straight draws possible with this flop that are a concern. If my continuation bet is called, I would say I'm probably up against an ace, a flush draw, or maybe something like J-T. T-8 is a remote possibility from those more-aggressive players who might call with T-8s. It is checked to me, I make a continuation bet of 425, and the big blind calls.

 Turn (1,500): This is both a good and a bad card for me. It is good because now I have a hand with showdown value, and bad because it completes a flush draw. I have position over my opponent, so hopefully the big blind will check again so that I can check behind and go for a cheap showdown. The big blind checks, and I check.

 River (1,500): Another good and bad card. The second ace makes it less likely that the big blind has an ace (since there is one less ace he could have in his hand), but that could easily give me a false sense of confidence in my hand. The big blind could still have a made flush that he was trying to check-raise the turn with, but it's also possible he has some busted draws with J-T or T-8. If the big blind bets, I will have to make a tough decision.

Fortunately, the big blind checks the river. Remember, my range of hands for the villain was an ace, a flush, or a busted draw. It makes sense to just check behind, as the hands I am beating will probably not call a value-bet here. If he does happen to have a made hand I beat, like T-9 or something, I'll just make a note that he's capable of calling continuation bets with little and adjust my game to him in the future. If he shows a flush, I'll note that he likes to try trapping when he should probably be value betting. I check behind, and the big blind shows K♠ 3♠ for a flush and wins 1,500.

Hand 74

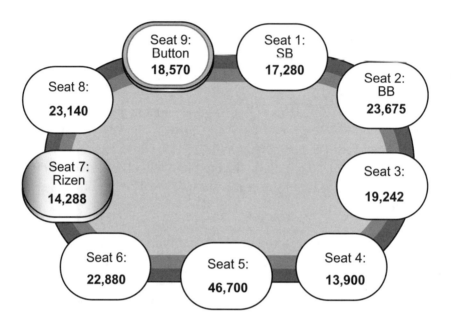

Setup: This is one of the biggest online tournaments of the year, with a $2,600 buy-in. The blinds are 50-100. The field is full of both big online and live professionals, as well as lots of satellite players who got into the tournament for a very small investment. The table has been pretty loose, with mixed play from very solid to very poor. I have a note on Seat 5 that says he likes to overbet his big hands on the river. I have already shown down several poor hands, having been on the losing end already in two or three big pots.

 **Pre-flop** (150): Pocket nines is a strong hand that plays best in big multiway pots where you can flop a set, or against a single opponent post-flop. Seat 3 raises to 300, Seat 5 calls, I call, and the rest of the table folds.

Flop (1,050): Although I have the best hand possible at the moment, there are a lot of turn cards I don't want to see, as there are multiple draws on the board.

Seat 3 bets 500, and Seat 5 calls. The under-the-gun player is most likely either on a flush draw, an overpair, or possibly a set. The middle-position player could have a wide variety of hands, but his smooth call suggests some sort of draw, or he may be slow-playing a lower set than me.

I have position in this hand, and if I make a moderate-size raise here, lots of good things could happen. If the under-the-gun player has a big pair or set, he could easily come back over the top with a big reraise and create a very tough situation for the middle-position player if he's on a draw. If the under-the-gun player has big cards, he will probably just fold, and the middle-position player can define his hand better for me. When he calls, he's probably on a draw, and if he comes out of the woodwork, he's probably slow-playing a smaller set, and I can try and get all the chips in the middle. As an added benefit, my opponents will likely check to me on the turn, and I can check behind if a dangerous card comes. This allows me to keep the pot size under control while also giving myself a chance to improve to a full house on the river. I raise to 1,800, Seat 3 folds, and seat 5 calls.

 Turn (5,150): This is a terrible card for me. Given my opponent's call on the flop, his most likely hand is a flush draw. Less-likely possibilities include a straight draw such as T-8, 8-6, or 6-5. One other small possibility is something like A♥ 9x for top pair and a backdoor-flush draw. At this point, though, the flush is the most likely possibility, so I am going to be hard-pressed to put many more chips in this pot unless the board pairs on the river. Fortunately, my opponent checks, and I get a free card to see the river.

 River (5,150): Yes! The board pairs, giving me the best full house possible, and I can play my hand as if I have the nuts since you can't really ever play a hand in fear of quads. My opponent bets 1,000, which is a really small bet into a 5,150 pot. It could very well be a blocking bet. With a blocking bet, he has probably made some sort of a made hand (probably the flush I put him on earlier) and wants to prevent me from pricing him out of the hand with a big bet. He may also think he's making a small value-bet and that I may pay off with a pair of nines, or something similar. Either way, it's doubtful he'll call an all-in raise, but it's very likely that if I give him better than 2-to-1 odds on his call, he'll begrudgingly put some more chips in. I raise to 6,000, and he calls, showing A♥ 7♥ for the nut flush.

Hand 75

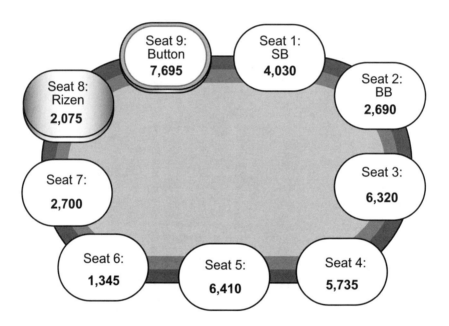

Setup: This is one of the big Sunday major tournaments with blinds of 60-120. This tournament has lots of satellite players, so the field is filled with weak players playing a much higher buy-in tournament than usual.

  Pre-flop (180): A pair of jacks is a great hand in late position. It is folded to me, and I raise to 360. Only the big blind calls.

Flop (780): This is a very awkward situation. I have second pair, a 1,715 stack, and a 780 pot. I could make a continuation bet here, but I am in a bit of a bind if I get check-raised. Although I have second pair, the board is such that my opponent could easily check-raise me with a draw or even a pair of eights. If I make a continuation bet, I will probably have to call a raise on this board. Conversely, I could check and try to keep the pot a little smaller and perhaps induce bluffs on future streets, but then I create the possibility of being outdrawn.

I tend to do a mix of both, but in this particular tournament filled with weaker satellite players, I'll often check behind in situations like this to try to keep the pot small. Players play poorly enough in these tournaments that there is just too much value to having a seat in the tournament, and so I tend to prefer lower-variance plays in the earlier stages. My opponent checks to me, and I check behind.

 Turn (780): The turn puts a few more straight draws on the board, and if my opponent is loose enough to call with 9-6, he got there. My opponent bets 240, which is a super-small bet in relation to the pot. This bet could mean anything from a draw to a smaller pair to a complete bluff. There is some merit to raising here and trying to take down the 1,020 pot right now, since it represents a significant boost to my chip stack, but I still hate getting all-in with second pair this early in this particular tournament. I decide to call the 240 to induce a river bluff and keep the pot small.

 River (1,260): The river is a decent card for me. While it's remotely possible he has a 5 in his hand, this card missed all the draws that were out there. Also, if he holds 8-7, he just got counterfeited. My opponent bets 720, a much bigger bet in relation to the pot than the turn. This sort of line (check-flop, bet small on the turn, and make a much larger bet in relation to the pot on the river) is often a busted draw. Players check the flop with either the intent of semibluff raising or calling and hoping to hit their flush. When you check behind, they feel obligated to bet their draw on the turn hoping you'll fold. Once they miss on the river, they attempt a bluff because you haven't shown any real strength either, and it's the only way they can win the hand.

I call the 720, and my opponent shows T♥ 9♠ for a turned straight draw that missed on the river.

Hand 76

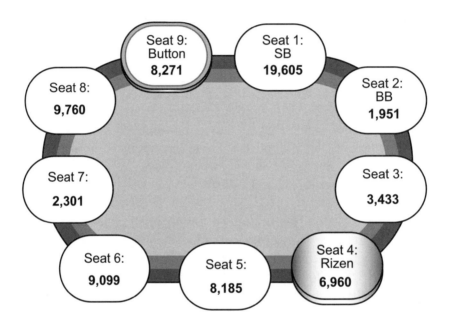

Setup: This is a nightly $150 buy-in tournament, and the blinds are 80-160. I just moved to a new table and have no significant reads on any of the other players.

  Pre-flop (240): Pocket jacks is a solid hand from any position. Seat 3 folds, and I make a standard raise to 460. It is folded to the small blind, who calls, and the big blind folds.

   Flop (1,080): Even though I have no definite reads on the other players, when the small blind cold-calls an early-position raise, I immediately figure he has something like a low to middle pocket pair, a middle suited ace, or something like A-Q, A-J, or K-Q. That's typically the kind of range that players think warrants a call but isn't strong enough to reraise. On this particular flop, that means I have to worry about a huge part of his range hitting. If my opponent bets into me in this situation, I'll just give up most of the time. I don't like continuation betting these flops with stacks of this size because my hand has a lot of showdown value and betting most of the time just causes players with two or three outs to fold. It is much better to save chips when against hands that I'm behind with only two outs and see how the action develops on the turn. With that in mind, my opponent checks and I check behind.

 Turn (1,080): I actually pick up a gutshot-straight draw, which helps a little bit, but most of the value in this hand comes from the times you get A-x suited and 77 to bluff here. The small blind bets 160, which is the minimum bet into this pot. In this situation, I would often consider raising to take the pot away, but given the range I've put my opponent on, there aren't a whole lot of cards that can hit on the river that will help him. I might as well give him another chance to put his chips in the middle when he is in a bad spot.

 River (1,400): This is a rather harmless-looking card (unless he has 55). The small blind again leads for the minimum, 160. Given the action on the hand to this point, the only hand in his range I am really behind is A-Q. Everything else that beats me, he would have played more strongly—with the possible exception of J-T, which is something I didn't put in his original range but is a possibility nevertheless.

If I had a better read on my opponent, this might be a good spot for a really small value-raise, but without significant reads, I take the safe route and call the 160. My opponent shows A-8 offsuit, which flopped bottom pair, and I take down a 1,720 pot. I also make a note that this player will call with weak hands out of position against early-position raisers, likely indicating that he has little understanding of position and may overvalue any hand with an ace.

Hand 77

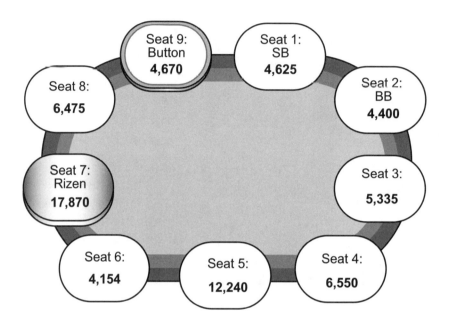

Setup: I just moved tables early in the second hour of a nightly $55K guaranteed tournament with a $150 buy-in. The blinds are 80-160.

  Pre-flop (240): K-J offsuit can be a tricky hand to play. It's the type of hand that typically plays best against a single opponent when you are in control of the pot. Seat 5 limps, and it is folded to me. I think folding is OK here, and I'm not a big fan of calling. Isolating the lone caller is a consideration. The size of my chip stack in relation to my opponent's means that I can afford to make an isolation raise here and still have lots of room to play post-flop. I raise to 720, and it is folded back around to the original caller, who calls the additional 560.

   Flop (1,680): This is a good flop for me. It is very rare that a player would just limp preflop and then call a pot-size raise with an ace. Most players at this level would have raised any big ace preflop to begin with, and wouldn't have called the raise with a small suited ace. It is checked to me. I bet 1,150, and the early-position player immediately makes the minimum raise to 2,300.

This type of betting line with a minimum check-raise is quite odd. The only strong hand that really makes sense here is 77. I think it's also possible he has something like J♥ T♥ or Q♥ J♥ for some kind of combination draw, or this could be a complete bluff. I could just fold here and save my chips for another situation, or I could flat-call and then reevaluate the turn. I always like to have a plan if I make a call like this, though.

If I call here and my opponent has 77, then he's likely to make a big turn bet on any card that misses a draw so that I don't draw out on him. If he's on a draw, once I call his raise he's more likely to either make a small blocking bet to control the price he pays for his draw on the turn, or just check, hoping for a free card. My plan is to call the flop and raise on a favorable turn card if my opponent makes a small bet, and fold if he makes a big bet. An unfavorable turn card would be any card that completes a flush or straight draw, which in this case is any heart, Q, J, or T. I call 1,150.

 Turn (6,280): Well, the 9♣ is about as benign a card as you can get here. My opponent bets 3,500; a relatively small bet in relation to the pot. This is the moment of truth: If my reasoning is correct, I can make a big raise here and use the threat of elimination to get my opponent to fold. Even if he did call preflop with some sort of small ace, the pressure will make it very hard for him to call. I raise all-in for 14,850, and after a little deliberation, my opponent folds. I rake in a nice pot, putting myself in a commanding chip position at the table.

Hand 78

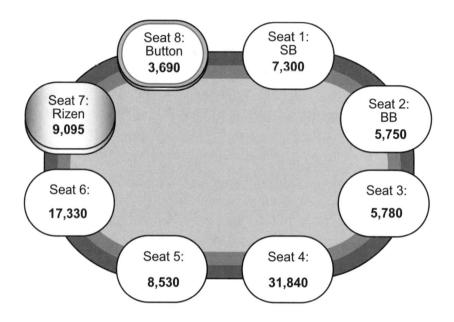

Setup: It is the second hour of a $30 rebuy tournament with blinds of 80-160. My image is somewhat loose and aggressive. I've been raising in position a lot, and the table has started to pick up on it some. I haven't shown down any bad hands at this point, but I am raising often enough that the table is probably getting suspicious. I have no substantial reads on any of the relevant players in this hand.

 **Pre-flop** (240): It is folded around, and I raise slightly under three times the big blind, to 460. The button folds, Seat 1 calls in the small blind, and the big blind folds.

 **Flop** (1,080): This isn't the best flop for me. I have a gutshot-straight draw and a backdoor-flush draw, but pretty much nothing else. Also, the flop texture is poor. I raised in position, and given my image, a lot of hands that call, such as Q-J, J-T, and even another Q-T, might decide to play back at me with

a gutshot draw. Lots of other hands like A-9, K-J, K-T, and even K-9 could easily have called, too.

The small blind checks. I make continuation bets the majority of the time against a lone opponent. Given my table image, the position I raised from, and the flop texture, there are a lot of reasons to check behind here. I can take the free card and possibly hit a J on the turn for the nut straight. With deep stacks, you should always be hesitant to put yourself in a position where your opponent could take you off a big draw to the nuts. Also, I could have a scare card like an ace come where I could take the pot away on the turn. My opponent may play back at me here, so I check the hand to reevaluate on the turn.

 Turn (1,080): Bingo! Not only have I hit the nut straight, but the turn completes a rainbow board, so I don't have to worry about redraws to a flush. My main concern here is trying to extract maximum value. The small blind checks. At this point, my goal is to bet an amount that will build as big a pot as possible without scaring my opponent away. A pot-size bet often looks too strong, and my opponent might fold a weak pair. A smaller bet might induce him to make a play back. I bet 600, and the small blind quickly calls.

 River (2,280): This is a bad card for me. Since I bet the turn representing a jack, this could scare a pair of nines or fives a bit. Given the action on this hand, it's highly unlikely I'm beaten by a full house, as I would have expected two pair or better to raise the turn, but it's a remote possibility. The small blind checks again. At this point, I have to try to figure out a good value-bet to get some action. Remember, I stated earlier that Q-J and J-T are definitely in my opponent's range here.

Stack sizes come into play, too. My opponent started the hand with 7,300 chips and is now down to 6,140 with a pot of 2,200. I think the best bet size here is slightly over half the pot. If my opponent has some sort of weak made hand like kings and jacks or nines and jacks, a bet of that size makes it easy for him to call because it won't be a super big blow to his stack. Conversely, if he does have Q-J or J-T, the bet looks weak enough that he's likely to come over the top for the rest of his chips. Betting over half the pot also gives him an opportunity to make a big check-raise bluff on the river if he completely missed with something weird like 8-7. In the end, I decide to bet 1,250. The small blind calls, and he mucks T-9. He flopped second pair and picked up an inside straight draw on the turn.

Hand 79

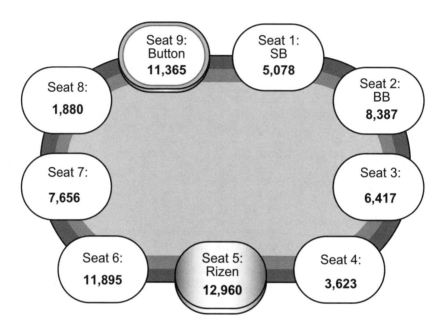

Setup: This is the weekly $1,000 tournament that draws together all the best online poker players each week. It is early with blinds of 100-200.

 **Pre-flop** (300): As long as the stacks are more than 30 big blinds deep, I often like to raise suited connectors if I'm opening the betting from early and middle position. This adds both variety and deception to my play. It allows me to represent strength post-flop and win a lot of pots by simply continuation betting. I will also hit some very concealed hands that my opponents will not be able to put me on for big pots. With less than 30 big blinds, it can be very hard to play suited connectors (and other similar hands where implied odds are the key to successful play) out of position. I'm not deeply stacked enough to win big pots when I do

hit a big hand, and when I hit a marginal one, it can be very tough to get away from easily without losing a significant portion of my stack.

It is folded to me, and I raise to 550. It is folded to the button, with whom I have extensive history. The button loves to play pots in position with a variety of hands and often calls down with moderate-strength hands. He is generally aggressive with his strong hands and occasionally bluffs with his weaker holdings. The button calls and the blinds both fold.

   Flop (1,400): I hit a pair, but the board contains many flush and straight draws. Even so, I have a solid read on my opponent, and I raised from a position of strength. I make a continuation bet of 1,000, and my opponent calls. As we discussed pre-flop, our opponent likes to call in position with a very wide variety of hands. This could indicate he's calling our flop bet with everything from a draw like A-Q, A-J, or Q-J, a flush draw, a pair like QQ-JJ, or even complete air just to try and take the pot away from us on the turn.

 Turn (3,400): My read tells me that my opponent would have raised this flop if he had flopped a strong hand, especially with all the draws on the board. I often give up betting this flop if I have been called after making a continuation bet. However, the king pairing gives me a good chance to represent a very strong hand. I bet 2,400, and my opponent calls.

 River (8,200): I am now playing the board, as my hand has no showdown value. The read on my opponent is very important here, though. I know he calls down with moderate-strength hands and plays his strong hands boldly. Knowing this, it is nearly impossible for him to hold a king, and very likely he called behind with a hand like J-J. He has only 7,415 chips left, and the pot is 8,200. I know he has a propensity to call with his medium-strength hands, so making some sort of *post oak bluff* at this pot with a 2,500 or 3,000 bet is not a good play. Given my read that he doesn't have three of a kind, it will be nearly impossible for him to call if I put him all-in. I put him all-in, and after some deliberation he folds.

Hand 80

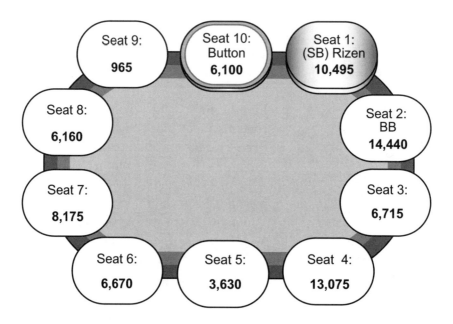

Seat 9:

965

Seat 10:
Button

6,100

Seat 1:
(SB) Rizen

10,495

Seat 8:

6,160

Seat 2:
BB

14,440

Seat 7:

8,175

Seat 3:

6,715

Seat 6:

6,670

Seat 5:

3,630

Seat 4:

13,075

Setup: I am in the second hour of a $30 rebuy tournament with the blinds at 100-200. I've been pretty active so far, and the table has started to notice. Seat 4 is a good player I know, but the rest of the table I've never played with before, and they seem to be mostly weak players.

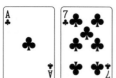 **Pre-flop** (300): Suited aces are marginal hands out of position. They are good hands if you are lucky enough to see the flop cheaply against some limpers. They can also be good hands when you are short-stacked to re-steal against late-position raisers. The action is folded to me. *A-xs* is much better than the average hand the big blind is sitting on, so I raise.

I raise to 600, and the big blind reraises to 1,800. The big blind is aware that I've been very active, and he could be reraising here with a wide variety of hands. Given my image, I could push all-in here and expect the big blind to fold with a high frequency. However, that's a very risky play with these stack sizes, as I am basically risking my entire 10,000 stack to pick up 2,400 (although I'll win a showdown sometimes, I'll almost always be a big dog when my opponent calls). I can also check-raise my opponents on many flops and win an even bigger pot that way. Folding is certainly an option here given that I can often be dominated on ace high flops, but with my loose image I expect to be getting played back at with a very wide range of hands. I call 1,200.

 Flop (3,600): This is the best flop I could ask for without it giving me a made hand. I have an open-ended straight draw plus the nut-flush draw. I could even have the best hand here with ace high. I am a favorite versus all single-pair hands, and I am not very far behind hands as strong as a set or even a made straight. Many times the big blind will be holding hands like A-Q or K-Q where he's going to have a hard time continuing if I put pressure on him. My hand is strong enough that it warrants a check-raise all-in here.

Because the big blind raised before the flop, hopefully I can trap him for a continuation bet with the intention of check-raising all-in. If he missed, he'll probably have to fold. If he calls, there's a very good chance I am a favorite in the hand. I check, and the big blind bets 3,600. I raise all-in, to 8,695. The big blind calls and shows AA. Note that even though my opponent has aces, I am actually a 55% favorite in this hand on the flop.

 Turn (20,990): I make my straight immediately, and the AA is drawing to one of the remaining three sevens for a chop.

 River (20,990): The river is the 3♠, and I win 20,990. Even a monster hand like aces is vulnerable to big combination draw hands. Also, even though my opponent had AA, his range was much wider than that, and many times I will take down this pot on the flop without having to show down my hand.

Hand 81

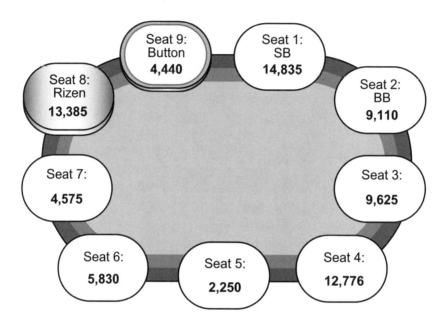

Setup: I am in the second hour of a $100 rebuy tournament with blinds of 100-200. It is just after the rebuy period, so most of my reads are invalid because most players play very differently after the rebuy period than during, when chips lost cannot be easily replaced with rebuys.

  Pre-flop (300): K-J offsuit isn't a great hand, but it's more than good enough to open from late position when it's folded around. Everyone folds to me, and I raise to 550. The big blind elects to call 350 more.

   Flop (1,200): Flops of all one suit can be very dangerous, especially when you have a hand like top pair or an overpair. A lot of players like to bluff at these flops, espe-
cially if they have the A♠. With the A♠, they often play very aggressively because they always have outs; this puts their opponents in a very difficult position, as they can never have the nuts without the A♠. If the stack sizes were smaller in relation to both the pot and the blinds at

this stage in the tournament, I would often bet here to protect my hand and take the pot down immediately. Given the relatively deep stacks for this stage in the tournament though, when the big blind checks to me, I check behind to keep the pot small and to reevaluate the situation on the turn.

 Turn (1,200): A great card. I now have three kings. My hand is also somewhat disguised, as my opponent probably believes I would have bet the flop with a king. My opponent leads for 1,000. While it's possible he has a flush, it's more likely he saw my flop check as weakness and is trying to buy the pot. He could also have something like A-8 that he thinks is good here. Another possibility is that he is now semibluffing with the A♠.

I raise to 3,600, and after some thought, the big blind moves all-in for 8,560 total. I think a little, and for 4,960 more it is still quite likely I have the best hand. Even if I don't, any K, J, 8, or 3 will probably make me the best hand. I call 4,960 more, and my opponent shows me A♠ T♦ for the ace-high flush draw. I just have to fade any non-jack spade on the river to win a nice pot. The river is the 8♥, giving me a full house, and I win an 18,320 pot.

Hand 82

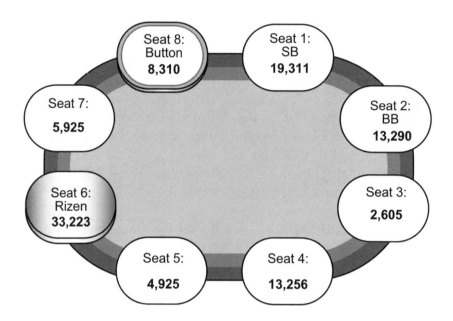

Setup: This is the nightly $100 rebuy tournament that attracts all the best online players. The blinds are 150-300 with a 25 ante. My table is filled with solid, tough players. The button, however, is a player I've never seen before in this particular tournament, and I have no reads on him.

 Pre-flop (650): I like to open with this hand when folded to. It can be somewhat tricky to play, but you can make a lot of deceptive hands and execute a lot of semibluffs with it. It is folded to me, and I make a standard raise to 850. It is folded to the button, who calls the 850. Both blinds fold.

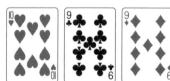 **Flop** (2,350): This is a good flop for me, but the problem here is stack sizes. The button has about 7,500 left. This is the kind of board I will often get raised on if a player holds K-Q and Q-J, and sometimes hands like 88 or 77. If I make a standard continuation bet in the range of 1,500 to 2,000, I'll have a

tough decision to make if he reraises all-in. If I check to him, he may bluff with a bad hand, or he may even believe his 88 is the best hand and bet and call a raise with it. I check here with the plan of raising a bet all-in. He checks.

 Turn (2,350): I now have a straight draw in addition to my pair. Most opponents would have bet 88 or Q-J when checked to on that flop, so I feel comfortable that I have the best hand here. My opponent could have slow-played any 9 or TT on this flop as well, but that is a risk I am willing to take, especially with these stack sizes. I bet 1,500, and my opponent quickly calls.

 River (5,350): When your opponent quickly calls, it's often a sign that he has some sort of drawing hand. The 3♣ brings in the backdoor-club draw, so I need to be a little careful here. If he has a four-card straight, though, my hand is good, and my opponent very well may bluff when checked to. Since my hand can't stand a raise, and there is the possibility that my opponent may bluff-raise this board, I check to the button, who makes a small bet of 1,500. I call the 1,500, and he shows K-J offsuit for the busted straight draw.

Hand 83

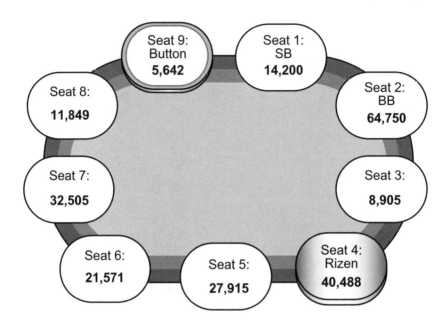

Setup: This is another hand from the same $2,600 buy-in tournament I discussed earlier in Hand 74. The play is still mixed, from very solid to very poor. However, my image has changed from earlier in the tournament and is now quite solid after winning some big hands and having someone at the table point out that I am a professional.

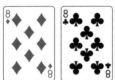 **Pre-flop** (600): As long as the stacks are fairly deep, I like to open-raise pocket pairs from any position. Pocket pairs tend to be easy hands to play out of position if you have to, and raising even small and middle pocket pairs from early position gives deceptive value to your hands. Early-position raises also get a lot of respect, so you can often represent big hands on the flop to pick up the pot. I raise to 1,100, and it is folded to the big blind, who calls the additional 700.

Flop (2,400): My opponent checks. This is a very scary-looking flop. There are two clubs on board, and I find that players often like to check-raise bluff paired boards. I have the advantage of position in this hand, and a hand with reasonable showdown value. It makes sense to see if I can get to a showdown cheaply in this spot. Checking can actually indicate some strength to my opponent, as he might think that either I'm slow-playing or I'm trying to keep the pot small with a hand like Q-x or better, and that I don't want to build a big pot with the pair on the board. I check to see what develops on the turn.

 Turn (2,400): The turn is a harmless card, although it brings another flush draw into the picture. My hand still has showdown value and could still be the best. The big blind bets 1,200, which is just half the size of the pot. A half-size bet seems a little suspicious, as most players will often bet more than that with their good hands, given all the drawing possibilities on the board. It looks a lot like a probe bet so that he can see where he stands in the hand. I call.

 River (4,800): I know that the big blind likes to bet big on the river with strong hands, so if he bets 4,000 or more, I can fold fairly confidently. If checked to, I might have the best hand, but betting doesn't make sense given that there aren't many hands I am ahead of that will call. My toughest decision will be if the big blind makes a bet in the 2,000 to 3,000 range. This is a board that's very tough to bluff at twice, so I'd have to figure he has a real hand if he bets again. Luckily, the big blind checks, and I check behind. The big blind shows 44, and I win a 4,800 pot.

Hand 84

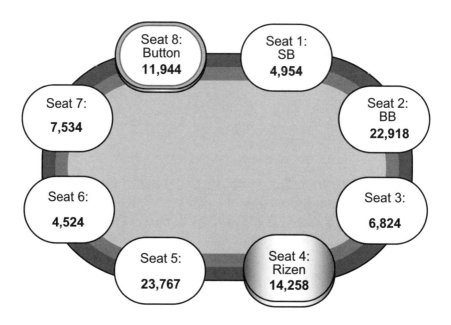

Setup: I am in the middle stages of a second-chance Sunday tournament with blinds of 250-500, and the ante is 50. The fields in these tournaments are usually tough due to the lack of satellites and the large buy-in, and they are generally filled with lots of aggressive, tricky players.

  Pre-flop (1,150): A-J offsuit is a questionable raising hand under-the-gun in a nine-handed or ten-handed game, but in an eight-handed game from *UTG+1*, it is a fairly standard opening hand. Seat 3 folds, and I raise to 1,299. In online tournaments, I often like to bet amounts that graphically "appear" much larger than they are. It is folded to the button, who raises the exact minimum to 2,098. Everyone folds back around to me. These situations are extremely tricky. Minimum raises are virtually always aces or kings at this stage in the tournament, although they occasionally represent a "misclick" (where your opponent accidentally clicked "raise," either without making the proper amount or just by randomly clicking the window to bring it into focus, a common habit of multi-table players).

Since there is no way to know if my opponent accidentally made the raise, I often assume this is either AA or KK here. There is 4,547 in the pot, and I have to call 799 more, giving me pot odds of nearly 6-to-1 and implied odds for my opponent's entire stack. The thing you have to be really careful of, though, is this: With a hand like A-J, you have to know what you are looking for. Since you hold one ace in your hand, it is twice as likely your opponent holds kings than aces if those are the only two hands we put in his range (there would be six combinations of KK and three of AA). Also, if your opponent does have AA, the likelihood of the case ace flopping is extremely low. So when you call here, you are looking to flop an ace, two jacks, or a straight, or you're done with your hand. If the flop comes jack high, you have to just fold, even though you have top pair top kicker. Here, the stacks just aren't deep enough to find out where I am, and even though I'm getting great pot odds pre-flop, I am also offering my opponent tremendous *reverse implied odds*, if I am willing to play for my whole stack with a jack-high flop. I call 799.

 Flop (5,346): This is exactly the flop I was worried about. I'll stick to my discipline and check and fold. I check, and surprisingly my opponent checks.

 Turn (5,346): Well, my opponent either has slow-played himself into trouble or did indeed misclick. Many players take the art of trapping too far, though, and it's very possible he checked behind with AA or KK to induce a bluff. What I like to do in these situations, where I'm almost sure my opponent either has a huge hand or has made an embarrassing mistake, is make a somewhat small-looking lead bet on the turn to feign weakness. If he has aces or kings, he'll think his trap was set perfectly and pounce. Additionally, if he misclicked "raise" here, he may interpret my weak bet as a steal attempt and turn his first mistake into a second one by coming over the top of me. Either way, my opponent has dug himself a hole, and I am going to hand him a bigger shovel. I bet 2,650, or just under half the size of the pot.

My opponent immediately makes a minimum raise to 5,300. This is virtually always aces or kings, and players who play this way are hardly ever capable of folding them once they've "set the trap." I move all-in for 12,110, and my opponent instantly calls all-in and shows KK. The river is the 8♠, and I win a 24,938 pot, nearly doubling up, and knock out my "trapping" friend.

Hand 85

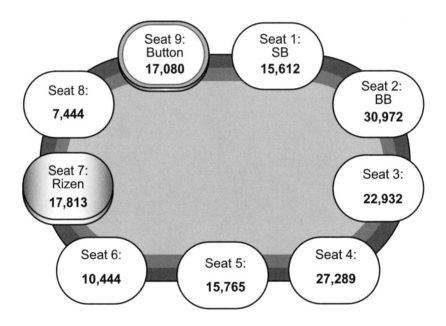

Setup: This is a nightly $150 tournament with a mix of good players and satellite players. The blinds are 300-600 with a 30 ante. I have extensive history with the under-the-gun player in this hand. He is a very good player, extremely capable of mixing it up and playing very aggressively. Usually, though, when he gets involved in a big pot he has a good hand.

 Pre-flop (1,170): A-Qs is a strong hand that I will play aggressively in most situations at this stage in the tournament. The under-the-gun player raises to 1,500, and it is folded me. I would often fold this hand to an under-the-gun raiser, but he made a small raise of two-and-a-half times the big blind, which gives me good odds to play this hand. The advantage of having position post-flop helps if I am dominated here. Also, it is very unlikely that a player behind will reraise here unless he has aces or kings, since there was an under-the-gun raiser and a caller.

   Flop (4,170): Gin! The perfect flop for my hand! The only question is how to play it for maximum advantage. The villain leads into me for 2,700. Given our extensive history, the villain in this hand knows I'm perfectly capable of raising this flop in position with a dry A♣ or as a complete bluff. The best way to win a big pot here is to make a raise of a size that will have my opponent believing he can make me fold by putting in a big reraise for the rest of my chips. Since my opponent raised under-the-gun, it's very likely he has a good hand here, and if I slow-play my hand just by calling, it will probably look more scary to him than if I raise. After putting the ante in and calling the flop, I have about 14,000 chips left. At 300-600 blinds, I want to leave enough chips behind after raising so that my opponent believes I may still fold. Raising half my remaining stack looks like I'm leaving myself room to fold. I raise to 7,000, and my opponent goes all-in for 21,402 after some thought. Obviously, I call, and he turns over K♠ K♦. He is drawing extremely thin. The turn and river come 2♦ 9♣, and I double up.

Hand 86

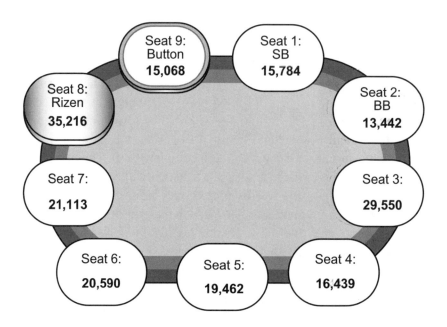

Setup: I am the chip leader at the table. There are 150 players remaining, and 120 get paid, so I'm not on the bubble yet but I'm fast approaching it. This is the $150 nightly tournament, so there are lots of satellite players who got in for $5-$10 who will be looking to cash. The blinds are 400-800 with a 40 ante.

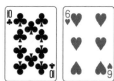 **Pre-flop** (1,560): It is folded to the player directly to my right, who raises to 1,600. Although I have a horrible hand, this is a great opportunity to pick up some extra chips here. With the bubble approaching, this player has 21,113 at the beginning of the hand, more than enough to hold on and make the money. I have the perfect stack size to make a reraise that will put lots of pressure on him while he is out of position, but the reraise amounts still allow me to make an easy fold if he comes over the top. I reraise to 4,800.

It is folded to the big blind, who goes all-in for a total of 13,402, and the initial raiser folds. I am getting a great price to call here, as there is 20,562 in the pot and I only need to call another 8,602 to give me 2.4-to-1 pot odds. The problem is that I am against the big blind, who has pushed over the top of a raise and a reraise with the bubble approaching. He surely has me completely dominated. He may have A-K, but it is more likely that he is sitting on an overpair. I am better off folding here to preserve my chip lead for better opportunities as the bubble approaches, rather than calling off another 8,602 to gamble with a player who almost certainly has me drawing very thin. I fold.

Hand 87

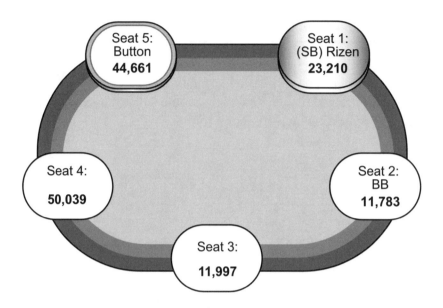

Setup: I am on the bubble of a $100 six-max tournament with blinds of 400-800 and a 100 ante. Currently, there are only five players at the table. Both of the big stacks at the table have been raising and re-raising mercilessly to take advantage of the bubble.

 **Pre-flop** (1,700): Pocket nines is a very strong hand in a five-handed game. My hand is even stronger given the bubble and the stack size of 30 big blinds.

It is folded to the cutoff, who raises to 2,400, and then it is folded to me. With 4,100 in the pot now, I have too many chips left in my stack to push, since my opponent will almost always only call with hands that dominate me or maybe A-K. If I make a pot-size reraise to 8,500, I increase the chance that he may decide to get frisky and think he can push all-in to take me off my hand, given that he thinks I am trying to make the money. A pot-size raise also leaves me the perfect amount left to bet if he calls, to push the rest of my chips in on any flop. At any rate, with the aggressive chip leader in this pot I am not folding my hand. I reraise to 8,500, prepared to play for all of my chips. The cutoff calls.

   Flop (18,300): A terrible flop for my hand, but having made the reraise pre-flop, I must continue with my plan to shove the flop. Looking at my opponent's possible range of hands, I think it's very likely he would have just moved in pre-flop with a hand like A-K, A-Q, and maybe even A-J. I find a vast majority of the time that when players call in this situation is it with medium pairs and random broadway hands (K-Q, Q-T, etc). Given that range of hands, this flop is likely to scare him. I will run into hands like A-T, K-Q, or K-J on occasion but there is too much money in the middle to back out now given that there are also a lot of hands that I am ahead of. I push for 14,610, and my opponent folds.

Hand 88

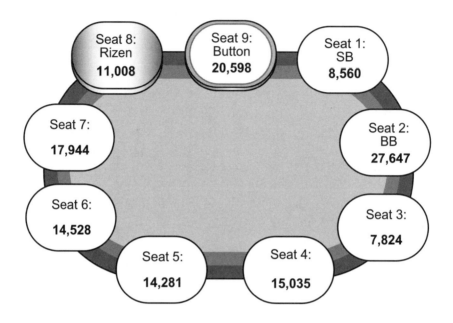

Setup: I am almost at the payout bubble in a nightly $100K tournament with blinds of 300-600 and antes of 30. This is one of the bigger regular daily tournaments with a mix of good players and satellite qualifiers. I have an average stack and have been fairly active near the bubble.

  Pre-flop (1,170): K-Jo is a solid hand from late position when no one else has entered the pot. It is folded to me and I make a modest raise to 1,649, which is fairly standard for this stage of the tournament. It is folded to the big blind, who calls 1,049.

 **Flop** (3,868): This is a really dry, ace-high flop, which is usually perfect for continuation bets. To my surprise, the big blind bets 1,800. This is an odd bet in that it is less than half the pot, and he is betting into the pre-flop raiser. Most opponents will check-raise a real hand in this situation. Some sophisticated players will lead with big hands here to trick their opponents,

but this player has done nothing to lead me to believe that he is the type of player to make that kind of tricky play. It is more likely that he has observed how active I've been on the bubble and is trying to push me off my hand, hoping I don't have an ace.

I actually see this move on dry, ace-high boards a lot, both live and online, and against most players you can take the pot here by raising. A push for a total of 9,359 chips is just a little over a pot sized raise here, which shouldn't seem too suspicious to the original bettor. I raise all-in to 9,359 and the big blind folds.

Hand 89

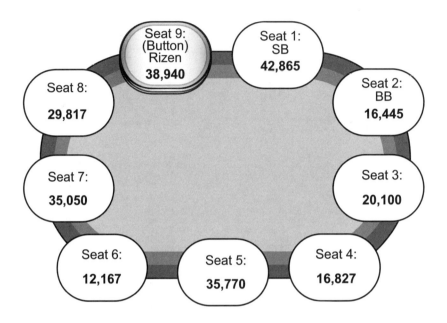

  Pre-flop (1,575): K-Q is a strong hand on the button if it's folded to me. Even against a middle- or late-position raiser, this hand can have a lot of strength. I'll be forced to fold if someone from early position raises or if there is a raise and reraise in front. It is folded to me, and I open with a raise to 1,800. The small blind folds, and the aggressive, defensive big blind calls 1,200 more.

 **Flop** (4,575): This is a flop that lots of players like to bluff at. It's very unlikely that this kind of flop would hit a raising hand, and lots of blind defenders like to defend with A-x, which would often give my opponent a gutshot-straight

draw and two overcards. My opponent checks, and knowing he likes to bluff and check-raise, I check behind for the free card.

 Turn (4,575): This is a great turn card. Against this particular opponent I am almost certainly ahead, and I'm very likely to get action since he'll often call on the end with mediocre cards. It's time to take a trip to value town and see how many chips I can extract from the big blind. He checks, I bet two-thirds the size of the pot for 3,000, and the big blind quickly calls.

 River (10,575): This is not the best river, as it puts a potential straight on the board with a 4. Knowing how aggressively this player plays, though, it is very likely he would have already pushed all-in with an open-ended draw unless he was slow-playing A-4. With my read on this opponent, I am perfectly fine getting all of my chips in the middle. The principle question here is how to extract the most value.

The big blind checks to me, and I decide to bet 4,000. The bet is small in relation to the pot (not even 40%) and will get a call from many worse hands. It may even induce my opponent to bluff-raise all-in on the river.

He does indeed raise all-in, to 11,570, and I call the additional 7,570. He shows Q♣ 6♣. He hit his 6 on the river! It's very unfortunate that my opponent hit his card on the river, but given my reads, I played the hand well. My check on the flop prevented him from making a big bluff raise with his gutshot-straight draw and allowed me to pick up the best hand on the turn. I then extracted value from a second-best hand that got there on the river. Sometimes that happens, but as long as my thought process and decision-making are solid, I will win money in the long run.

Hand 90

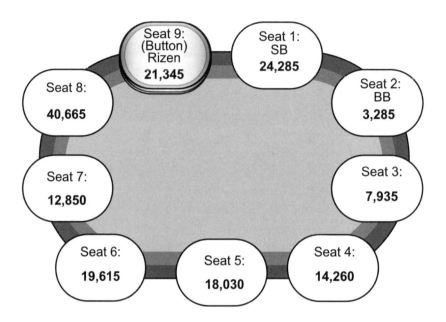

Setup: It's a nightly $20K guaranteed tournament with a $120 buy-in, and I am on the pay bubble. The blinds are 300-600 with 75 antes. Seat 8 is the largest stack at the table and has been routinely attempting to use this as leverage to pick up pots by raising and betting.

  Pre-flop (1,575): A-J is a strong hand in late position. It is folded around to the aggressive cutoff player, who raises to 1,600, which is standard for him. With my 21K chip stack, a reraise could work, but in the past the cutoff has shown that he is more than willing to come over the top of reraises on the bubble to threaten someone's entire stack. A-J is strong here, but I'm not sure I want to play it for all my chips preflop with around 35 big blinds. Flat-calling here and then picking my spots post-flop is a reasonable play; the only downside is that calling sets up a potential squeeze play from the blinds. The big blind, though, has only 3,285 in chips; his stack is too small to squeeze. I call 1,600, and both the blinds fold.

Flop (4,775): I didn't hit my hand, but this is also the type of flop that rarely hits my opponent. Boards with one face card and two low cards often miss most players. He could have a club draw or T-9 for a straight draw, but without a king on this flop, it will be very tough for him to go on with the hand if I raise his continuation bet. The cutoff bets 2,400.

A raise to about 7,000 looks right here. It's not so big that I can't get away from the hand if he comes back over the top, and it is strong because it almost looks like I want him to call. At the same time, I leave enough behind for a threatening turn bet if I need to. The threat of future large bets can often be just as intimidating as the big all-in bet itself while getting the same desired effect as an all-in push. I raise to 7,000, and my opponent folds, leaving me the pot and also sending the message that I won't just let him run over the table during the bubble period.

Hand 91

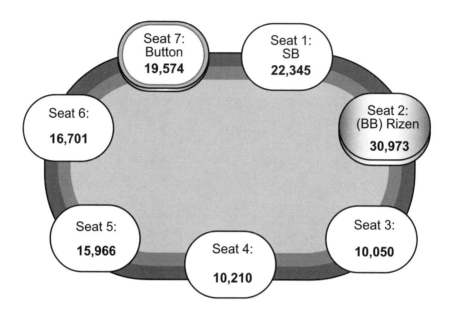

Setup: I am close to the money bubble of a $100 tournament with blinds at 400-800 with a 50 ante. I have a tight/solid image at this point and have only shown down winning hands thus far.

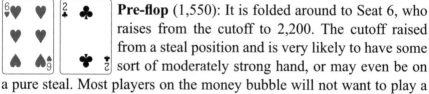 **Pre-flop** (1,550): It is folded around to Seat 6, who raises from the cutoff to 2,200. The cutoff raised from a steal position and is very likely to have some sort of moderately strong hand, or may even be on a pure steal. Most players on the money bubble will not want to play a hand for the rest of their chips unless it's a very solid hand. Given my image and my chip position, this is a good opportunity to try a re-steal. Because the cutoff started the hand with just under 17,000 chips, a raise to 7,200 seems about right.

A raise of this size accomplishes a few things. It's big enough that he can't smooth-call for implied odds with hands like suited connectors or low pocket pairs. It's also big enough that the cutoff should know that he is basically pot-committed if he plays the hand, given that he must call about a third of his stack. His best options are either to go all-in or to fold. If he does decide to smooth-call, he should have a very strong hand, and I would fold with anything short of two pair on the flop. The raise is also small enough that I can easily fold to a reraise because I haven't priced myself in. This is an excellent bubble play because it maximizes the pressure on my opponents while minimizing the losses for me when I run into a real hand.

This is a risky play. I am risking 6,400 to win 3,750. However, given the bubble and my opponent's range of hands, he should fold more than enough to make this a profitable play. However, note that my opponent is in the cutoff, where many players play a wide range of hands. I would almost never make this type of play against a player in early position nor, in most cases, against a player in middle position.

Hand 92

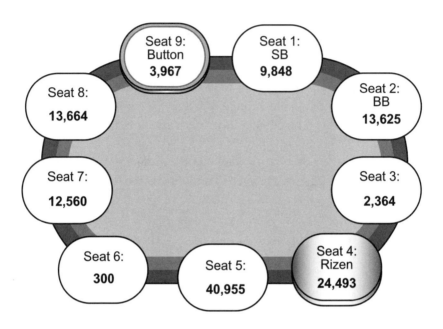

Setup: This is a Sunday $200 rebuy tournament that often brings together one of the toughest fields in online poker. I am in the middle stages of the tournament, with blinds of 200-400 with a 25 ante. Seat 5, the chip leader, is a very good, well-known player who knows how to use his chip stack to push people off hands. I've tangled in several pots with him, with neither of us really getting the better of the other.

  Pre-flop (825): Obviously, the second-best hand in poker is nice to have from any position. It is folded to me, and I make it 1,099. The chip leader flat-calls my raise, and everyone else folds.

   Flop (3,023): Well, I really didn't want to see one of the aces come out on the flop. The question is whether to check in the hopes of getting to a cheap showdown, or to bet my hand aggressively. In position, I often like to play this sort of situation for a cheap showdown when I can, but out of position I am going to have a really hard time controlling the size of the pot. Because I raised from early position, it is very unlikely that my opponent has AA or A-K, as he would not want to encourage other callers with those types of hands by flat-calling. A-Q is a possible hand, though. The most likely non-ace hands are pairs (not including AA/KK) and suited connectors. Given that his range does not include lots of hands with aces based on my read of the situation, it makes sense to bet. I likely have the best hand, and if I give control of the pot to my opponent out of position, I am much more likely to lose the pot. I bet 2,000, and my opponent calls.

 Turn (7,023): This is actually a good card for me. The second ace on the board leaves only two in the deck, which makes it much less likely that my opponent holds one in his hand, especially given the narrow range I put him on. That being said, this is also an excellent bluff-raise card for him, because it makes it less likely that I hold an ace as well. I will often lead here a second time with the ace for that very reason, but check when I have a strong non-ace hand. This can induce bluffs from my opponents while making sure I don't get moved off the best hand. It also helps control the size of the pot so that I don't lose a huge pot when my opponent does have an ace.

I check to my opponent, who bets 3,200. This is a small bet in relation to the pot, which smells of weakness. At the same time, a good player will often do this, knowing it looks weak. A good player looks ahead and knows that if I call, there will be a 13,423 pot, and I only have 18,194 behind. This allows him potentially to put a lot of pressure on me on the river.

This is really a tough spot for me. Raising here doesn't make much sense because I will only be called by hands that completely dominate me, and there aren't really any draws on the board to price out here. On the other hand, if I call, I may be facing an even bigger river bet, which will put me in a real bind. Folding seems really bad, though, given the size of the pot and how often I am ahead. I decide to call 3,200 and reevaluate based on the river action.

River (13,423): This river card brings in the K-Q draw, but since I have two of the kings, it is unlikely that this hand is out there. It brings in TT as well, but most players would have checked behind on the turn with TT because it has so much showdown value. I am stuck in a very similar situation as I was at the turn, in that if I bet, I am only likely to induce action from a better hand. I might also get moved off my hand if my opponent raises.

The best choice here is to try to induce another bluff on the river by checking, and then making a decision once I see the size of the bet. I check, and my opponent bets 2,750. This is a very confusing bet because it's so small. On the river, a bet like this usually indicates a strong hand and is designed to entice a call or even a raise. Sometimes this is also a value-bet by someone who may think his jack is good, or it may even be a post oak bluff, where the person is making a weak bet designed to look strong in the hopes that you will fold.

The pot odds are now just too favorable, and if my opponent holds an ace or some sort of JJ or 77 for a full house, he really should have tried to build a much bigger pot at some point. I call the 2,750, and my opponent shows 7♠ 6♠ for aces and sevens that picked up a flush draw on the turn. I win the pot, but I was fortunate that my opponent let me get to a showdown so cheaply.

He should have checked behind after he picked up the flush draw on the turn to go with his pair. Instead, he called the flop with bottom pair so that he could try to take the pot away from me on the turn when I checked. After he picked up a draw and I checked, he felt the need to follow through on his flop plan by betting, but made a weak bet so that he didn't get moved off his hand easily. This is a good example of why you should reevaluate your situation on every street. Just because you call on the flop in order to take the pot away later doesn't mean you can't switch gears when the turn card turns out to be much more favorable for you.

Hand 93

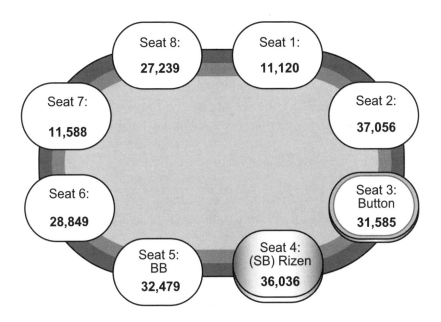

Setup: It is later in the same $200 rebuy with blinds of 500-1,000 and antes of 100. The villain is the same player, except this time in the big blind.

 Pre-flop (2,300): A-Q is a very strong hand in the right situations and depending on how the action unfolds in front, I could easily do anything from folding to playing for all of my chips. In this case, it is folded around to me. In a blind-versus-blind situation, I will definitely play for all of my chips preflop here, but I'm too deep to shove, so a standard raise is in order. This late in a tournament, a standard raise is often slightly less than three times the size of the blind, but since I am out of position on this hand, I raise to 3,000, and the big blind calls.

Flop (6,800): I flop a gutshot-straight draw with an overcard. This is a dangerous flop, though, as lots of hands in my opponent's range could have hit this flop. K-J, Q-J, Q-T, J-T, and 44 are all hands the big blind would call with that would like this flop. That said, there are a lot of hands he will fold, and even if he calls, I could very well make the best hand or move him off a hand on a later street. Also, recall from the previous hand that he floated me with bottom pair earlier and tried to take the pot away on later streets. So even if I get called and miss my hand, I may be able to take him off his hand on a later street if I am willing to fire more than one barrel. I bet 4,000, and my opponent calls 4,000.

 Turn (14,800): The turn card doesn't change things much. I still have an overcard and a gutshot-straight draw, and my ace high might even be the best hand. Looking back on my history with this player, though, he has floated me on the flop with poor hands before, and in previous hands with him, I checked my medium-strength hands on the turn. If he's the thinking player I believe him to be, he should view a second bet from me as indicative of a very strong hand. Given the combination of his wide flop calling range and his perception of my tight turn betting range, this is an excellent place to fire a second barrel. If called, I still have outs. I bet 9,500, and the big blind thinks for a long time before folding K-J face up. I win a 14,800 pot.

Hand 94

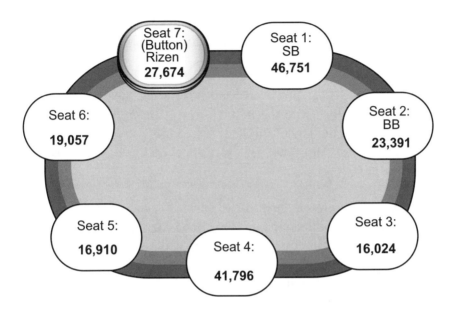

Setup: I am in the later stages of a $100 freezeout with blinds of 600-1,200 and 125 antes. Most of the table has been playing reasonably well; no one sticks out as particularly poor or particularly good.

  Pre-flop (2,675): Suited broadway hands in the middle and later stages of tournaments can be powerful reraising and semibluffing hands, as they hold up reasonably well in all-in situations before the flop and play well on the flop when called. You can semibluff a lot of pots post-flop when you flop a flush or straight draw with overcards and have a lot of outs if you are called.

In this case, it is folded to me on the button, I raise to 3,199, and the big blind calls.

Flop (7,873): This isn't a good flop for me as I have only a gutshot-straight draw and a backdoor-flush draw. That said, it should be a very scary flop for my opponent as well. Surprisingly, my opponent leads into me for 2,400, which is only one-third of the pot.

First of all, if he had an ace in his hand at this stage, he probably would have been reraised before the flop. If he was playing his ace tightly, then he surely would have "checked to the raiser" to make sure he got a continuation bet out of me. This sort of bet really seems like a weak queen or a club draw.

Two playing lines present themselves. One is to go ahead and raise right here and try to take the pot down. That line is perfectly reasonable, but this is also a good spot to *float* the flop, or call his bet in position with the intention of winning the pot on a later street. The float has several advantages here. One is that I may hit a K or a J on the turn and end up with the best hand; whereas if I raise the flop and get reraised, I will be forced to fold my hand and lose all my equity in the pot. Another is that my opponent will get a chance to further define his hand on the turn. Most players who bet one-third of the pot on the flop have a very hard time following through with any sort of meaningful bet on the turn without having an ace here. I decide to call.

 Turn (12,673): This is a very benign turn. It's highly doubtful he has 99 here, as he probably would have reraised with it preflop. My opponent again bets 2,400, this time about one-fifth of the pot. A one-third pot bet on the flop and then a one-fifth pot bet on the turn just screams weakness. This is a good spot to go ahead and take the pot away. By just calling on the flop and raising the turn, you are representing a very big hand, and it will be extremely difficult for your opponent to call without an ace, which he is very unlikely to hold for all the reasons discussed above. I raise to 18,000, putting my opponent all-in. He folds and I win a nice pot.

Hand 95

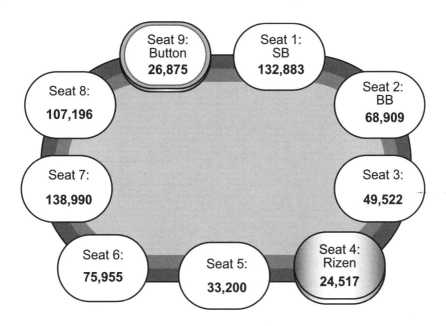

Setup: I have just begun the fourth hour of a big $500 Sunday tourna-ment. The blinds are 600-1,200 with 150 antes. The table is playing quite loose-passive, with lots of players calling preflop and generally playing very straightforward after the flop. My image is on the tight side, having shown down only big hands and not having any of my bluffs caught so far.

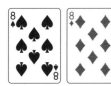 **Pre-flop** (3,150): Pocket eights is a strong hand, and I will often open for a raise even in early position. However, Seat 3 under-the-gun acts first and limps into the pot before me. Pocket pairs play best if you can get a big multiway pot and spike a set, or if you can get it heads up preflop. Given that the under-the-gun player has already called, calling behind him should induce at least a few more callers behind, building a pot. Also, the fact that the initial caller is under-the-gun has a bit of a "freezing" effect on the entire table, as often an early-position call signals a big hand. Tricky players will sometimes limp with their premium hands in early position, hoping someone raises so that they can

come back over the top and win a big pot. I call 1,200, Seat 7 calls, and it is folded around to the big blind, who checks.

   Flop (6,750): This is actually one of the better flops for me that doesn't have an 8. Most players like to limp with pocket pairs, suited connectors, and suited aces. While it's very possible someone is on a flush draw, a queen is a pretty innocuous card that isn't in my opponents' ranges for the most part. Some players will limp with hands like K-Qs and Q-Js from early position, though, so there is some cause for concern.

The big blind and Seat 3 both check. At this point, I like my hand, but at the same time I must be careful, given that I could very well be in big trouble with few outs. I want to choose a bet amount that will give me a good chance to win the pot while also defining my opponents' hands more precisely so that I can make better decisions on later streets. The goal is to minimize my losses when I'm behind, while still having a chance to take down the pot. I decide to bet two-thirds of the pot, or 4,800. Everyone folds to the player under-the-gun, who calls.

 Turn (16,350): My opponent checks. The turn card probably doesn't change a whole lot. It's unlikely my opponent is on a king-high flush draw or called with just a bare king in his hand. His most-likely holdings are a flush draw, a weak queen (something like Q-T or Q-J), a middle pocket pair, or perhaps even a big combination draw like A-4s or 5-4s, though most players would raise the flop with such a strong draw. It's remotely possible that my opponent holds AA, 33, or 22 as well, but most players would have check-raised those hands on the flop to prevent me from outdrawing them. The hands I am ahead of in his range I am not in fact that far ahead of, except hands like 77 and 66, and the hands that beat me have me completely dominated. At this point, it is in my best interest to keep the pot small and try to get to a cheap showdown, so I check.

River (16,350): Again, this card probably doesn't change the result of the hand if my read on the situation and this player is accurate. I expect my opponent will bet both his stronger hands for value (a pair of queens or better, probably) as well as his missed draws since betting is the only way he can win this pot. He will probably check most of his medium-strength hands to try to see a cheap showdown, or he may make some sort of a small blocking bet to prevent me from making a much larger bet to price him out of the pot. My opponent bets 4,800. I am getting 4-to-1 pot odds, so I only need to win more than 20 percent of the time to make calling here profitable. My opponent has made my decision easy because he could be bluffing more often than 20 percent of the time, given the range of hands I have put him on. I call 4,800, and my opponent shows A♠ 7♠ for a missed nut-flush draw.

It was critical in this hand to trust the initial read on the flop. Many players will look at the two overcards on the turn and river and give up on their hand. The range of hands on the flop that I put him on never changed because the action never dictated that it should. This, and the fact that my opponent made a weak river bet, allowed me to win a nice-size pot.

Hand 96

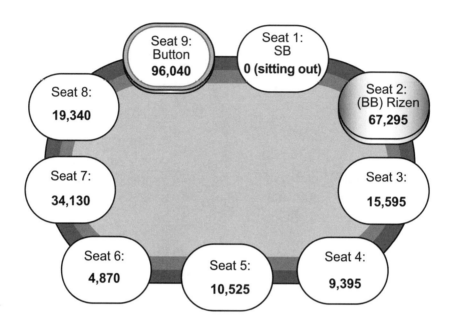

Setup: I am near the payout bubble in a yearly online championship event with a $500 buy-in. Many players in this event are satellite qualifiers, so the payout bubble is exaggerated even more than normal by the fact that the first payout level is 10 times or more than what many of these players paid to qualify. The blinds are 600-1200 with a 50 ante. The button seems to be an amateur player who has widened his range as the chip leader on the bubble. The small blind is currently sitting out.

 **Pre-flop** (2,250): This hand can be played many ways depending on the action in front of you. Here, the action is folded to the button, who opens for 3,040.

Given the opening bet, two playing lines present themselves: Against a very aggressive bubble player, I would tend to call here because I can win a big pot when they overplay their hand post flop trying to abuse the bubble. This type of player is also more likely to four-bet a wide range of hands preflop effectively forcing me to fold.

However, in this case, my opponent is a more typical tight-aggressive player who is probably playing out of his comfort zone with a big stack on the bubble. His four-bet range is probably limited to the very best premium hands, so a three-bet ought to have a high success rate. If he calls, he is less likely to pay me off if I hit a big hand, compared to a loose-aggressive opponent capable of making moves after the flop. By calling, I will often end up folding the best hand in a small pot given the difficulty of playing out of position.

I hold one of the few stacks at the table that can really hurt my opponent. While I could call profitably here, a better play is to reraise, and put pressure back on the initial raiser. I am on the bubble with a chance to increase my chip stack by 10%, with a hand that plays well out of position. I reraise to 10,120 and the button folds.

Hand 97

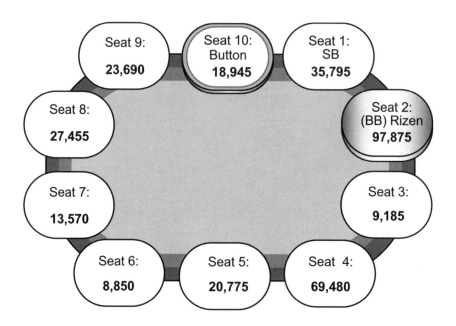

Setup: This is a hand a little later in the same tournament discussed in the previous hand and we are still near the payout bubble. The blinds are 800-1600 with a 150 ante.

 **Pre-flop** (3,900): Obviously, this is not a very strong hand. In fact, it's a slightly below-average hand against a completely random hand. Scat 3 goes all-in for 9,185. It is folded around to me. Many players will muck here without a second thought, but with Seat 3 only having 5.5 big blinds, he's very desperate and will often push any two cards here rather than get blinded out. There is 13,085 in the pot after the blinds, antes, and the short stack's push. I must call 7,535 more, so I am getting pot odds of just under 2-to-1.

With a shorter chip stack, I would never consider calling here, but with a large chip stack, I can accomplish two things by calling. First, if my opponent pushes with his top 20 percent hands (which may be a low estimate for some online players), I am getting just slightly less than the odds I need to call. Against a completely random hand, I am 48.22 percent to win, and against a top 20 percent hand, I am 31.67 percent to win[4]. I need a 36.5 percent win rate for the call itself to break even from a chip perspective.

Assuming my opponent's range is fairly wide, calling here is about a chip-neutral play. On average, when you call, you will end up with about the same amount of chips as you would if you fold, but calling will increase your variance. However, there is another consideration: If I call here near the bubble and my opponents see that I will call them with Q-3o, then regardless of the outcome of the hand, the table is likely to be VERY cautious against me for the remainder of the bubble period, knowing that I am willing to put their tournament on the line with any two cards. It will give me a maniacal image, one I should be able to utilize to pick up many more chips as long as the bubble lasts a while longer.

I call, my opponent shows J-2o, and neither of our hands improve. I eliminate an opponent and add 13,085 to my stack. The next three times I have the big blind on the bubble, all of my opponents fold to me.

---

[4] These types of calculations can be done using a poker odds calculator found at many sites on the Internet, including www.InternetTexasHoldem.com.

Hand 98

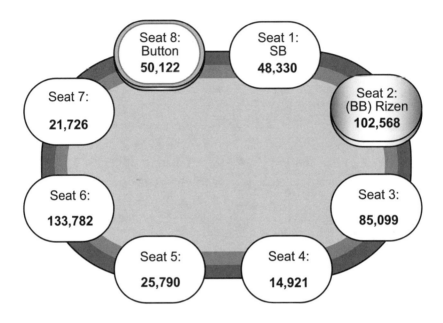

Setup: It is in the late-middle stages of the same $200 rebuy tournament discussed earlier, with blinds of 1,000-2,000 and 200 antes.

 **Pre-flop** (4,600): This is not a particularly strong hand, but in the middle to late stages, it can be a good blind defense hand that you can semibluff a lot of flops with when you have a large stack. It is folded to Seat 4, who pushes for 14,721, and then it is folded around to me. At first glance, this seems like a very easy fold with 10 high, but let's look a little more deeply into the situation. There is 19,321 in the pot, and I have to call 12,721 more, so I only have to win the pot 39.7 percent of the time to break even. With only seven times the big blind, an M of 5, and the big blind hitting him in two hands, his range should be pretty wide.

If I give him a theoretical range of any ace, any pair, any two broadway cards, and suited connectors greater than 6-5, then I win 40.1 percent of the time. As discussed in the previous hand, making calls in these types of situations can be very valuable to my image, as my opponents will be more reluctant to get involved with me in future pots unless they have a solid hand. Now, I want to make it clear that I wouldn't be making this play if the chips were more significant to my stack. If I had a stack similar to the small blind's stack, calling would risk 25 percent of my chips. I would often fold in these very chip-neutral situations because the amount of chips I lose can significantly damage my ability to win future pots. For example, you may not have any fold equity by reraising, and you may not be able to effectively check-raise post-flop.

In this particular example, I am only risking 12 percent of my stack, which will not alter how I play future pots. Taking a chip-neutral higher-variance path can be profitable when it allows you to establish a specific image that you can exploit later in the tournament.

I call 12,721, and my opponent shows A♥ K♣. The board runs A♠ J♣ 3♠ 9♠ 3♣, and I lose a 32,042 pot. Just because my opponent had A-K doesn't necessarily mean that I was wrong about his range. In fact, if for some reason he had showed me his hand prior to me calling, I was still 39 percent to win the pot, making the play only a very slight loser and still giving me the image benefits mentioned before.

Hand 99

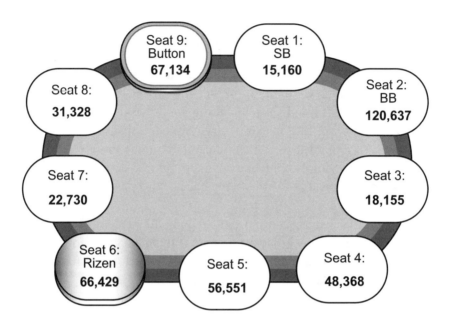

Setup: I am deep in a $200 major Sunday tournament. The blinds are 1,000-2,000 with a 250 ante. We are nearing the payout bubble, and this particular tournament is filled with satellite players who got into the tournament for much less than the buy-in, often $20 or less, so the first-level payout is a very significant return on investment for these players. The play at the table is generally reasonable but timid.

 **Pre-flop** (5,250): A-T offsuit is a reasonable hand from middle position, but not a super-strong one. Once you consider that I am on the bubble and that players are playing more timidly, it becomes an easy hand to open with. It is folded to me, and I open the pot with a raise to 5,199. Everyone folds to the big blind, who calls the bet.

Flop (13,648): I didn't hit, but this is the type of flop that isn't likely to hit my opponent either. It's a great board texture to make a continuation bet with. However, before I get the chance to do so, my opponent bets into me for 8,000. On this type of board texture with no draws out there, if the big blind really had a queen or a 7, wouldn't he go for the check-raise? This is a common misplay by a big stack near the bubble in tournaments with lots of satellite players or other players who aren't used to playing this deep very often. They know they're supposed to be using the bubble since they're the big stack, but they don't really know how, so they make weird plays like this as bluffs because they're "supposed to." If this were a sophisticated player, he would lead with big hands as well, but nothing to this point has shown me that level of sophistication, so I'll attack the weakness with what very well might be the best hand and raise to 26,500. The big blind folds as I reverse the "bubble abuse" he was trying to put on me and use it against him.

Hand 100

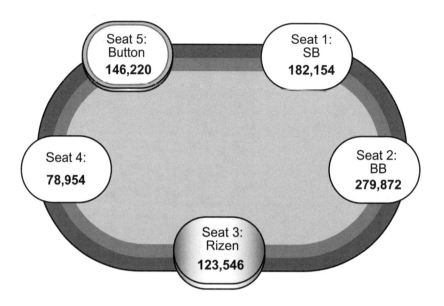

Setup: I am on the payout bubble of a $50 rebuy tournament. The blinds are 2,500-5,000 with a 600 ante. Only nine places play, and 10 players are left. The players have been playing the bubble aggressively with many steals and re-steals.

  Pre-flop (10,500): Q-Jo is not a spectacular hand, but it is a reasonably strong hand five-handed, and it is worth trying to pick up the large number of chips in the middle. I raise to 12,499, and it is folded to the big blind, who calls.

   Flop (30,498): This is one of the better flops I can hit without actually having a made hand. I have two overcards and an open-ended straight draw. My opponent checks. I could take a free card here, but my hand is very strong and my opponent will miss often. There are also a lot of chips in the pot already.

A continuation bet here is definitely warranted, but I have to be careful how to size the bet. With 110,447 chips left, ideally I want to make my bet size such that if I am raised, I can three-bet all-in and have fold equity. Betting the full pot is too much, because a bet of 30,498 will put more than 60,000 in the pot with around 80,000 behind, and if my opponent decides to raise, he will be pot-committed. My hand is strong, but a large part of its strength comes from the fact that I can make my opponent fold.

A smaller bet, in the half-pot range, will give me the flexibility to either take down the pot right now or possibly three-bet all-in with fold equity. I bet 18,000, and my opponent check-raises to 40,000. With this being the bubble and seeing lots of aggressive play, this could be anything from a complete bluff to top pair. He bet an amount that also looks as if he's leaving himself room to fold. I still have a lot of fold equity here with a three-bet all-in, and even if I am called, I have eight outs and could have as many as 14. It's also remotely possible my opponent has J-8 or 8-7, where I may even be ahead. I raise all-in to 110,477, my opponent folds, and I add 57,999 to my stack.

Jon "Apestyles" Van Fleet

Hand 101

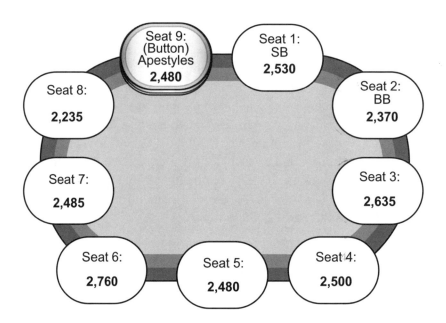

Setup: I am at the very beginning of a $215 freezeout tournament with the blinds still at the first level of 5-10. I don't recognize anyone at the table, and I haven't played any hands yet, so I'm assuming my opponents do not have any impressions on my play yet. There also haven't been any significant hands among the other players for me to gain reads on them.

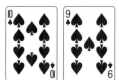 **Pre-flop** (15): Seat 8 in the cutoff makes a pot-size raise to 35. This particular tournament structure is very deep, especially at the initial blind level where everyone starts with a stack size of 250 big blinds. When all players have 200 big blinds or more, hand values change. Suited connector and small pair hands have more value than hands like A-K or other big card hands, which normally favor smaller stacks. This

is due to the tremendous implied odds opponents have to out flop you. Given the size of the stacks at the table, pairs and suited connectors have the potential to flop monsters where one can play huge pots; whereas when playing big pots with just top pair, top kicker, you will often find yourself in trouble against most, or at least reasonable, opponents.

Given my stack depth and the fact that T♠ 9♠ plays well, and also because my opponent is raising from late position, probably with a wide range of hands, reraising is a great play. You can also call here, but I like reraising for a couple of reasons. Mixing suited connectors into my reraising range adds deception, both on this hand and for future hands while I am at the same table. Only reraising big hands at this point is very exploitable and transparent.

My general philosophy at this point is to avoid putting in all of my chips without the goods while also applying pressure on my opponents since they will be hesitant to play large pots without nut hands. Many players, including advanced ones, play too tightly and cautiously in the early stages of a tournament. Because players are playing so tightly and passively, this is an excellent time to start accumulating some chips by applying pressure on your opponents in position and utilizing superior post-flop skills.

I make a standard three-bet to 120. Seat 1 in the small blind calls, and the initial raiser in Seat 8 folds his hand.

 Flop (285): The small blind checks. It's unlikely that the small blind is going to be cold-calling a three-bet in that spot with raggedy aces. However, it is quite reasonable for a decent player simply to cold-call strong aces like A-K or A-Q due to how deep the stacks are, as opposed to four-betting them. I have no information on this player, but I assume his range includes strong broadway cards and medium to big pairs. He could also have suited connectors and smaller pairs, but most players would opt to fold those hands in face of a raise and a reraise.

The fact that I caught a piece of this board isn't important because this is not the flop I am looking for when I play suited connector hands. Betting here is basically a semi-bluff. He really needs an ace to continue in the hand, and I may induce him to fold better hands like JJ or TT. I decide to make a continuation bet with the intention of folding to a raise. I will probably shut down if called, although making another bet on the turn or river isn't terrible since he is often holding QQ-TT given the pre-flop and flop action.

I bet 225 for around 80 percent of the pot, and my opponent folds, winning me the 285 pot.

Hand 102

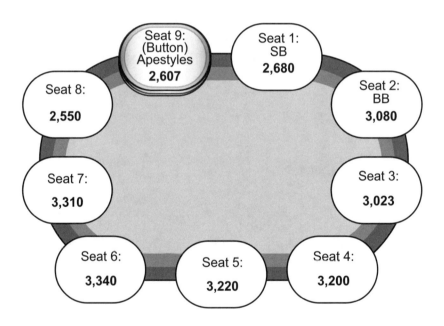

Setup: I am still at the very first level of a $1,060 tournament with the blinds at 10-20. There are a few solid regulars at the table in Seats 3, 5 (Rizen!), and 7, but I don't really know what to expect from the rest of the table yet.

Pre-flop (30): The action is folded to me and I make a raise to 80. The big blind calls.

   Flop (170): Seat 2 checks to me. This is a great flop to make a continuation bet on. Against a decent-to-good player, you usually aren't going to see many aces in his range. This is because it's generally bad to call with weak A-x hands out of position, and he's probably going to reraise the stronger aces like A-J+ pre-flop. However, I don't have much of a read on this player or any history with him, so I can't conclusively rule ace-rag out at this point. Because the board is dry, coupled with the fact that aces probably comprise a very small part of his out-of-position calling range, I can expect to have a high rate of success by representing an ace with a continuation bet. I also induce folds from most of the pocket pairs that beat me, and my hand is basically a bluff at this point.

I bet 133, and Seat 2 calls me; my bet failed this time. Right now, I am putting him on a flush draw, a pair of eights, maybe TT-99, a slow-played set, or a pair of aces with a medium or weak kicker.

 Turn (436): Seat 2 checks. While a second barrel here should cause a small part of my opponent's range to fold (such as TT-99 and 88), it's probably going to fail against the majority of his range. It's unlikely that I'll get him to fold a flush draw or a pair of aces, and I am certainly not going to be comfortable three-barreling even a good river card against an unknown player. When bluffing in general, it's preferable to have four or more outs that can improve to a lock hand. With 33 here, I can't play for stacks even if I river the 3♥, since the flush completes and, in some rare instances, he could even have a better set. I check behind.

 River (436): Seat 2 checks again. After check-calling the flop and checking this turn and river, it definitely seems like his hand is weak. He's most likely sitting on a weak ace or a busted flush draw. Betting could make 8-x and higher pairs fold, but they are a smaller part of his range than A-x hands at this point.

I am beating missed flush draws (unless they include a K or a 5), so there's no point in betting.

From a strategic perspective, I try to avoid marginal multi-street bluffs when deep-stacked or in the first level. This is because the blinds and pot sizes will be significant portions of our stacks soon, and I like to have a tight table image to capitalize on later.

I check behind, and Seat 2 shows a surprising A♦ Q♠, a fairly weak line from pre-flop all the way to the river.

Hand 103

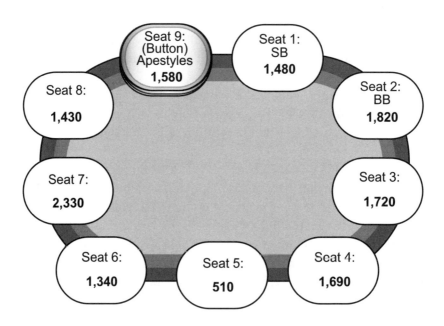

Setup: I am in the very early stages of a $109 freezeout, and the blinds are 10-20. I've only taken down one pot so far with a raise and a flop continuation bet. It's too early in the game to really be getting reads, but Seats 2 and 5 have already shown themselves to be bad players.

Pre-flop (30): I raise three times the big blind to 60. The big blind calls.

   Flop (130): Seat 2, who happens to be an extremely loose and passive calling station, checks. This board is really coordinated. Regardless, I am probably still ahead, and a lot of turn cards could make the board texture even uglier for my aces. I do have the A♥, so that limits his flush draw range. I decide to make a continuation bet of 111 for value, and Seat 2 calls. I am only a dozen or so hands into the tournament and this player has been incredibly loose, so I can't really narrow down his hand range much. At this point, he could have any pair, any straight draw, or any flush draw.

 Turn (355): Seat 2 checks. This is an absolutely horrible card. It completes the flush draws, a lot of straight draws, and even gives what were once single-pair hands like J-T, T-9, and T-8 two pair now. Despite how loose and bad my opponent is, there's no reason to make a bet here to get any value. The only thing betting would accomplish here is getting me into a situation where I would have to fold my ace-high flush draw. Worse hands probably fold (or bluff-raise, which I have to fold to), and most better hands either check-raise or call. I check, hoping to hit the flush on the river.

 River (355): Seat 2 checks again. This river is interesting. Since I know Seat 2 is a passive and weak player who probably isn't tricky at all, I interpret his river check as fear and generally rule out any suspicion of him "trapping" with a higher straight or made flush. If I'm confident that opponent is playing the board as well, the only thing I can do is try to get him to fold by representing the king or flush in order to win the pot. To get folds in this situation, my bet should be large enough (probably at least two times the pot) to make calling very difficult, yet also small enough to look like I am trying to get some realistic value out of it. Because this player is so bad, he will probably perceive an enormous bet as stronger than a two-times-pot bet. A bet around three times the pot seems sufficient. This sort of play actually works better against strong players who realize calling big overbets just for a chance to split the pot is bad, although you are vulnerable to being rebluffed by an observant opponent if you overuse the play and/or do not balance your range by betting the same amount with your made hands.

I fire 1,000, and Seat 2 instantly calls with 7♣ 5♠ for the split.

Hand 104

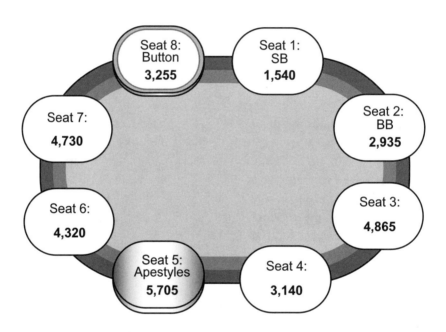

Setup: I am in a $320 freezeout tournament with the blinds at 15-30. I just moved to this table and only have history with Seats 1 and 3, both of whom are aggressive regulars. Since the blinds are still so small, the table still has big enough stacks to be playing a lot of post-flop hands.

Pre-flop (45): I make an open raise of three times the big blind to 90. Given the large stacks at the table, I am going to be open-raising pairs from any position. Seats 6, 7, and 2 flat-call.

  Flop (375): This is obviously an excellent flop because I have hit the set, and especially because there are three other players on a king-high board. While there is a club draw out there, at least I don't have to worry about too many big draws, as the best they can do is have a flush draw with a gutshot at this point. Given that there is a good chance someone is sitting on top pair here, coupled with the possible flush draw that I want to charge to play, I should be betting out here the majority of the time.

If I check-raise rather than make a continuation bet, opponents with weaker kings like K-J or K-T are going to be very alarmed as I'm often going to have hands like A-K or AA when I make that move. Betting out also disguises my hand strength on this board texture more than a check-raise. It's probably best to make a larger bet in this spot because kings are almost always going to be calling. Flush draws are probably calling any reasonable bet, so I charge them more with a large bet as well.

I bet 300, 80 percent of the pot, and only Seat 6 calls the bet. He probably has a medium-strength king or a flush draw he's playing weakly. A set of nines is also possible but unlikely. It would be pretty bad for him to be calling with just a pair of nines here considering I made a continuation bet into three other players, but anything is possible in this game.

 Turn (975): Almost any turn other than a club would've been just fine, so I am still in great shape here. Because I put him on either a flush draw or a pair of kings, the only move here is to keep betting. If I go for a check-raise, I might let him off his hand much too easily, and I'd really hate to let a flush draw peel off a free card or let kings with kicker concerns check behind and call just one river bet. With a set, I am looking hard for ways to double or stack my opponent. I bet 730 for 75 percent of the pot. Unfortunately, Seat 6 just flat-calls again rather than raising. The range I assigned him on the flop still holds true.

River (2,435): This is one of the best rivers I could've hoped for. My hand is extremely well disguised at this point, and my opponent could easily put me on a flush draw. The river improves weak kings to trips now, which should be excruciatingly difficult for my opponent to fold. I am very confident that I have the best hand, as I would expect him to raise the turn with a set of nines and raise the flop with K-9. I need to evaluate the options that will get me the most chips. If I make a big pot-size bet, all the flush-draw hands he might have will obviously fold whereas trips will either flat-call or push, depending how strong their kicker is and this player's tendencies.

By checking, I can induce bluffs some of the time from missed flush draws but also check-raise those trip king hands, which he is almost certainly going to be betting on the river for value. It's unlikely that he'll be able to fold most kings he could have like K-Q, K-J, or K-T in the face of a check-raise, so I get to stack him this way. The only downside to checking is that I let a pair of nines check behind, but this is really a small part of the range I expect him to have, if at all. Check-raising clearly seems to be the superior play. I check, and Seat 6 bets 1,675 (after thinking for a while) for 69 percent of the pot, leaving himself 1,525 behind. I pause for a little while so as not to betray my hand strength, and then raise all-in.

Seat 6 folds his hand. I can only guess that I induced a bluff from a flush draw here.

Hand 105

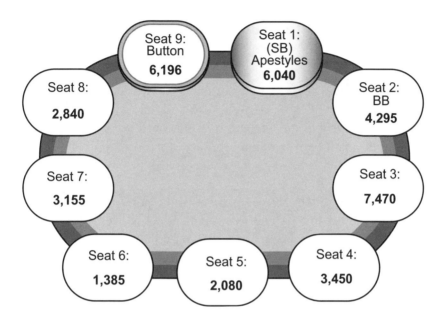

Setup: I am in the second level of a $320 freezeout with a $150K guaranteed prize pool. This particular structure has deeper stacks and much slower blind levels than your average tournament. With the blinds still only at 15-30, you'll notice that most of the table is pretty deep-stacked. I currently have a solid, aggressive image and have only shown down a set that I doubled up with earlier. There are a couple of aggressive players in Seats 3 and 9. Seats 4 and 7 have been playing exceptionally tight-passive, and I've only noticed them in a couple of pots.

  Pre-flop (45): Seat 4 raises four times the big blind to 120. Even though I have a big hand, I have to consider my opponent's tendencies and image before deciding which action to take. In this case, Seat 4 has been playing extremely tight and is raising from the second-earliest position at the table, thus making him very likely to have a top-tier hand. By three-betting him with jacks, I'll have to fold to a four-bet, which is liable to happen frequently given how close I think his range is to only premium hands. If I do three-bet and he flat-calls, I'll be playing the pot out of position and likely getting significant action only from hands that have me crushed. Flat-calling my big pair and playing deftly post-flop definitely seem superior to reraising. I call.

 Flop (270): Excellent, I've flopped a boat and it's very possible my opponent has a monster that I can get tons of value from. I could take a variety of lines given how strong my hand is and the strength of hands he'll be giving me action with. The decision here is rather arbitrary, but I decide to stay in line with the pre-flop action and go for a check-raise.

I check, and Seat 4 bets 180, 67 percent of the pot. I raise a little over three times the bet to 570, and my opponent deliberates a little before calling. He may have been considering folding TT-88 (if he even continuation-bets those hands in the first place) to my check-raise here, and calling overpairs to the jack like KK or QQ. However, most of the time I can expect him to have A-K or A-Q for trips with a strong kicker. It'll be extremely rare for him to have A-J or AA, and I'm really excited about this board since I can expect to stack him frequently.

 Turn (1,410): Yikes, this card could cause me some trouble since A-Q and QQ now got there, which comprise a significant portion of his flop calling range. I still need to bet here, though, so that I can get value from KK and A-K. Based on the other hands I've observed Seat 4 playing, I can probably expect him to flat-call both of these hands. Bet size is an important consideration here because I want to get value from KK rather than scare it away with a big bet. Around 50 percent of the pot seems like it would be enticing. I bet 780, and Seat 4 raises all-in to 2,760—very quickly.

This is a very tough spot. I flopped a huge hand, but the turn card really diminished the equity I have against my opponent's tight range. If he can only be doing this with strictly AA, QQ, A-K, and A-Q, then the jacks actually do have 39 percent equity[5], which merits a call in this spot given the amount already in the pot.

However, based on how passively Seat 4 has been playing and the speed at which he shoved, he's probably not going to be showing up with A-K very often. If I eliminate A-K from the above range, my hand has only 2% equity. It hurts to fold, but because of my read and his timing tell, I think it's the right play.

---

[5] 39 percent was computed using a poker odds calculator. However, in the heat of the action, you can roughly determine your equity by looking at the number of hand combinations you beat versus those you lose to. In this hand, there are eight possible A-K hands, six A-Q hands, one AA hand, and three QQ hands. I beat 8 out of 18 of them, or 44 percent, which is close to the poker odds calculator (the difference is the river card, which could counterfeit my full house).

Hand 106

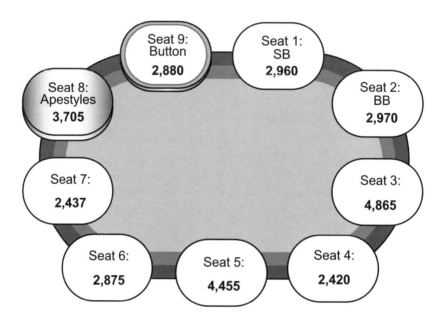

Setup: I am in a $162 freezeout tournament with the blinds at 15-30. I drew a really weak table and have been playing aggressively, picking up lots of pots from weak players. The only other player I've noticed being aggressive is Seat 7.

  Pre-flop (45): Seat 7 raises three times the big blind to 90. Seat 7 has been playing over-aggressively and raising frequently from late position. I really want to exploit his loose tendencies. While flat-calling to try to outplay him post-flop in position is a fine option, (especially with a hand like K-Jo), I decide to isolate him in position with a reraise since the stacks are deep.

He'll most likely fold, but in the event he calls, I still have position and will be able to pick up the pot a lot of the time with continuation bets on a good board. I will proceed cautiously if I flop top pair, as there is a significant threat of being dominated. Even though he's an aggressive player, he's not going to be able to check-raise my continuation bets cheaply. The pot will be 600 if he calls my reraise, and my bet will be around 450, leaving him 1,710 more to raise. My plan is to take the pot down pre-flop or post-flop if I miss, play for stacks if I flop two pair or better, and proceed cautiously if I flop top pair. I reraise a little over three times his raise to 277, and he calls instantly.

Although it's still possible he has a monster he's trying to play craftily rather than four-bet, the very short amount of time he took to call indicates something different. Usually when you have a big pair like aces or kings and your opponent three-bets, you're going to take a little time either to feign that your decision required some consideration or to really consider whether or not to four-bet as opposed to flat-calling.

   Flop (599): Seat 7 checks. This is a good flop for my hand; I hit top pair and there isn't much else going on with this board. However, there are a few problems with betting here. Even though I do have top pair at the moment, my kicker is pretty weak and I won't be able to stand much heat from my opponent. I do not want to play a huge pot here without more information to go on, and by checking behind I don't have to deal with an uncomfortable check-raise. I also disguise my hand and create an opportunity for my aggressive opponent to take a stab at the pot on the turn. I may get value from hands on the turn that would otherwise fold to a flop bet. Also, there are no reasonable flush or straight draws, other than gutshots and the unlikely 8-7. This is one of those situations where I am usually either way ahead or way behind and the only card I really don't want to see is an ace. I check behind.

 Turn (599): Seat 7 checks again. This turn card is pretty harmless. I decide to now fire 420 with my top pair for value. Seat 7 almost instantly raises my bet to 1,340. Right now he's representing (or at least trying to represent) either a strong king or better. While these hands are possible, there are a few factors here that indicate he holds nothing.

He instantly called pre-flop and instantly raised my turn bet. This doesn't really make sense. If he has an extremely strong hand as he's representing, he would most likely feign a little weakness before each of his decisions. Also, he just doesn't seem good enough to check a hand like AA, KK, A-K, 9-9, or K-Q twice. Another factor that might result in him running a bluff here is that he knows I am aggressive, and I've also detected a sort of annoyance from him concerning my table dominance. Considering that his line and timing tells don't really appear consistent with what he's representing, the fact that I've been playing aggressively, and the large turn raise three times my bet, I think there's more evidence that he's bluffing rather than actually holding a big hand. I push all-in for an effective 1,233 more.

Seat 7 instantly calls with A♣ T♥ and rivers the A♦ to win the 5,745 pot.

Hand 107

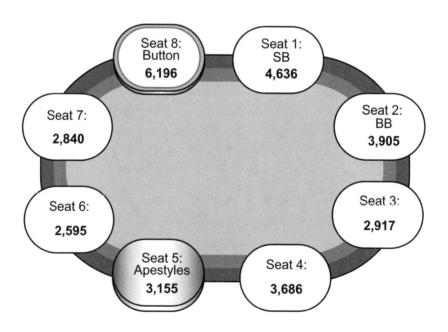

Setup: It's the second level of the Wednesday $320, $150K guaranteed prize pool. I haven't played many hands, and I have been taking down pots without showdown. The blinds are 15-30, so everyone at the table is deep-stacked. The cutoff is a loose, aggressive regular who has raised a few pots and then given up after his continuation bets were called.

  Pre-flop (45): I have a premium hand in middle position, and make a standard opening raise of about three times the big blind to 99. The loose, aggressive player in Seat 7 flat-calls, and the big blind comes along as well. I assume the cutoff's range here is fairly wide but is weighted toward suited connectors, small-to-mid pairs, and mid-strength high-card hands such as K-Q, Q-J, and J-T. I would expect big hands such as A-K, A-Q, or JJ+ to reraise in this spot, but it is possible he has flat-called with them. I have no reads on the big blind as he has not been playing many hands.

   Flop (312): This is an excellent flop for me, and I probably have the best hand. I have flopped top pair top kicker on a fairly unthreatening or "dry" board — not many hands hit this board hard, there is no flush draw and only a few probable straight draws. After Seat 2 checks, I make a standard continuation bet of 214, which is about 70 percent of the pot; any bet between 50 and 75 percent of the pot is fine here. The intention of this bet is to get value out of weaker kings like K-Q, K-J, and K-T, which are a large part of my opponent's range of cold-calling hands, and also to keep the initiative in the pot. He could also be cold-calling pre-flop with straight-draw hands like Q-J, J-T, T-8, and 8-6 that I want to charge him, as they have up to around 35 percent equity against me (assuming they stay until the river). The only hands I am really worried about in this spot are 99, 77, 9-7s, and the rare K-9s. There is also a slight possibility that Seat 7 flat-called with AA or KK in position to trap. Since I am holding an A and a K, the odds of this potential trap are greatly diminished.

Seat 7 raises nearly five times my bet to 999. With such a large bet, he has basically told me that he is committed to the pot because it's half his stack. Ugh, what could he have on this kind of board? Seat 7 is aggressive, so he would almost definitely be re-raising pre-flop if he had A-K as well. If he had K-Q he might raise, but certainly not five times my bet with a player to act behind him. K-Q, K-J, and K-T will usually flat-call the flop, and when they do raise it would probably be about three times my continuation bet, so I can rule out those hands. The most likely hands he would have that dominate me are 99, 77, and 9-7s. However, it's unlikely he would play such strong hands so fast and hard on such a dry board, with the exception of 9-7. So basically, he might have two pair or a set, but it's fairly unlikely.

By a process of elimination, I am putting him on straight draws with a lot of equity such as J-T, T-8s, or 8-6s. I have about 65 percent equity against this range and will be happy to get it all-in with him.

But wait … now Seat 2 reraises to 1,784, which is the minimum allowed raise. This strikes me as a super-strong play for several reasons. First, Seat 2 is re-raising a stack-committing raise from Seat 7. Second, he's re-raising the minimum amount, which is a play a lot of (inexperienced) players make when trying to get value with their absolute monsters. This raise is basically telling us he has 99 or 77 in this spot. For good measure I'll include K-9s and 9-7s, even though he rarely has K-9s and probably just shoves two pair instead of making a minimum reraise.

Given my reads, I am basically dead in this hand, and with this in mind, I fold my top pair, top kicker despite excellent flop texture. In fact, I ran an odds simulation after the fact, which shows my equity as only 7 percent against the ranges I've assigned these two players. One interesting thing to note here is that even if I think both opponents are absolutely nutty enough to do this with K-Q, my equity is only about 30 percent if I include K-Q in their ranges, and given the pot odds, about a break-even or slightly bad hand to get all-in with. I fold.

Seat 7 ends up shoving in the rest of his stack with J♥ T♥, and Seat 2 calls with 9♥ 9♣.

Hand 108

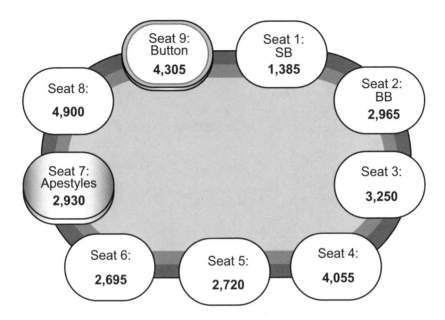

Setup: It's the second level of the Wednesday $320, $150K guaranteed prize pool. The blinds are 15-30. I've only played two or three hands so far, and there hasn't been enough action to really establish any sort of image. Seats 3 and 8 are the only regulars who have played with me in other tournaments; the rest are unknowns.

 Pre-flop (45): J-Ts is a great hand for post-flop play, especially considering the current deep stack sizes. Right now, everyone has at least about 100 big blinds, with the exception of one player in the small blind who's sitting on 40 big blinds. It's folded to me, and I raise three times the big blind to 90. I raise here not to "steal" the blinds like I would in later stages, but to build a pot in position with a hand that plays well. It's folded to the big blind, who calls.

 **Flop** (195): The big blind checks. This is one of those dry (hits very few hands) boards that are great for continuation betting. I bet 135 or about 70 percent of the pot. This bet is profitable purely as a bluff if he folds about 40 percent of the time. Unfortunately, the big blind calls.

I am unfamiliar with this player, so it's hard for me to put him on a hand range at the moment. Against most players, late position versus big blind hand ranges can be very wide. Assuming he is a "typical" player, he most likely has:

1.) small-pair hands like 77, 55, 33, and 22 that most players
   won't reraise pre-flop
2.) bottom-pair hands with 5-4s, 4-3s, and A-4s
3.) straight draws with 8-7s or 7-5s
4.) flush draws
5.) JJ-88

It's possible that he has trips or better, but given how deep-stacked we are, he will mostly be check-raising or betting on the flop with hands like this. Absolute monster hands (7-6, 66, 6-5, 44) also comprise a considerably small part of this range in general. Solid-aggressive players would probably check-raise or donk-bet (leading into a raiser) with any kind of draw. Since my opponent is completely unknown to me, I won't assume too much and will stick to the above range.

 Turn (465): This turn card is interesting. There are only seven or eight suited A-x hands he would've flat-called pre-flop that have flush draws on the flop. Given our stack sizes, he is probably three-betting A♦ K♦, A♦ Q♦, and possibly A♦ J♦ before the flop, and he can't have A♦ 6♦ or A♦ 4♦ because the flop contains these cards. Given all the other combinations of flush draws, small-pair hands, and straight-draw hands he could have, the seven or eight suited hands with an ace that he might be holding are a very small part of the current range I've given him.

He really shouldn't be able to continue in the face of a sizable turn bet for several reasons. First, straight-draw and small-pair hands won't be able to continue because I could easily have an ace or better; plus, I have position on him. The only information he has on me is that I raised pre-flop and made a continuation bet on the flop. A8-AK, AA, and suited A-x hands are most certainly within my range here. Small pairs should really hate this turn card because of that fact. Second, if I bet about 65 to 80 percent of the pot, and he has something along the lines of K♦ J♦ for a flush draw, he's going to have to call a very good portion of his stack on a paired board. This should be scary because he could be drawing dead already. He can certainly put me on the A-x of diamonds flush draw, since I bet the flop and the turn. His flush draw might be dead to a higher flush draw and he has no pair outs. He's out of position and just can't think he has any reasonable implied odds if he hits on the river, as his hand is fairly obvious. The only hands that a bet will definitely fail on are flopped monsters trying to trap me and A-x flush draws.

At this point it's pretty clear that a large part of his range is going to be forced to fold if I fire on the turn. This concept is known as "firing a second barrel" (firing the flop and turn as a bluff), and the A♣ is a fantastic card to do it on in this spot. Not only should my bet be large enough to deter him from calling again, but it should also be convincing enough that my hand is solid and in line with what I'm representing. When double-barreling, important factors to consider before deciding to fire again include: your opponent's hand range, your image, your opponent's image and how he will likely react to the turn card. Remember that double-barreling can be a huge leak in your game if you don't consider the specifics of the situation.

I bet out a respectable 326 (70 percent of the pot), and the big blind, after a short period of deliberation, mucks.

Hand 109

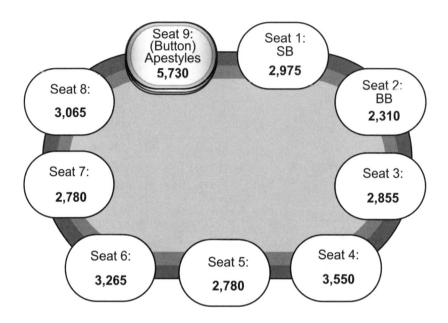

Setup: It is the early stages of a $1,060 freezeout tournament with the blinds at 20-40. I was fortunate to double early on, and my image is very strong at the moment. I don't have much history with any player at the table, and there hasn't been enough action to really establish reads on their play.

 **Pre-flop** (60): Seat 4 limps in and Seat 6 raises his limp four times to 160. Against an early-position limper and then a raise, I flat-call on the button with plenty of implied pot odds to hit a set with my pocket tens. Three-betting would be risky, given that either one of my opponents could four-bet, effectively taking me off my hand. The blinds fold, and the original limper calls as well.

Flop (540): The limper in Seat 4 checks to Seat 6, who makes a continuation bet of 400, 74 percent of the pot. Raising Seat 6 here is a bad idea for several reasons. First of all, I'm only likely to get it all-in against hands like better pocket pairs than mine or flush draws with two overcards. Despite having the T♥, I still just have around 50 percent equity against flush draws with two overcards, and I am absolutely crushed when my opponent has a better pocket pair. Against a range of A♥ K♥, A♥ Q♥, K♥ Q♥, and TT+ I have around 16% equity. That range is consistent with a player who would raise an early-position limper before the flop and then shove over my raise on the flop. If he would actually give me action with lower pairs like 88 and 99, my equity rises to around 39 percent. Without reads, however, it's hard to assess whether or not he'd stack off with those types of hands.

By flat-calling, I can re-evaluate my situation on the turn rather than get into an ambiguous flop spot. I call the 400. Unfortunately, Seat 4 check-raises both of us to 1,240. This most likely indicates a flush draw with one of those A♥ J♥ or K♥ Q♥ type hands that I mentioned earlier. He might have limp-called with 22 and now has a boat. If he's really crazy, he could also be going nuts with a 66-99 pair hand that he thinks is good. Surprisingly, Seat 6 shoves all-in over that raise as well. Considering the pre-flop action and all the flop action ahead of me, my tens aren't shaping up well at all. It's very likely that at least one of my opponents has me totally dominated. Even if both of my opponents are nutty enough to be doing this with a variety of hands, I would still rarely get my money in here. I have to fold my overpair.

Seat 4 calls Seat 6's all-in. Seat 4 has 5♣ 4♣ for trips, and Seat 6 has K♥ K♣ for an overpair. The turn comes 5♦ with the river 5♥, and Seat 4 takes the 7,150 pot with a boat.

Hand 110

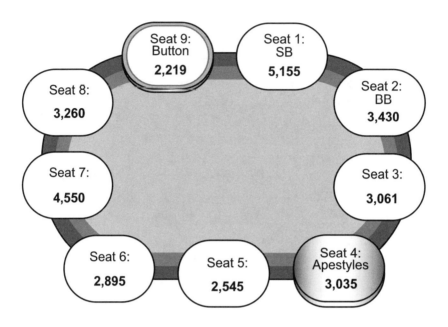

Setup: I am in a $55 freezeout with the blinds at 25-50. I haven't really been able to make anything happen yet, but my stack is still doing fine at 60 big blinds. My table has been pretty tight for the most part, with Seat 7 the only one playing rather loosely and aggressively. I've been getting garbage and haven't found any spots to make moves, so my image should be fairly tight as well.

  Pre-flop (75): I open-raise to 150. Seat 1 in the small blind pauses for a while and then reraises three and one-third times the big blind to 500. Seat 1 has been playing very few hands the entire time and, if he's been paying attention, should also perceive me as tight. I can't get all-in pre-flop with A-Q and expect to do well against a tight player's calling range. A-Q also doesn't fare well post-flop, especially in a large pot, and this is becoming one. The pot will be 1,050 on the flop, and I'll have only 2,500 chips behind. Considering how tight my opponent is, the suspicious amount of time he took before re-raising, and the rather large reraise size considering our stacks, it really seems like he has a big hand here.

If he makes a continuation bet post-flop, even on the driest flop textures, I am going to have a hard time pushing without a hand since I'm expecting to get called by pairs frequently. If he checks, I will have to either bet a significant portion of my stack on the flop or turn in an attempt to win the pot, or play the check-down game. Neither of these options is appealing, and it seems that given all the above factors and our awkward stack sizes, there isn't much I can do here. I'll still have 2,885 chips behind if I fold, so I can remain competitive in the tournament without making a speculative play with A-Q in this sticky spot. It's frustrating to fold the best hand I've seen in this tournament, but I am behind with only 30 percent equity against his estimated range of TT+, AK+. I fold.

Hand 111

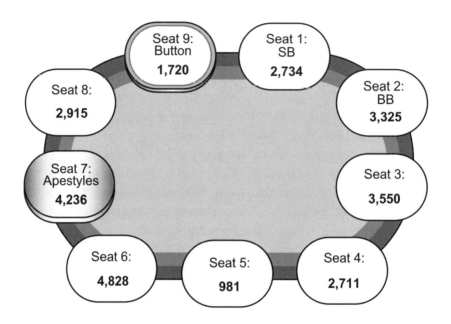

Setup: It is the early stages of a $320 tournament, and the blinds are 25-50. There are a few aggressive regulars at the table in Seats 6, 8, and 9. Seats 1 and 4 are the only really tight players. Right now I have a solid, aggressive image and have been picking up pots consistently.

  Pre-flop (75): Seat 4 raises three times the big blind to 150. Seat 4 has been playing very tightly and is also raising from early position, so I am definitely paranoid about a big hand. At the moment, I am most likely looking at a raising range of 6-6+, A-Q+. He's only sitting on a stack of about 54 big blinds, so if I three-bet, he could four-bet a very large part of his stack, putting me in an awkward spot considering how tight he is. When you get in 54 big blinds pre-flop early in a tournament with J-J versus a tight, early-position raiser, you are usually behind. But raise-folding a hand as strong as J-J is terrible with these stacks because it kills the value of our hand. It'd be better to raise him with a hand like T-9s if I am going to fold to a four-bet. In situations where your opponent will most likely either shove or fold, re-raising good hands that aren't quite strong enough to call all-in is a bad option because you are essentially turning your hand into any two random cards. My opponent could flat-call here pre-flop, but he'll most likely shove or fold instead.

There's also less value in raising J-J here because it causes the hands I can extract value from to fold. He's probably going to fold A-J and maybe A-Q to my three-bet, so he'll most likely shove or flat-call with A-K or big pairs he intends on trapping me with post-flop. If he does flat-call and check the flop, I'll end up making a continuation bet on most flops. I am really only getting worse hands like A-K to fold most of the time (depending on the flop, of course), while better hands will be check-raising all-in, putting me in another difficult situation for almost 65 percent of my stack.

When the flop does come with an A or a K, his range is going to be way ahead of me, not to mention the fact that I won't be able to proceed past a continuation bet. If he specifically has A-K, an A or a K will flop about one-third of the time. If he doesn't have an A or a K, the stat is 42 percent and I'll frequently be faced with a scare card where I am unsure where I am at in the hand. With my tight perception of this player, it really seems like three-betting here has little to no merit. By flat-calling, I keep the pot small against a strong range, disguise my hand strength, and have large implied odds with the potential to flop a set and stack his monsters. I call the 150, and everyone behind us folds.

   Flop (375): Seat 4 makes a continuation bet of 300, 80 percent of the pot. This is a great flop for my hand since I am basically racing against his calling range. Even against a tight range of 88+, A♣ K♣, and A♣ Q♣, I have about 48.5 percent equity. It's good to remember that an underpair against two overcards and a flush draw (15 outs) is basically a coin flip. Throw in single club A-K and A-Q combinations, and my equity actually increases a little to 49 percent. He'll also fold a large percentage of the time when I raise. It's clear that I am not going anywhere in this hand. I raise a little over two-and-a-half times his bet to 800, and he instantly shoves for 1,761 more. I call.

Seat 4 has T♣ T♥. The turn is the J♦, leaving him drawing dead. I pick up the 5,497 pot.

Hand 112

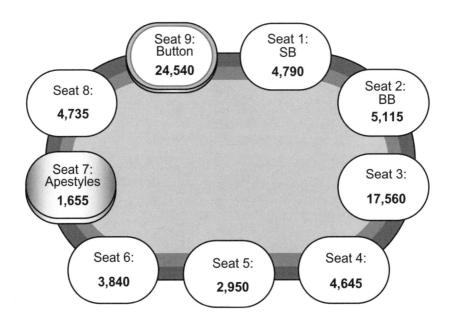

Setup: I am in another $215 freezeout tournament with the blinds at 40-80. I was doing well, playing solid poker for a while, until Seat 3 hit a set to my overpair, leaving me with a stack of 21 big blinds. Seat 3 is an aggressive regular, and Seat 9 is an extremely loose, aggressive player. The rest of the table has been pretty quiet, playing tight and conservatively for the most part.

  Pre-flop (120): With around 21 big blinds, my stack is a little too big to be open-shoving here, especially considering there are no antes yet. I certainly want action, and by open-shoving I am going to let a lot of hands that would otherwise three-bet or call my bet fold too easily. I open-raise three times the big blind to 240. Seat 9 flat-calls on the button. Seat 9 is a loose and aggressive player, especially when in position, so his hand range will be very wide here. Unless the flop comes an absolutely terrible T♠ 9♠ 8♠ or a similar board, I will probably look to get my stack in with him regardless of what kind of bet he throws at me. My hand is strong, and I can't let an aggressive player run over it just because I missed the flop.

 Flop (520): This is actually one of the better flops for me. It's very dry, or tough for his wide range to have a piece of. Even if Seat 9 shows up with a 77-22 type hand, my A-K has even more equity because I can hit an 8 or a variety of running cards (depending on which pair he has, of course) to make my ace high the best hand.

Pairs are somewhat unlikely, though, since I think he would just get it all-in with me pre-flop with his stack. The majority of the time he has simply missed this flop or has had a gutshot with J-T or T-9. I am not folding, so I want to exploit his tendencies as often as possible, rather than betting and letting him get away from worse hands. By checking to him here, I can expect him to bet very often in an attempt to just take the pot right there. I check intending to shove over his bet, or re-evaluate on the turn if he checks behind for some reason. Seat 9 fires a large bet of 82 percent of the pot for 426.

I push all-in for 989 more, and Seat 9, after some deliberation, folds.

Hand 113

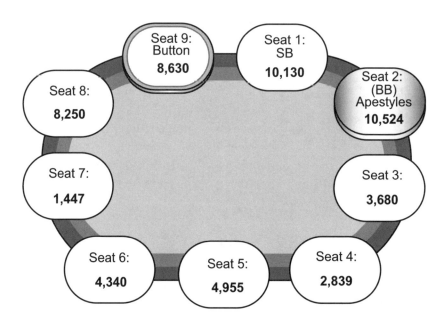

Setup: I am in a $530 major Sunday tournament with the blinds at 40-80. I was fortunate enough to double with a strong hand already, and my table image is currently solid and aggressive. The table has been pretty loose so far, most likely due to the deeper stacks this specific tournament structure yields. However, Seats 3 and 6 have been playing extremely tight, while the rest of the table has been playing many hands and flops. Seat 4 has been playing aggressively and recently lost the stack he had accumulated on a three-barrel bluff (firing the flop, turn, and river).

  Pre-flop (120): Seat 4 limps, as does Seat 7. I am obviously going to raise my strong pair here, and since there are two limpers, I need to make my raise size a little bigger than my normal preflop raise. I raise four-and-a-half times the big blind to 360. Seat 4 flat-calls, and Seat 7 folds. Seat 4 could have a really wide range of hands here. He's been loose and aggressive from the onset and is possibly on tilt right now after his big bluff failed. It's going to take some especially nasty flops for me to concede my hand to him at this point.

Flop (840): I am disappointed, as most players are, when overcards flop to their stronger pairs. My opponent could limp pre-flop with K-Q, K-J, K-T and maybe even worse suited kings, depending on how tilted, if at all, he is at the moment. Regardless, I am not going anywhere considering how strong my hand is, how many draws are out there, how bad my opponent's image is, and finally the fact that he has only about 2,500 chips left behind in his stack with the pot at 840.

Since I am choosing to run with the hand, I really need to figure out how to exploit his playing tendencies. If I bet a smaller amount, I often induce bluffs from weaker hands; but if I make a large bet, I let him off the hook and likely lessen the weakness of his range if he chooses to continue. I bet 480 for 57 percent of the pot, intending to call a shove. After a little deliberation, Seat 4 calls.

Well, I didn't induce a shove with my small bet. It's possible that he's floating me (calling to see what I do on the turn and bluffing me later), but it's also very possible that he has a pair of tens or kings. There are plenty of T-x hands that play well post-flop that he could've been limping with pre-flop (A-T, Q-T, J-T, T-9, T-8s). If he had any draw, most likely he would've shoved, especially since his stack size was ideal to raise all-in with a draw .

 Turn (1,800): This is a great turn because it doesn't complete any draws or improve any reasonable flop-calling range my opponent could have. My assessment on the flop was that he is somewhat likely to be floating me, so I like to check here to let him bluff into me. By firing again, I am also very likely to cause a pair of tens to fold, whereas checking will give him more confidence in his hand either on this street or at least the river.

By betting, I am letting my opponent off the hook too easily and paying off a pair of kings much more often than anything else. I check, and my opponent checks behind after a few moments. If he was floating, he probably would've made a bet on the turn rather than check again to try it on the river. It's unlikely he's slow-playing a king this way, considering his stack and the board texture, but I can't conclusively rule it out.

By deeming both of these parts of his range unlikely, the more likely scenario is that he's sitting on a pair of tens.

 River (1,800): This is a fantastic river as it doesn't complete any draws, and now it's even less likely that my opponent is sitting on a king since there are only two left in the deck. It also makes my hand look less believable in his eyes if he has a pair of tens. My opponent has only 1,999 left in his stack, which happens to be just a little bigger than the pot. A lot of factors are going my way here: My hand looks less believable on the river, I am fairly confident he has a pair of tens, my jacks figure to be good, he seems tilted and likely won't be able to fold a ten in this spot, and his stack is just 10 percent bigger than a pot-size bet. I decide to put Seat 4 all-in for his remaining 1,999 to try to get value from my hand.

Seat 4 calls quickly with A♥ T♠ for second pair, top kicker, and I take down the 5,798 pot.

Hand 114

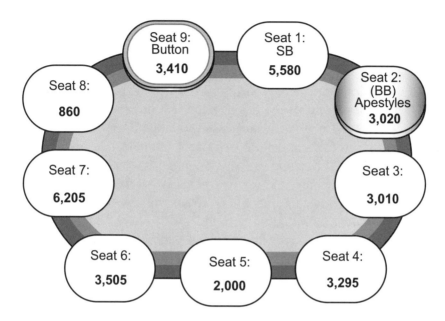

Setup: It is the early stages of a $55 $20K guaranteed tournament. The blinds are 50-100. I've been fairly inactive so far since there haven't been any real opportunities for me to move my chips. As a result of this and the fact that I have no history with the players at the table, my image is pretty tight right now.

  Pre-flop (150): My first decent hand in a while, and Seat 9 on the button raises to 350. Seat 9, a solid but fairly loose-aggressive player, has been active at the table so far. I've seen him raising in late position and making standard continuation bets on the flop. I am definitely playing this hand, so let's analyze some of the options.

Right now, I am confident that I am ahead of his opening range when he's on the button, but I will almost definitely be behind his four-betting range (at best, a 65:35 dog and at worst around 70:30), given that he is a solid, thinking player. A three-bet will have to be an amount around 1,100 or an all-in (the latter looks weaker). I'll be getting over 2-to-1 on a call if he four-bets me, making a call almost mandatory. I can't raise-fold a hand with as much value as A-J, in which case I might as well have total air. It's definitely +EV (positive expected value) to three-bet here or push, since he's folding so often, and in fact I do reraise a decent percent of the time here. However, there are good alternative options that may produce better results.

If I flat-call, I'll have 2,670 left in my stack. If he makes a continuation bet of 70 percent of the pot or more, I'll have a good stack size to check raise all-in if the board texture is right. This option is interesting in contrast to three-betting, because if I three-bet, hands like A-K and A-Q are probably going to shove over me. By flat-calling and then check-raising all-in on dry flops, I can actually get those hands, as well as small pairs some of the time, to fold. Due to how light I think he's raising the button, it would be burning chips just to check-fold every flop I miss. Also, if I actually hit a flop, I'll have the opportunity to get it in as a big favorite and double up. Since I have a pretty good stack size, and considering that three-betting is risky, I decide to flat-call, intending to check-raise all-in on a lot of flops.

   Flop (750): I check, and my opponent bets 750. This is exactly the kind of board I was looking for because a lot of his hands will now have to fold. It's a rainbow flop, so he can't have big draws like overcards with a flush draw. A-K and A-Q will almost definitely have to fold to a check-raise. Lower pocket pairs like 2-2 through 7-7 (not including set hands, of course) will hate calling with two overcards on the board.

A general rule to remember: Two live overcards usually have around 25 percent equity versus an underpair, given they have six outs. I assume that 9-9, any set or overpair, and any T-x or 8-x hand is calling (although 8-x will not always continuation bet), which I only have 19 percent equity against overall. The best-possible scenario is my opponent holding Q-J or J-9 and calling my shove, where I'd be a 65% favorite. After combining these estimated calling ranges, I figure to have around 27 percent equity as demonstrated:

A-J offsuit versus 88+, 44, ATs, A8s, KTs, QTs+, J9s+, T8s+, 98s, 87s, ATo, A8o, KTo, QTo+, J9o+, T9o, 98o[6].

For this play to be profitable, I need Seat 9 to fold around 60 percent of the time. Not only is this a reasonable expectation, but I believe he's actually folding much more often than that, based on how often he's raising. Most of the time my opponent has missed the flop completely or just simply has a hand he can't call with.

Looking at the math:
When he folds 60 percent of the time, I win 1,500 without showdown (.6 x 1,500 = 900).
When called, I win 3,070 11 percent of the time in total (.11 x 3,070 = 338).
When called, I lose 3,020 29 percent of the time in total (.29 x -3,020 = -876).

Each scenario added up yields a +362 expectation (Chip EV = +362).

Assuming my opponent folds 60 percent of the time, I have over three big blinds in positive expectation, which means I estimate the flop shove to be a nice winning play.

I shove over the top of his continuation bet for 2,670 total. Seat 9 folds.

---

[6] Using a poker odds calculator, you can enter this range of hands against A-J offsuit, which will show that A-Jo wins 27 percent of the time.

Hand 115

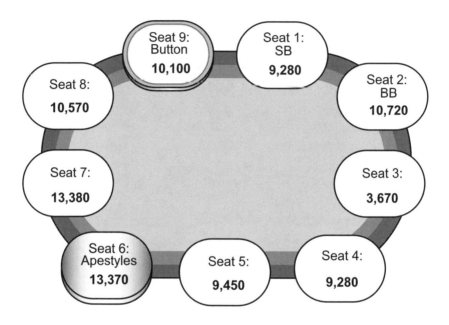

Setup: I am still in the very early stages of a $530 buy-in Sunday freezeout. The blinds are 60-120. The only two hands I have shown down so far have been the nut straight and top pair. My table has been playing tight poker for the most part, with the exception of Seats 1 and 2.

  Pre-flop (180): I open-raise three times the big blind to 360. Seat 8 calls, and everyone else folds.

 **Flop** (900): This is a dangerous flop for my hand. If I bet and get action on this flop, I am really going to be in a tough situation. Seat 8 has played tight, aggressive poker so far, and A-T, K-Q, K-J, Q-J, and T-9 are most definitely in his range here. If I bet, the worst hands I will probably get value from are random flush draws, K-T, Q-T, and maybe J-T, which aren't too far behind. The

number of combinations of these hands is also a lot smaller than the above range that crushes me. There's a flush draw out, and a few combo draws with flush and straight draws are possible given that I don't have the A♣ or K♣. I would feel more confident with A♣ or K♣ because then it would be impossible for my opponent to have hands like K♣ T♣ or any suited ace of clubs, which has a lot of equity.

Betting here creates problems for two reasons: First, the hands that will give me action will have a lot of equity, and second, my opponent is aggressive. The combination means that betting gives me little value. Checking also gives him the opportunity to bluff worse hands, and it gives me the chance to get to a cheap showdown. I check, intending to call a bet, and he checks behind.

 Turn (900): Because he checked behind on the flop, I am positive I had the best hand on the flop. Most opponents wouldn't slow-play a straight with that kind of board, and checking two pair would be horrendous. This turn card is terrible for my hand, though. If he did check behind a hand like Q-T, J-T, or T-x, he's now gotten there. It's also nearly impossible for me to bet and get value from anything worse, since there's a one-card straight on the board. It's possible he could be sitting on a flush draw with something like 7♣ 6♣, but some opponents would bet a flush draw when checked to on the flop. Also, this is such a small part of his range that there is just not enough reason to validate a bet. I check, and he checks behind again.

 River (900): This is a harmless river card. Because there hasn't been any action on previous streets, it's very likely that I have the best hand, and it seems a value-bet is definitely in order here. He could have checked behind a ten for a straight to try to trick me into thinking a one-pair hand might be good, which is why betting and folding to a raise is the appropriate play here.

I bet 480, and he folds.

Hand 116

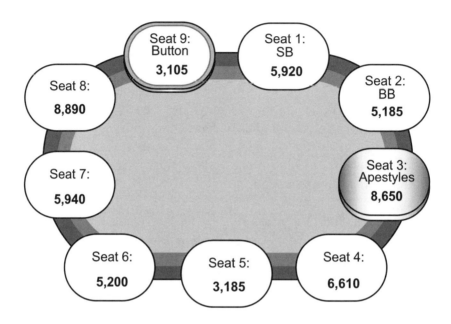

Setup: I am in the early stage of a $55 freezeout tournament with the blinds at 75-150. I've been running the table for the most part, and the only hands I've shown down so far are monsters (top pair with A-K and a set of nines). I love the table right now because it seems to be full of bad unknowns and my image is solid. The table is a mixed bag, as about half are playing really tight and the other half very loose.

 Pre-flop (225): I make a standard raise of three times the big blind to 450. The loose Seat 6 calls. Seat 7 stalls for a bit and then reraises a little over two-and-a-half times the bet to 1,200, leaving himself 4,740 behind. Seat 7 has been playing very tightly the entire time. Because Seat 6 is so loose, I am not really worried about what he has; essentially, he isn't even in the hand since he is folding almost 100 percent of the time if I come over the top. The only hand I have seen Seat 7 go to a showdown with so far is QQ, which he got all his chips in pre-flop against A-K at the 15-30 level to double up. Since then he has just been raising occasionally uncontested.

I know Seat 7 is playing a very tight range here for several reasons. First of all, I've noticed that he's been playing very tightly and has only shown down one monster that he fast-played pre-flop. If he has been paying any attention to the table, he should also perceive me as very solid. Second, he is reraising an under-the-gun raiser. Under-the-gun raising ranges should be significantly tighter than other positions at the table, and thus more highly respected. Third, the time he took before his reraise was suspicious. When players have AA or KK, they will often take a little time before reraising to feign a weaker hand, trying to give the impression that their decision required consideration. The amount he raised is also interesting. He only raised a little over two-and-a-half times the last bet, with a caller behind, when three-and-a-half to four times the previous bet is typical with an effective 40 big blinds. Most players would probably raise more if they had A-K, as they don't want callers (especially not two callers).

If I consider all these factors, this raise size really seems like a monster pair, most likely AA. Against an A-K, JJ+ range, I only have 30 percent equity. Based on my read, though, he probably has a range more like JJ+, which I have slightly less than 20 percent equity against. Our deep stacks mean I am not committed to moving all-in, yet I'm also not deep enough to have appropriate odds to call for a set. Although I have direct implied odds to hit a set, I actually need more than 10-to-1 since I will not always win his entire stack. This is because on ace-high flops I won't stack K-K or Q-Q, I'll have a lower set occasionally, and I won't ever be 100 percent certain of his range. It's important to be able to recognize scenarios when big hands just simply aren't good anymore.

I muck my hand, as does Seat 6. Seat 7 doesn't show his hand.

Hand 117

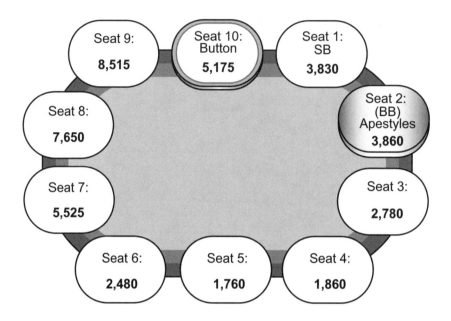

Setup: I am in the early middle stages of a $215, $200K guaranteed freezeout at the 75-150 level. I haven't been able to play many hands because of table activity and dynamics. I've been aggressive post-flop in the hands I have entered, but my opponents seemed to have good hands each time. At the moment, my post-flop image definitely isn't as solid as I'd like.

 **Pre-flop** (225): The action is folded to the small blind, who completes. Normally when a player limps in the small blind, I will raise him with a wide range of hands. In this particular situation, my hand is terrible, and even though I'd raise it sometimes, here I check behind.

I choose not to raise here for several reasons: One, the hand is terrible; two, the stack sizes make a raise here a bit awkward for play post-flop if he calls; and three, some players like to limp and then shove all-in from the small blind with a stack size between 15-25 big blinds.

Flop (300): I miss completely, and the small blind checks. When the small blind limps, I can basically put him on almost any two cards that aren't totally unconnected and trashy. Despite the slight coordination of this flop (some straight draws and flush draws) and my bad image, I can typically fire a bet at any flop and be a favorite to take it down since his range is so wide. Note that even marginal pairs like 6-4 will have a hard time continuing. I bet 225 or 75 percent of the pot, which only has to make him fold about 43 percent of the time to be a break-even play by itself. He calls.

 Turn (750): Right now, I am putting him on some kind of weak pair. Most players would bet out or check-raise on the flop if they had top pair, a flush draw, or a strong straight draw. He most likely has second or third pair with gapped cards at this point (something like J-9, 9-8 to 9-5, T-6 etc.).

This turn is a bad card for me to fire on again without a special read. Pairing the top card makes it a lot harder for me to represent a king since I'd have to have trips now. If I bet the turn, I am probably going to have to fire another barrel on the river since he's almost always calling the turn as well in a blind-versus-blind situation. Right now, I have no clue how this player would react to a third bet on the river with second or third pair, and it would also require me to bet a large part of my stack. I check behind.

 River (750): This is an interesting river card. My opponent fires 250, which is 33 percent of the pot. It's possible he played something like K-x passively on the flop, with the intention of trapping (despite the draws) and check-raising the turn. However, his river bet is really strange. A bet so small could mean two things. He may have a pair of nines and is trying to get some kind of value from a lower pair like sixes. A more likely scenario is that he is making a small "blocking" bet so that he will not have to call a bigger bet from me if he checks with his weak pair and I bet.

It is pretty hard for him to have a hand that beats me, given his play so far, and I am pretty sure I am ahead in the hand. There is a possibility of K-x, or Q-J, Q-T, or J-T, which all had gutshots on the flop, but this possibility is quite small given how the hand has played out and the wide range of hands I have put him on.

From his standpoint, it will be very hard for him to put me on a hand that beats him, as the flush draw missed. He must assume that I would have bet trips on the turn. Remember also that I have a semi-reckless post-flop image. Given the fact that I am probably ahead and that my opponent could easily expect me to be bluffing, I decide to make a thin value raise.

Because a raise looks like a bluff, I raise three times his bet to 750, hoping to get value from a pair of nines some of the time, or even a pair of sixes. Obviously, I'll fold to a reraise. Arguably, there is a slight chance I will be called by a better Q, but his hand range is weighted toward 9-x and 6-x hands.

Warning: Do not start blindly raising river bets with second pair! This hand was unorthodox and included a number of factors such as previous table image, history, and hand-reading skills to find value. The other lesson in this is that if you bluff with reasonable frequency, you should also be able to find more value in your marginal hands.

He calls a lot lighter than I thought, with 6♣ 5♥.

Hand 118

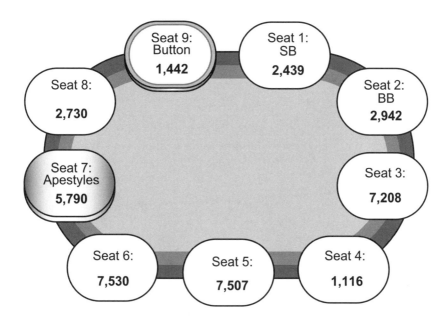

Setup: I am still in the early stages of a $162 freezeout tournament. The blinds are 75-150. I doubled up a level or two ago when my A-K held against A-Q all-in pre-flop. With a 40 big blind stack, I still have enough room for some post-flop play, which is what I'll examine in this hand.

Pre-flop (225): It gets folded to Seat 5 (a solid regular), who open-raises a little over two-and-a-half times the big blind to 400. Seat 6 folds. Reraising pre-flop in position is out of the question; my hand is ahead of his opening range but far behind his four-bet all-in range. Also, I have position and consider my post-flop abilities to be superior. My plan is to get my stack in with top pair or better and to outplay him a certain percentage of the time post-flop (depending on a combination of flop texture and bet sizing).

Flop (1,025): Seat 5 makes a continuation bet of 500 for a little less than half pot. This particular player's continuation bets normally are on the small side. As such, I am not going to treat them as unusual or anything special. One interesting thing about tight, aggressive (mostly straightforward) players is that you can often just "float" (flat-calling to try to take the pot on a later street) their flop continuation bets. They will essentially let you know whether or not they have anything with a turn bet or check. I could raise here to something like 1,300 to exploit his continuation-betting frequency as well. However, the downside to this move is that I don't have that little extra bit of information that a turn bet or check would give me. One interesting thing to note is that a call appears stronger than a raise to many players. This player is hardly ever going to be two-barrel bluffing me, so I decide my best move is to call and re-evaluate on the turn since he will bet if he is strong and check if he is weak.

Keep in mind that I am floating for several reasons:
1.) I want to exploit (outplay) my opponent's continuation-bet frequencies, inducing him to fold better hands on the turn.
2.) My hand very well might be good.
3.) I have the added equity of possibly hitting the gutshot, and my ace might be a live overcard which could improve to the best hand.

One thing that's nice to have when floating is well-disguised backdoor draws or gutshots to the nuts. The implied odds are huge a lot of the time when you actually end up making a hand. What I decide to do on the turn depends on the turn card in combination with the opponent's action. I call.

 Turn (2,025): Seat 5 checks. On a scale of 1 to 10, the J♠ would be a 10 and the T♦ would be a 5 or 6. In some ways it's good, because now if Seat 5 suspects me of flat-calling a 10 in this spot, he might think his QQ or JJ is now utterly hopeless. It's a bad turn card because, playing the way he is, he might very well check in this spot with a king (that he won't fold), fearing I flat-called with a ten. This play mostly serves to control the pot and/or to get to showdown more cheaply. His turn check or bet would be a much more reliable indicator of hand strength if the turn came a blank 3♠, for instance. Despite all these factors, he really isn't going to have a hand here a majority of the time with just a pre-flop raise and a continuation bet. I bet, expecting pairs QQ-JJ, 99-66, and 44-22 to fold. I am also causing worse hands to fold, which isn't necessarily a bad thing, as they often have equity against me. Checking with the best hand also makes me susceptible to river bluffs. If he calls, I am giving up on rivers that don't improve my hand.

I stick with my flop plan and fire a bet of 1,200, which is the bet size I'd make if I were trying to get value with trips or a strong king. Seat 5 folds.

Hand 119

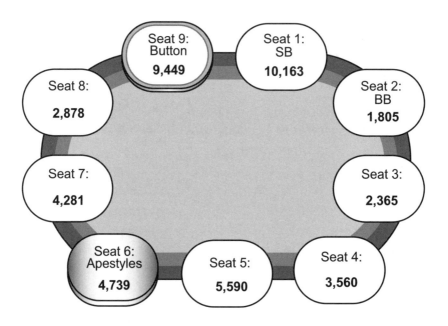

Setup: I am in a $1,050 freezeout tournament with the blinds at 100-200. My table has been playing very conservatively. Seats 1 and 9 have been playing loosely but still passively for the most part. I've been raising pre-flop frequently and stealing the blinds, but I also just called a few tiny value bets from Seat 5 with a weak hand that the table probably saw. A late-position raise I made also got shoved on by Seat 7 recently, so my image definitely isn't good right now. I plan to wait for better hands or better spots for a little while.

  Pre-flop (300): This hand came at a great time considering how bad my image is right now, and as such, it's much more likely I'll be getting action. I raise to 565, as I have been doing at this level, and Seat 1, the big stack at the table, flat-calls my raise from the small blind. I've seen Seat 1 call a lot of hands pre-flop from 5-4s to Q-T, so it's going to be hard to put him on much of a range here.

Flop (1,330): Seat 1 checks. This is a solid flop for my hand, and I want to make a bet that looks like a standard continuation bet just trying to take down the pot. Since I've seen my opponent flat-call with suited connectors before, it's very possible that my opponent holds connected cards that made pairs or open-ended straight draws with hands like T-9, 9-8, 8-7, 7-6, or 7-5. With a weak-looking bet, I might induce a check-raise from him when he holds air and I can also expect to get value from decent pairs like TT, 88, and 77 most of the time. A set is certainly a possibility here, but I am going to go broke on this kind of flop regardless, since I can be getting action from so many worse hands. I make a continuation bet of 865, 65 percent of the pot, and my opponent calls. At this point, he most likely has a decent pair, like 88, 77, J-9, T-9, 9-8, or 7-6.

 Turn (3,060): Seat 1 checks. Despite being an overcard to my pair, this turn card is actually pretty meaningless. It would only help my opponent if he had a very specific hand, such as K-9. I expect him to be reraising A-K pre-flop rather than playing it out of position, and it would be just way too weird for him to float the flop out of position with a K-Q, K-J type hand. I'm still pretty certain that I have the best hand, unless of course my opponent is slow-playing a set.

Against a regular opponent I have history with, I might two-barrel here to make my hand look like a bluff, as he would expect me to bluff if I had air and represent the king that peeled off on the turn. This would also serve to balance my ranges long-term versus a regular to make me less predictable and harder to play against. Since I have no history with my opponent, though, firing again here is fairly bad and likely to make him fold those pair hands I put him on earlier (this is why it would be a good two-barrel card). By checking behind and then betting the river, my hand really looks more like a bluff to the average tournament player, and I'll be more likely to get value that way.

River (3,060): Seat 1 checks again. If Seat 1 had a set, he would almost certainly make a small value-bet here, or even put me all-in because I checked behind on the turn. I can basically rule out sets and kings now that he's checked to me on the river. I am very confident his hand is weak and in accordance with the range I assigned him on the flop (88, 77, J-9, T-9, 9-8, or 7-6).

This river card is convenient, as it doesn't improve any of those hands to my jacks. Since I checked behind on the turn to make my river bet look more like a bluff, I need to figure out what amount is most likely to get called by those hands. I currently have 3,309 left in my stack, which is a little more than the amount in the pot. Against a good player I am going to be making standard value-bets and value-bet bluffs (bluffing by making a smaller bet that looks like a value bet rather than a large pot-sized bet or overbet) of around 60 to 70 percent of the pot. I don't figure this player to be very good, so in combination with how bad my image is and how weak my hand must look to him after checking behind on the turn, it really seems like a shove here would appear very weak.

I push all-in for 3,309, and Seat 1 calls with 7♦ 6♦ after thinking for 10 seconds or so.

Hand 120

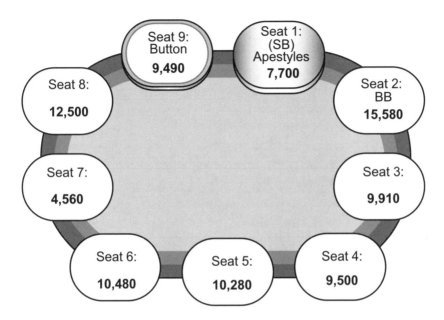

Setup: I am in a $530 major Sunday tournament and was doing well until I lost with pocket aces when I got all-in on the flop against the nut-flush draw. That was two hands ago. I love this table, though, since it's full of absolutely fishy players. My image should be solid as I've been playing that way, but it's possible a few players might suspect me of being on tilt after that hand. Seats 4, 5, and 6 have been exceptionally loose and passive the entire time. The blinds are 100-200.

  Pre-flop (300): The loose-passive player in Seat 4 limps in early position. It's folded to me. A-J offsuit is a decent hand, but pretty terrible to be playing out of position, especially against a loose calling station. If I raise, Seat 4 will almost certainly call, and I will have to make a continuation bet out of position against someone who is not going to give his hand up often or easily. I decide just to complete the small blind. The big blind checks.

Flop (600): This is obviously a great flop for me. I have top pair, top kicker, and there isn't much going on with this board at all except a possible flush draw and a gutshot-straight draw. Betting out first to act in this pot is definitely a viable option given the flush draw and Seat 4's playing style. However, if Seat 4 is willing to call a bet, he is probably going to bet this flop himself when checked to. By check-raising I get more money in the pot and can get a lot more value out of him on later streets.

He definitely won't have a hand here most of the time, but when he does, this seems like the best way to get maximum value. Also, by check-raising the flop and betting the turn, I inflate the pot so much that my opponent is going to have attractive odds on the river to call when I finally push. This is great, since I have a hand I intend on playing for my entire stack. I check, looking to raise either the big blind or Seat 4's bet. The big blind checks, and Seat 4 bets about 67 percent of the pot, or 400, as I hoped he would. I raise three times his bet to 1,200. The big blind folds, and Seat 4 calls. Right now, I am putting Seat 4 on some kind of pair. He most likely has K-J, Q-J, J-T, 9-7, 8-7, or 7-6. He could also have some small pocket pairs in this spot like 99, 88, 66, or 55, or a flush draw. My opponent could also be sitting on a set with 77 or 33, but this is a small part of his range. I can expect him to reraise with a set rather than calling. If he has a set and I lose, so be it.

 Turn (3,000): Although a few of the hands I put him on earlier now get there, this is a good turn card for me as I am still way ahead of his range. It's also a good turn card because it won't scare him off the pair he seems to be attached to. The only play here is to follow through with my check-raise by betting to get more value. Since this player is such a calling station, along with the fact that he really doesn't seem to want to give his hand up, a large bet definitely seems appropriate. A large bet is also great because if he does have a flush draw, he won't have the correct pot or implied odds to draw to it, as I'll only have about 3,000 to 3,500 left in my stack. His pot odds on the turn are exactly 2-to-1, and even if he stacks me every single time he hits his flush on the river, he is only getting 3-to-1 implied odds. With just a flush draw, he needs better than 4-to-1. There are some exceptions however, as flush-draw hands that picked up straight outs now have the odds to continue. I bet 3,000, leaving 3,300 behind, and he calls. I intend on shoving any river, even if one of the worst cards hits the river, such as K♥ or Q♥.

 River (9,000): Well, the flush draw got there. I am not going to stress out if he has it, though, because for the majority of his range, he was not getting the correct implied pot odds to continue on the turn. I can still get value from top-pair hands, which probably are the biggest part of his range anyway when he limps in early position and takes this line. Since I am not going to fold my hand on the river for just 3,300 more, check-calling would only make sense if I suspect he might bluff in this spot. Attempting a bluff in this situation is not very likely, so checking doesn't make sense. If I check, he will simply check behind hands I have beaten and bet the hands that beat me. Shoving is a much better play, as now I give my opponent an opportunity to call with a worse hand.

I shove for 3,300 in a 9,000 pot, and Seat 4 surprisingly folds.

Hand 121

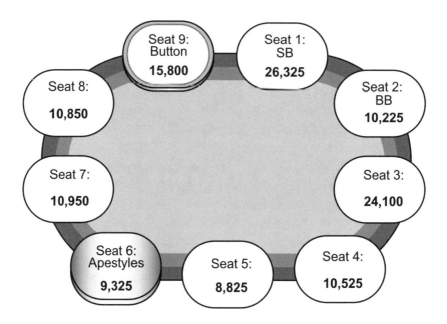

Setup: I am in the early stages of a $215 major tournament on Sunday, and the blinds are 150-300. I have a tight image at this table, and I am basically sitting on the starting stack since there hasn't been a good spot to pick up chips yet. Seats 1 and 3, the big stacks at the table, have been playing aggressively. The rest of the table is a mixed bag of overly tight, moderately loose, and generally weak players.

  Pre-flop (450): I raise to 789. The small blind in Seat 1 calls.

   Flop (1,878): Seat 1 checks. There is an overcard on the flop, so I am a little bit worried, but it is a dry and mostly unconnected board. Seat 1 is the chip leader at the table currently and has been playing aggressively to get that lead. On this board right now, I am either way ahead or way behind, and betting here doesn't seem to be as good as checking. If Seat 1 has a smaller-pair hand that I beat, which is fairly common given he flat-called out of the small blind, he only has two outs to improve, and I can extract value from him on the turn. Most hands I have beaten only have two or three outs, with the exception of the unlikely hands A-5, A-4, A-3, A-2, 7-6, 6-5, and 5-4, so there's not much danger in giving a free card. Second, I know Seat 1 is aggressive, so I am definitely worried about getting check-raised here with worse hands, thus putting me in a tough spot. I'd have to make a continuation bet of around 1,200, in which case Seat 1 would raise to around 3,600, a significant portion of my stack. He's likely to do this with air as well as a king, so it's a very difficult situation to deal with. On the other hand, if I check, I can induce calls or bets from worse hands, and even induce bluffs on the turn from an aggressive opponent sensing weakness. Considering these factors, I decide checking is the best play.

Turn (1,878): Seat 1 bets 900, a little less than half the pot. This turn card is pretty harmless. While this little half-pot bet might be a strong hand attempting to induce a call, it's more likely that he's just being aggressive and taking a stab at the turn since I checked the flop. Judging by the size of his bet and his line so far, it could also very well be a sort of value-bet from pair hands like TT-88 that he now thinks are ahead. I am not going to raise here for the same reasons I gave for not betting the flop: It lets worse hands off the hook too easily, and only better hands are going to call. I call.

River (3,678): Seat 1 checks to me. I am almost positive I have the best hand right now. I have given the impression of weakness here by checking behind on the flop and flat-calling the turn, so if my opponent had a strong hand, he would probably be betting for value rather than going for a speculative river check-raise. While it's most likely he was just taking a stab at the turn, I have to consider an appropriate river bet size that gets value out of those smaller-pair hands that sometimes showdown. A half pot seems like it would be enticing to a TT or 99.

I bet half the pot, 1,839, and Seat 1 folds.

Hand 122

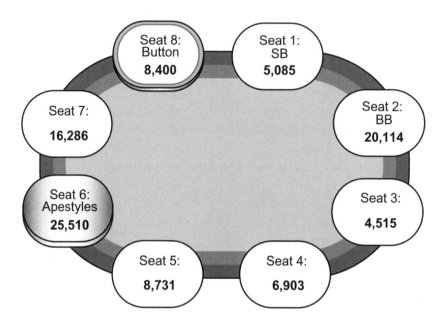

Setup: It is the middle stages of a daily $109 freezeout tournament. The blinds are 150-300 with a 25 ante. I have the biggest stack at the table and feel like I am on my game, making the right moves at the right times. The players at the table were fairly loose in the early levels, but as the blinds have increased, they have tightened their play. Seat 2 has been the exception. His stack is in good shape for post-flop play, and he seems to have no problem using it to limp and call. The table has yet to show any sign at all of adjusting to my frequent stealing. With this in mind, I am going to continue to be greedy and use my big stack to abuse their tight play and accumulate even more chips.

  Pre-flop (650): The action is folded to me. When considering stealing, it's crucial to evaluate the stacks and players behind you before coming to a decision. In this instance, I've noticed that all the stacks behind me are big enough that I am not committed to calling any shoves, that they have been playing really tightly, and that they haven't adjusted to my stealing at all. Seat 2 is the only one who is likely to play a pot and will definitely do so with a wide range of hands, even out of position. Seat 7 in the cutoff seems solid but more on the nitty side, and I expect him to cold call sometimes with decent hands, in position. All in all, this seems like a perfectly fine spot, so I open-raise for a little over two-and-a-half times the big blind to 755. It's folded to Seat 2, who calls. I don't really mind, though, because his post-flop play is so weak and our effective stack sizes aren't going to make for awkward post-flop decisions.

Flop (1,900): This is a great board for continuation betting against a big blind's flat-calling range, especially against typical or more standard players. Typical players will be reraising their premium aces and not calling ace rag here out of position, as it plays very badly post-flop. This is true for several reasons. First, and probably most important, you generally have to flop an ace to continue against an aggressive player, which means you'll be getting pushed off the best hand frequently. Second, when you actually do flop top pair, you won't get much action and will hardly be able to get any value out of your hand. Last, when you actually get action, chances are your ace is completely dominated and you're going to have to pay off some value bets. Against this player, though, I am definitely not ruling out ace rag from his calling range as he's been pretty loose. Despite this fact, his range is still so wide that I can usually take the pot with a bet.

He really needs to hit this flop to continue in the face of a bet, or at the very least have a small pocket pair like 66 to make a speculative call with (which I actually have around 35 percent equity against since I have six pair outs, besides the fact that another ace would double-pair the board, making my king high the best hand). I bet 1,100, or 58 percent of the pot, which is the amount I'd probably bet with a real hand. Balancing bet sizes against bad and unperceptive players is often unnecessary though. He calls.

Turn (4,100): I am not happy with his call, but I am still happy with the bet and play since I'm confident that I have reasoned correctly. Right now, he most probably has a pair of aces with ace rag or is slow-playing trips. Essentially, I have to give up. However, this turn card isn't totally meaningless. If he saw my play for what it was (a steal and a standard continuation bet), he definitely could have called my flop bet with a pocket pair like 77 or 66 as mentioned earlier, which I now have beaten. Betting here would be a very poor play, since the bet will not cause better hands to fold or worse hands to call, an important concept in no-limit play. I check behind.

 River (4,100): My opponent quickly fires a bet of a little less than half the pot, or 1,800. He almost definitely doesn't have a 77 type hand in this spot. Turning a hand like that into a bluff on the river, especially with a bet this small, is a sophisticated play that this player just isn't capable of. If he does have a small pair hand, he's going to be checking the river praying that I check behind. I am going to fold to almost any bet sizing on the river, but the speed and size of this bet in particular especially validated my read.

I fold, and Seat 7 wins the pot.

Hand 123

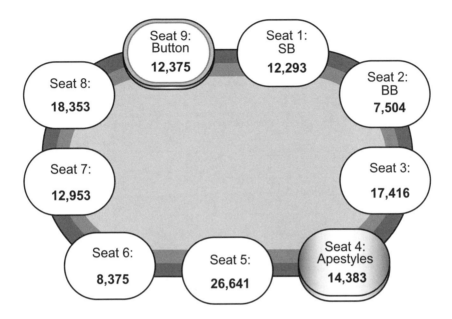

Setup: I have a solid stack in the middle stages of a $55 rebuy tournament, and the blinds have just gone up to 150-300 with a 25 ante. Seats 1, 6, and 7 are the only regulars at the table, although I find Seat 1 has a rather straightforward and transparent game and doesn't think on high levels. The table has been playing tight and aggressively for the most part, and my image is the same.

 **Pre-flop** (675): The player under-the-gun folds. I make my standard raise of two-and-a-half times the big blind to 750, since the blinds are getting higher. Given that the average stack size at the table is around 40 to 50 big blinds, it would also be fine to make a raise here of three to three-and-a-half times the big blind. With deep stacks, I'm raising to build a pot. When the stacks are smaller, I prefer smaller raises to steal cheaply. The action is folded around to Seat 1 in the small blind, who calls. The big blind folds. Because Seat 1 is out of position and a regular whom I know is fairly solid pre-flop, I am putting him on small to middle pocket pairs, maybe some upper-suited connectors like

9-8s, and bad broadway cards that he wouldn't reraise such as K-Q, K-J, Q-J, Q-T, J-T, etc.

   Flop (2,025): Seat 1 checks. This is one of those dry flops that won't be hitting him very hard. With that in mind, and considering I have a good hand, even with the overcard, betting here doesn't seem to accomplish much. If I bet, he is likely to fold most of his range, with the exception of queens and maybe some middle pairs. If I check, I disguise my hand and maybe induce either bluffs with nothing or bets and calls from worse made hands. Although I am giving him a free card, it's worth it considering these factors, plus the low probability he has of improving his hand. Normally, checking behind such a dry board would set off alarms in a good player's head; however, based on what I've seen, I don't expect this level of thinking from him. I check.

 Turn (2,025): A fairly harmless turn. I am hoping to induce some bluffs here, but Seat 1 checks again. I am very confident that I have the best hand now, as he would almost certainly bet a queen. Either he doesn't feel like firing a bluff at me, for whatever reason, or he has a hand with some showdown value that he doesn't feel comfortable betting (A-J, A-T, or 99-55, for instance). Since I've disguised my hand on a pretty harmless board, my opponent might very well call some bets with hands that have showdown value. By not making a continuation bet the flop, and then betting the turn, it could definitely look like a stab at the pot to him. I decide to make a value bet around 60 percent of the pot, or 1,200. Seat 1 calls.

 River (4,425): He checks again. By calling the turn and checking the king river, I have narrowed down his range to mid-pairs, ace high, and a very passively played queen. K♣ is extremely unlikely to have hit him since it makes no sense for him to get to the river with one, and it would be pretty terrible not to bet out if he did have it. However, it's a bad card because now it's going to be even harder to get more value out of him. Since I am confident I have the best hand most of the time, and because I have narrowed his range to hands with showdown value, it only seems appropriate to try to get more value. Also, I bluff here often enough when an overcard hits that I can bet my decent hands for value as well. It is important to evaluate all the factors before making thin value-bets like this.

I bet 50 percent of the pot for 2,200 and Seat 1 calls with 9♣ 9♠.

Hand 124

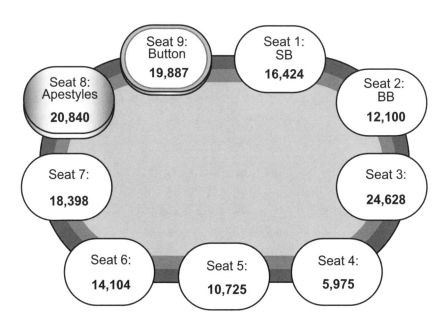

Setup: This is a weekly $215 buy-in $1 million guaranteed tournament. The blinds are 200-400. I was just moved to this table, so my opponents shouldn't have any special reads on how I am playing. Seats 4, 5, and 9 at the table are regular tournament players.

  Pre-flop (600): I open-raise two-and-a-half times the big blind to 999. Seat 9 on the button, an aggressive regular, calls. This isn't surprising, as he's an aggressive player with position and we have around 50 big blinds in our respective stacks. I can probably expect him to play tricky post-flop by raising my continuation bets or floating lots of flops. Both blinds fold.

Flop (2,598): I flop top pair. My opponent would have reraised pre-flop most of the time with A-K and probably A-Q, too. He could have A-J or 22, but I am confident I have the best hand the vast majority of the time at the moment, given the width of his range. His range most likely includes connected cards like T-9, small to medium pairs like 66, or broadway cards like K-J, and probably doesn't consist of many ace rag hands (if any at all). Usually I prefer betting my hands for value rather than playing passive lines. Betting here isn't necessarily bad, but I will be in a tough spot if I am raised on the flop. Checking also serves to control the pot size. I am more likely to get value from this particular opponent by not betting. Since he probably expects me to bet when I hit here, coupled with the fact that he's an aggressive player looking for spots to pounce on, I decide to check to induce some bluffing. He bets 1,600, 60 percent of the pot. I call.

 Turn (5,798): This turn is pretty harmless. He might put me on a jack that could fold, and since there still isn't much value in betting, I try to induce a second barrel play from him and check. He checks behind and seems to have given up.

 River (5,798): This isn't the greatest river, but it's still unlikely that he's made a better hand than mine. Considering that there are no draws on the flop, the fact he checked behind on the turn, and the considerable size of his stack he'd have to bet, he isn't going to be bluffing this river very often. It's very possible he played a jack this way, so I might as well try to get some value.

I bet 2,899 for half the pot, and Seat 9 folds.

Hand 125

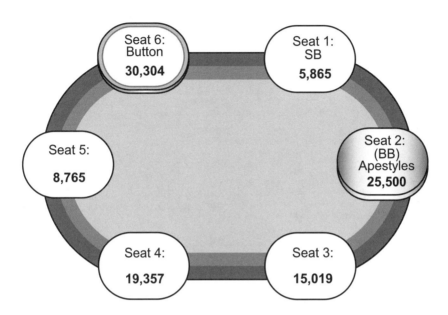

Setup: I am in a $77 6-max tournament with the blinds at 200-400 and a 25 ante. I haven't been at the table too long, but I can already tell everyone is playing aggressively. In short-handed games, you'll find the good players raising more hands and playing more pots, playing as if they are always in late position. While I have noticed the aggression, I haven't made any moves to profit from it yet, but I intend to look for opportunities to do so.

  Pre-flop (750): Seat 4 raises three times the big blind to 1,200, and everyone else folds. I have decided that now is the time to exploit the table's aggressive tendencies. While making plays with position is obviously preferable, it's actually not that difficult to play out of position and make small moves. If you play out of position, you have to play aggressively; otherwise you will be check-folding a lot of flops and giving away money. I could three-bet here, but this would create some stack tension considering I am playing an effective stack of 40 big blinds.

Q-J flops well and is ahead of most players' opening range, so it is OK to occasionally call here. Another merit of simply calling rather than three-betting is that post-flop I can get big hands like A-K down to A-J to fold when they miss, and maybe even some pair hands depending on the texture of the board. If I three-bet, either I'll be inviting calls that put me in tricky post-flop situations, or I'll be four-bet a lot of the time since 6-max is by nature a more aggressive game.

I decide to call, intending to check-raise a lot of the flops that will frequently miss my opponent's raising range.

 Flop (1,550): King-high boards are great to bluff, especially when they are dry and really unconnected. Not many hands hit this board at all and I am definitely going to follow through with my plan to check-raise him here. I check, and Seat 4 bets 1,200, around 77 percent of the pot. Given his wide opening range and high frequency of continuation bets, it's unlikely that my opponent has a hand at this point. Check-raising should take down the pot with a high frequency. I make a small raise of a little over two-and-a-half times his bet, to 3,100, and he folds.

While this is a very standard play, it's certainly one you should be using even more often in aggressive short-handed games. Note that I also did not get out of line at this table prior to this hand, so my image allows my bets and raises to garner more respect.

Hand 126

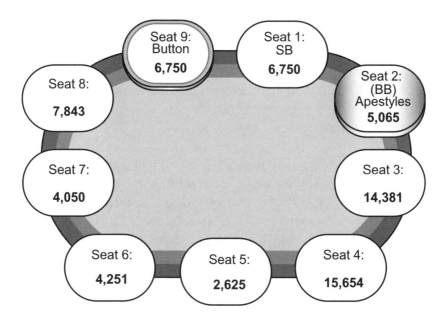

Setup: It is the middle stages of a $109 freezeout tournament with the blinds at 200-400 and 25 antes. I haven't had many opportunities to pick up chips and have an awkward stack size. With a stack size of around 13 big blinds, or an M around 6, I can't be open-shoving with too wide of a range; it is just too much risk to pick up 825. I also do not have a lot of re-steal fold equity, since the raiser I three-bet will be getting very good odds to make a call. Basically, I am forced to mostly play tight.

One of the few exceptions is when there are one or more weak limpers, since there is more money in the pot and I have plenty of fold equity. Seat 9 has been playing weak/tight, open-limping and minimum-raising a fair amount.

Pre-flop (825): It is folded to Seat 9 on the button, who open-limps. The small blind folds. Open-limping the button is usually a sign of a weak player with a marginal hand. At this blind level with his stack size, I would expect him to be raising hands he intended to get all-in with. I haven't been in a situation yet where I raise a small blind or a late-position limper. This unknown player has no reason to expect me to be aggressive in this spot and trap me. Against some players I would be suspicious that they might be open-limping with a big pair, but I've seen this particular opponent limp too often.

There's 1,225 in the pot currently, and I have 4,640 remaining. My A-9 is way ahead of his limping range, so even if he makes a stubborn call with his hand, I'll be in decent-to-good shape. I expect him to fold at least 50 to 60 percent of the time, and when he does call, I should expect to be a small underdog with at least 40 to 45 percent equity against his calling range. He might even limp and call with a dominated ace. Even if I have a hand like 8-7s, I'm going to be close to a coin toss against his range if he calls, and he's going to fold a large percentage of the time.

In summary, I increase my stack by about 25 percent around 50 to 60 percent of the time when he folds, and I double up around 40 to 45 percent of the time when he calls. These numbers are estimations, but it shouldn't take an EV calculation to see how profitable and standard this play is with even any two cards.

I push all-in for 4,640 more, the button mucks, and I increase my stack by about 25 percent without a showdown.

Hand 127

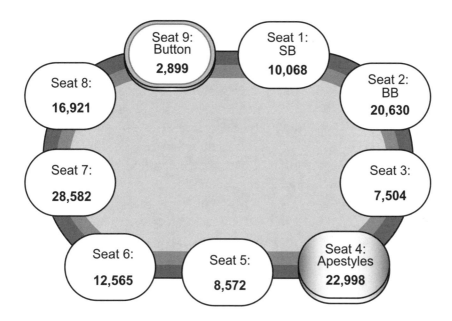

Setup: I am in the middle levels of a $109 freezeout tournament with the blinds at 300-600 and 50 antes. I have the second-largest stack at a fairly passive/nitty table, and I've been using it to my advantage. There is only one regular tournament player, in Seat 5. Seat 6 seems to be the only loose player and has been cold-calling a lot and playing very passively post-flop, despite having a bad stack for doing so.

Note also the blind and ante structure: In many tournaments, the antes are only 5 percent of the big blind. In other tournaments, the antes can be as high as 12.5 percent. With a substantial ante, it's in my best interest to be playing a loose, aggressive style pre-flop.

Let's look at an example to demonstrate this concept. Say you have 500-1,000 blinds. In some tournaments, the ante might be 50, whereas in others it might be as high as 100. In a ten-handed game, the pot size with the first structure is 2,000, while in the second it is 2,500. You win 25 percent more with 100 antes every time your steal is successful (plus, you win more post-flop with your continuation bets). Larger antes favor aggressive play since there is more money to be won in the pot with the same bet sizes pre-flop. In this particular hand the antes are 8.3 percent of the blind, which is relatively high compared to most tournament structures.

  Pre-flop (1,350): I raise approximately two-and-a-half times the big blind to 1,525. I plan on stealing the blinds and antes pre-flop a good percentage of the time with this play, since early-position raises get more respect, especially at this table where most of the players are so tight. Picking up the blinds in favorable conditions like this is crucial if you want to build a large stack.

When cold-called, I have an excellent hand for post-flop play, and if any reasonable stack comes over the top of my raise, I can easily muck my hand. The only player I have to call is the button, since I will be getting enormous pot odds.

The loose player in Seat 6 cold-calls my raise. It is likely that he would three-bet his premium hands, so he is probably cold-calling with connected cards, suited gappers, and medium to bad broadway cards like K-J or Q-T. I am not too unhappy about his flat-call since I am going to be able to take the pot down on the flop with a continuation bet the majority of the time, given my read.

However, the short stack in Seat 9 shoves over the top of my raise for 2,849 total. Seat 9 has gotten short-stacked by playing very tightly and blinding down, rather than losing his chips post-flop. Seat 9 certainly has a strong hand since he definitely knows he has no chance of causing either of us to fold for only 1,324 more. Given the pot odds, though, his hand strength is fairly unimportant. Right now I am getting about 4.3-to-1 on a call and therefore would need around 19 percent equity versus this player's range. Even if Seat 9 is only raising JJ+, A-Q+, which is probably tighter than his actual range, I have 30 percent equity against this range, which mandates about 2.3-to-1 pot odds. I almost have the correct odds to call even if I am against AA, as Q-Js has 19.1 percent equity against AA. With a slightly wider range of hands such as 88+ and A-T+, my equity is 35 percent, and I only need 1.9-to-1 pot odds.

However, I still need to worry about Seat 6. The best way to handle Seat 6 is simply to push all-in, putting a lot of pressure on my opponent to fold. There is a slight chance that Seat 6 might call, but given my read, it is fairly unlikely. He will probably call about 5 to 10 percent of the time. In summary, although I know I am behind against Seat 9's range of hands, there is +EV because of the excellent pot odds I am getting.

Flat-calling is basically out of the question. If I call, I know Seat 6 is going to be in the pot, and this makes post-flop play very awkward for me. Unless I hit the flop, I probably won't bet into the protected side pot. Also, my equity is greatly decreased when Seat 6 enters the hand with the type of range I put him on earlier.

I shove over the top, and Seat 6 mucks instantly. Seat 9 has A♥ J♠ and takes the pot after flopping an ace. Although I lost the hand, I had 31 percent equity against A-J, justifying the play given the large pot and small amount I had to call.

Hand 128

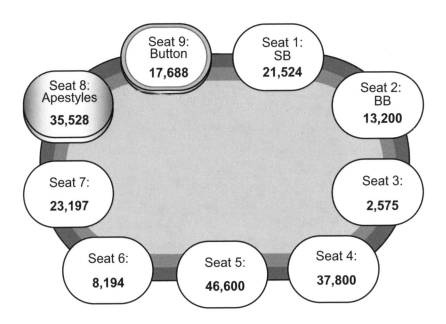

Setup: I've made it to the middle stages of the Sunday $215 1 million guaranteed tournament. The blinds are 300-600 with no antes. I am sitting on a cozy 60 big blind stack and looking to use it to my advantage. Overall, the play is poor at the table and I assume that most of the players are satellite winners. Seats 1, 4, and 5 are playing loose pre-flop and generally weak post-flop. The reasonably solid players are in Seats 2 and 7.

  Pre-flop (900): The loose player in Seat 4 limps in. The action is folded to me, and I raise a little over three-and-a-half times the big blind to 2,200. Raising three-and-a-half to four times the big blind over a limper at the higher blind levels is standard. Because this player is so weak and my hand plays well post-flop, I am raising to isolate him and play a pot heads-up as I have an advantage on later streets. Our stacks are both healthy enough to make continuation bets without being pot-committed, and my opponent will normally fold to a continuation bet on the flop.

Seat 2 in the big blind reraises to 6,600, and Seat 4 folds. Seat 2 has been playing very tightly and solidly ever since his stack got down to around 20 big blinds. Some advanced players with guts might recognize my raise as an isolation play and play back at me with a weak hand, but I am pretty sure he isn't the type of player to make that kind of move. Given my read on him, there really is no reason to think he's doing this with weak cards. Against an 88+, A-Q+ range, I actually have 36 percent equity, but my pot odds aren't sufficient because my opponent is basically pot-committed for his whole stack, as he has put in half his chips. There's only one move.

I fold, and Seat 2 wins the pot.

Hand 129

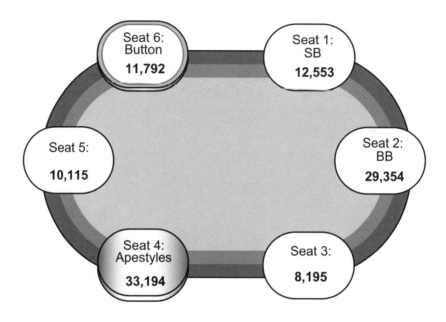

Setup: I am in a $109 6-max tournament with the blinds at 300-600 and a 50 ante. Since I got to the table, I have been running it over with aggressive play. My continuation bets and check-raises have frequently been successful, and my opponents haven't shown that they can fight back yet. I am going to keep taking advantage of the table's poor post-flop abilities and continue to play aggressively so as to accumulate chips.

 Pre-flop (1,200): I open-raise a shade more than two-and-a-half times the big blind to 1,525. When the blinds get a lot bigger compared to the stacks, it's important to lower your raise size to around two-and-a-half times the big blind. This allows you to avoid being frequently committed when smaller stacks re-shove your raise; it's also important for the simple fact that your opponents still respect raises of this size. When the stacks get much smaller compared to the blinds, it becomes increasingly difficult for other players to make moves against you without committing their entire stack to the pot. Most importantly, assuming you are playing an aggressive style taking lots of pots without a hand, if you can make your bet and raise sizes smaller with the same amount of success, then the plays become more profitable overall.

The action is folded to Seat 1 in the small blind, who calls. One interesting thing to note about Seat 1 is that he's been playing pots with me recently, and I've picked on him especially. He hasn't shown the ability to play back at me, and he also doesn't seem to be a very strong player. I am glad to play a pot post-flop in position against him with a hand like J-Ts.

   Flop (3,650): Seat 1 checks. Although the middle cards are a little more connected than optimal, rainbow A-x-x boards are great to make a continuation bet on when your opponent is just calling out of the blinds, as it's unusual for them to be playing many A-x hands out of position. It's very unlikely that my opponent is going to play back at me in this spot, so I can make my continuation bet smaller. His folding frequency is likely to stay the same, thus increasing the EV of my bet in general. If he does have a hand like 9-8, he's almost definitely going to be calling a larger bet, too, considering how often I've hammered him. Note that against an observant opponent who will pick up on tendencies like this, it is important to keep your continuation bet size consistent with both bluffs and made hands.

Bearing this in mind, I make a smaller continuation bet of around half the pot. I bet 1,907, and my opponent calls. Right now he probably has a pair of aces or a pair of eights. He normally wouldn't check-raise an ace here for two reasons. First, he might just be a weak-passive player whose staple play is pushing the call button. Second, he knows that I've been aggressive against him, and he might very well be trying to trap me or induce me to bluff and fire another barrel. If he is trying to take advantage of my aggressive play, he would likely bluff by check-raising the flop. The alternative would be to go for a strange out-of-position float line like calling the flop with the intention of betting the river as a bluff, if I check behind on the turn. It's really unlikely this player is capable of that kind of move, and if he is, I really can't do anything about it anyway on this board. He hasn't played back at me yet, and I am going to be giving up this hand on most turns.

Turn (3,814): Seat 1 checks. This is a very promising turn card. I've now picked up a flush draw and also a double gutshot with the K and 9 being outs to the nuts as well. I suspect Seat 1 has a real hand, so betting this turn doesn't accomplish much. If I bet, he's likely to call or raise if he has a pair of aces, which puts my huge draw in a weird spot. A bet really is only going to make a pair of eights hand (9-8, 8-7, and maybe T-8) fold, which is a much smaller part of his range than the spectrum of aces (AJ-A2) that he might have. Although I have around 30% equity against an AJ-A2 range, it's much more optimal to check behind and take the free card here. If I hit the backdoor draw, it's going to be extremely deceptive, and he's likely to perceive a raise from me on the river as a bluff rather than a made straight or flush. I'll still get a lot of value when I hit, so it's a much better alternative to betting and getting all-in here as a 30 percent underdog for the purposes of only causing a pair of eights to sometimes fold. I check behind.

 River (3,814): Seat 1 bets 2,400, 63 percent of the pot. Amazing! This is the best river I could've hit, and my opponent seems to be value-betting the river as well. The nut-straight I now have is one of the most deceptive I could've hoped to hit. If a king came on the river, my opponent could have been afraid of K-Q making two pair, and a club on the river would stand-out compared to the 9. The only possible flop draw I could've hit would be T-7 or 7-5, but those are trashy hands that he shouldn't be expecting me to have. My opponent views me as aggressive, and this coupled with the likely strength of his hand means I should definitely be making a large value-bet since he will frequently call. I choose to raise three-and-a-half times his bet, to 8,400.

He thinks for a while and then folds. I was fairly confident of getting a call here, and I don't really know what to put him on now that he has folded. It would be unusual for him to fold an ace or to bet an 8 here, especially after making that small of a bet.

Hand 130

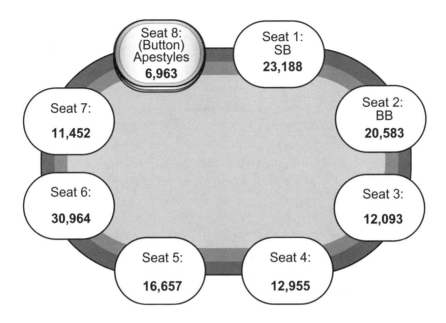

Setup: It is the middle stages of a $109, $15K guaranteed freezeout tournament. The blinds are 300-600 with a 75 ante. I was doing well for a while, but then QQ ran into KK, which reduced my stack to about 12 big blinds. The antes are really adding up, and my stack is great for shoving because of them. There aren't any regulars at the table, which has been playing pretty loosely overall, with the exception of Seat 3, who has been very tight. My image is solid, and I've yet to make any kind of a steal or re-steal play although I've been searching for them.

 **Pre-flop** (1,500): Seat 4 open-limps (something I rarely do with antes in the pot), and Seats 5 and 6 call behind. After all the blinds, antes, and limps, there is 3,300 (about 40 percent of my stack) in the pot. Seats 4 and 5 have been playing exceptionally loosely pre-flop and passively post-flop. I know that Seat 6's limp is weak since he had previously raised Seat 5's limp with KK (when I unfortunately had QQ). After he raised Seat 5's limp, I reraised three times his raise on the button,

and he called his 5,000 chips all-in; a typical late-mid tourney "cooler," there was no way to get away from it.

With this past hand in mind, I can be fairly certain that Seat 6 is weak in this spot, since he'd raise their limps with his premium hands. Therefore, it is unlikely he would call if I shove. My hand is great for shoving over limps because it's rarely ever dominated by a limp range, and actually does have the potential to dominate. If I shove A-4, for instance, I can be dominated by hands like A5-AJ and 55-88, which is what these players are likely to limp and call with, if they recognize my steal. With 77, the only hands that dominate me are 88 and maybe the occasional 99. Some players do limp big pairs from early position, but my read on Seat 4 was that he was limping with a very wide range.

It'd be pretty hard to speculate what exactly these players are limping with, but I can definitely create some limp and call ranges. Essentially, I am shoving 77 for value, but I am happy if everyone folds; increasing one's stack by nearly 50 percent without a showdown is never a bad thing. Based on experience, the ranges I am likely to see limping and calling me are probably 99-22, AJs-A5s, K-Q, Q-J, and AJo-A7o, although the bottom end of this range may be a little loose. I am ahead about 57 percent of the time heads up against that range with 77. Many opponents will limp and call with fewer hands, so this is really the worst-case scenario. There is also the possibility of someone waking up with a hand in the blinds, but I can't worry about that unless I think shoving is a borderline play. In this case, shoving is clearly a profitable play.

Doing an actual EV calculation would be tedious (due to the number of players and ranges involved) and unnecessary as common sense comes into play here. Since I am nearly always ahead, or at least coin flipping (50 percent equity), this is a standard shove. Combine that with the huge number of chips already in the middle in relation to my stack, and it is basically a no-brainer.

Seats 4 and 5 will probably fold the majority of the time, but just for fun, let's see how my hand holds against both. I am going to assume that Seat 4 will call with the aforementioned 99-22, AJs-A5s, KQ-QJ, AJo-A7o range, but after Seat 4 calls, I'll assume Seat 5 will only call with a tighter range like 88-99, KQ-KJ, and AJ-AT. Against these two ranges I have nearly 35 percent equity, which is fantastic in a three-way pot, especially given the blind and ante overlay. So even if I am called by both players, my hand is in good shape. Most of the time I actually will just take the pot pre-flop, since their hands are obviously weak.

In summary, I am increasing my stack by about 40 percent around 45 to 60 percent of the time when they fold, and I more than double around 57 percent of the time when called by one player. When called by both, I am more than tripling up 35 percent of the time. Finding good shove/steal spots like this is absolutely crucial to winning in online tournament structures.

A lot of inexperienced players would flat-call in this spot and try to get it in when they had an overpair or a set, which is actually a pretty terrible play given how great this pre-flop spot is and how rare those post-flop spots are going to be.

I push all-in for 6,288 more in a 3,300 pot. Seat 4 folds, and Seat 5 calls with 8h 8s. Seat 5's hand holds, and I am knocked out of the tournament. Seat 5 happened to be holding one of the few hands in his calling range that had me dominated. I am not unhappy with my play or analysis and focus on the next tourney.

Bubble Section

Setup: The rest of my hands go through every single hand in a single tournament up until the bubble bursts, to demonstrate how to ravage and exploit a bubble situation. This is a $1,060 buy-in $1 million guaranteed tournament, and I am 15 players away from making it into the money. First-place payout is $353,185 and players making the money get at least $2,054.

Tournament fields with this high of a buy-in on Sundays usually consist of a higher percentage of amateur satellite winners than your regular Sunday tournament. These types of players are really going to be sweating the amount of money they're playing for, as the bubble payout will represent anywhere between 10 to 100 times the amount of their satellite buy-in. Most satellite players in these situations will tighten up their play considerably in an attempt to glide into cashing.

Fortunately, I am in excellent position in this tournament as I happen to be the chip leader at the table among some pretty decent (10 M) stacks. With these stack sizes, it's going to be very tough for them to play back at me. Because of these two factors, I'm in a great position to be playing ultra-aggressively, using their fear against them to amass chips without showdown.

Hand 131

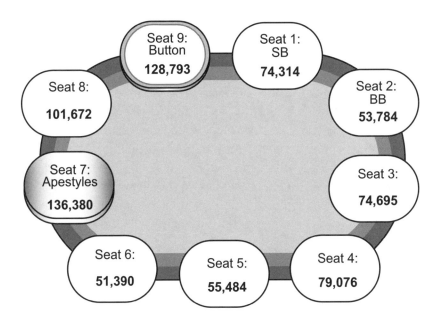

The blinds are 1,200-2,400 with a 120 ante.

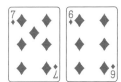 **Pre-flop** (4,680): Seat 6 makes a minimum raise to 4,800. Seat 6 is in middle position and only min-raising with a 20 big blind stack. I've seen him make this raise and fold before, and interpret his raise as a weak steal attempt more often than a real hand. I want to take advantage of this tell and reraise to 14,400.

Obviously, this isn't a standard play for me; there isn't much standard about bubble play anyway since it's mostly timing and frequency. Because it's the bubble and because of how weak I believe my opponent truly is here, I can expect a fairly high rate of success by playing back at him.

I'll have to fold to a shove by anyone behind me, including Seat 6 himself, since I'll be getting a little less than 2-to-1 on a call. If he had raised two-and-a-half to three times the big blind pre-flop, I would not have made this reraise because then I would be committed to call an all-in if he shoved. For example, if he made a raise of three times the big blind, to 7,200, and I reraise to 20,000 and Seat 6 then pushes, I would be faced with calling 31,270 to win a pot of 75,950. This is 2.4-to-1 pot odds.

When making moves like this, it's important to confirm that you aren't committed to all-ins behind you. As a rule of thumb, you're almost always committed pre-flop if you're getting more than 2.2-to-1 odds. The reasoning behind this is that you are generally not more than a 2-to-1 underdog against a player's hand range, unless of course his range is incredibly tight (9-9+, AQ+) or you have a junk hand on the lower end of the spectrum, such as 3-2 offsuit. I recommend playing with the free program *Pokerstove* to get a good idea of equity versus hand ranges.

Everyone folds, and I add 9,480 to my stack.

Hand 132

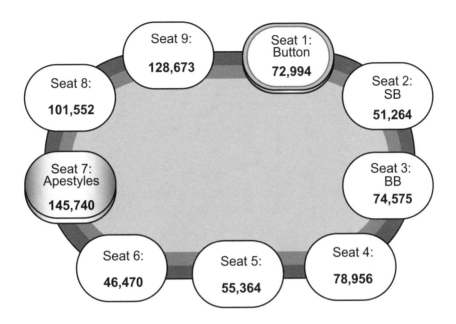

The blinds are 1,200-2,400 with a 120 ante.

 **Pre-flop** (4,680): Seat 5, an aggressive regular, raises to 7,200. I have a terrible hand, and I reraised my last hand. It's important to monitor my raising frequency in order to maintain at least some illusion of legitimacy when I make moves. Considering Seat 5 is in early position, my abysmal hand, and the fact that Seat 5 is a good regular and most likely aware of my bubble strategy, I choose to fold.

Hand 133

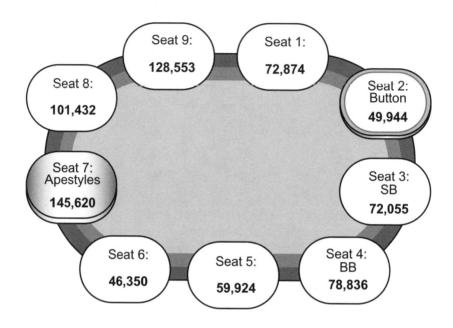

The blinds are 1,200-2,400 with a 120 ante.

  Pre-flop (4,680): I am in middle position and raise a little more than two-and-a-half times the big blind to 6,450. Seat 9 reraises to 16,800 from the hijack position. Even though I have a fairly strong hand, I have no choice but to fold. There's no reason to play this hand out of position post-flop or to four-bet a marginal holding here against one of the few players who can do some very serious damage to my stack. I can still count on winning many uncontested pots in the future, and it's important not to get frustrated when one of my moves fails, as it sometimes will.

I fold and make a mental note of Seat 9's reraise. If he persists in causing me trouble, I'll know he's up to something and will start fighting back.

Hand 134

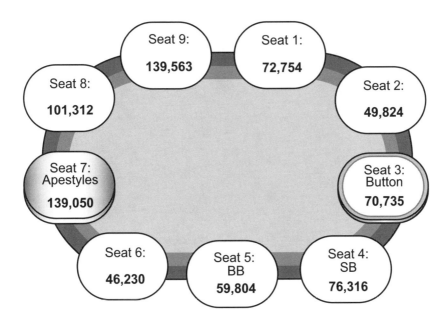

The blinds are 1,200-2,400 with a 120 ante.

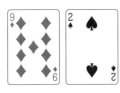

Pre-flop (4,680): Even though my plan is to raise a lot of unopened pots, I am not going to be doing it in early position very much and certainly not with a hand this bad. I fold.

Hand 135

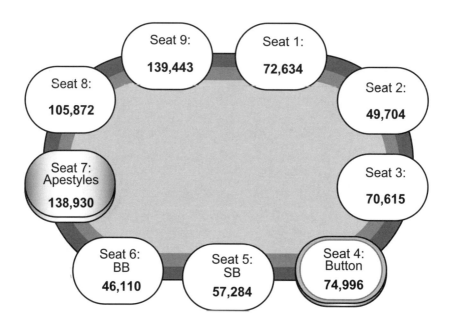

The blinds are 1,200-2,400 with a 120 ante.

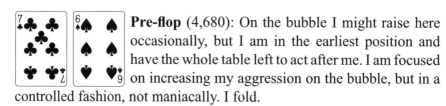 **Pre-flop** (4,680): On the bubble I might raise here occasionally, but I am in the earliest position and have the whole table left to act after me. I am focused on increasing my aggression on the bubble, but in a controlled fashion, not maniacally. I fold.

Hand 136

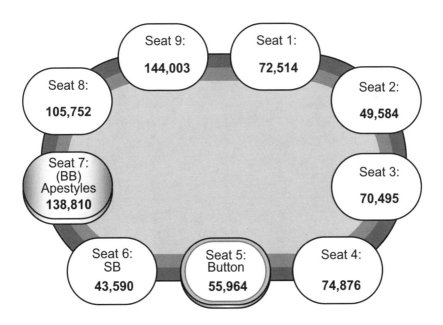

The blinds are 1,200-2,400 with a 120 ante.

 **Pre-flop** (4,680): Seat 5 raises to 7,200. He is an aggressive regular making a button raise. This would usually be a good spot to re-steal if it weren't for the fact that my hand plays so badly against any calling range. For example, J-Ts is usually around a 2-to-1 underdog to most calling ranges, while 7-3o is closer to a 3-to-1 underdog. While circumstances are usually more important than cards, I prefer to steal with hands with more showdown value, like middle-range suited connectors/gappers (J-9s, 9-8s, etc.).

Re-shoving 7-3o here is probably a losing play, so I make an easy fold.

Hand 137

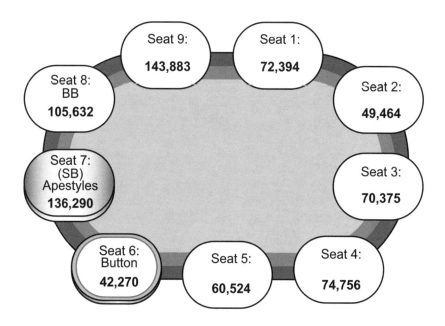

The blinds are 1,200-2,400 with a 120 ante.

  Pre-flop (4,680): The action is folded to me. I raise three times the big blind, to 7,200. I generally open-raise three to four times from the small blind, rather than my usual two and a half times, so as not to give the big blind incentive to call in position. It's a big mistake to raise with weak hands only two-and-a-half times the big blind from the small blind, because the big blind will frequently call, leaving me with awkward decisions post-flop. The big blind also reraised me already during this orbit, so he's unlikely to do it again so soon without a hand. I don't always raise in this type of situation, but since everyone, including the big blind, is playing much tighter (along with the fact that he's already reraised me), I decide to raise.

I raise to 7,200 from the small blind, and the big blind folds, I collect 4,680 from the pot.

Hand 138

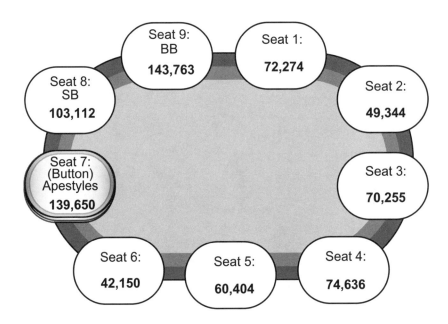

The blinds are 1,200-2,400 with a 120 ante.

 **Pre-flop** (4,680): The action is folded to me on the button. This is an easy raise as both the small blind and the big blind have really large stacks. This is important because they're probably feeling pretty snug in the tournament and won't want to risk busting out before the money with such healthy stacks. If they do reraise, I'll even consider four-betting all-in since I'll have fold equity against what is most likely a re-steal play, since they wouldn't even be getting 2-to-1 on a call. I will most likely just fold to a reraise though. Always remember when making moves to look at the players behind you paying close attention to their stack sizes and have a plan for their possible responses. Just like in chess, poker players always need to be thinking several moves ahead. I raise around two-and-a-half times the big blind, to 6,100. There are arguments for different raise sizes, and I do occasionally make larger or smaller raises pre-flop. Generally, it's best to pick a raise size to stick to

for each level, because it's easy and also cannot be exploited since the bet size offers a tell in itself.

I raise to 6,100, and everyone folds. I collect 4,680 from the pot.

Hand 139

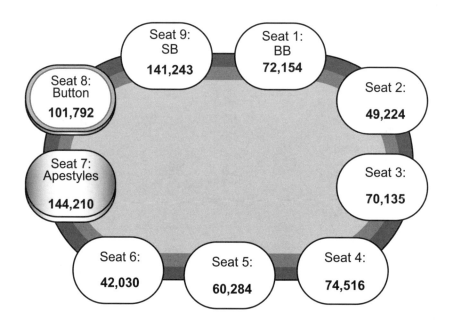

The blinds are 1,200-2,400 with a 120 ante.

  Pre-flop (4,680): I am in the cutoff seat, and the action is folded to me. I would usually consider slowing down here because I've been so active, but we're getting even closer to the money and I've even noticed a few players bragging about getting here through a low-limit satellite. They're probably just dying to get into the money intact, and now I basically have a license to pillage certain areas of the table. I choose to raise my standard 6,100 again. If Seat 1 shoves, I'll be forced to fold due to his stack size. However, Seats 8 and 9, who have large stacks, offer a range of possibilities: They might just call my raise, and I can see a flop with a hand that flops well. If they play back at me and reraise, I could certainly fold or even four-bet all-in. Whether or not I execute a four-bet all-in (as a bluff, mind you) depends on timing tells and reraise size. I will most likely fold to a three-bet from either player in the absence of any extra information.

I raise to 6,100, and everyone folds. I pick up my third pot in a row, collecting 4,680.

Hand 140

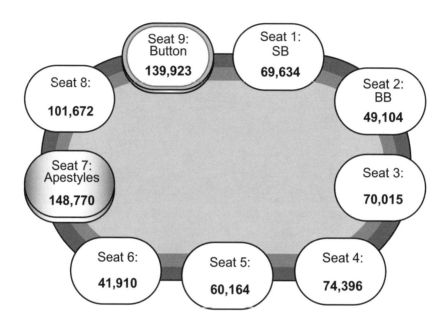

The blinds are 1,200-2,400 with a 120 ante.

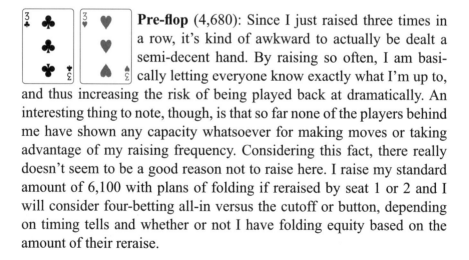

Pre-flop (4,680): Since I just raised three times in a row, it's kind of awkward to actually be dealt a semi-decent hand. By raising so often, I am basically letting everyone know exactly what I'm up to, and thus increasing the risk of being played back at dramatically. An interesting thing to note, though, is that so far none of the players behind me have shown any capacity whatsoever for making moves or taking advantage of my raising frequency. Considering this fact, there really doesn't seem to be a good reason not to raise here. I raise my standard amount of 6,100 with plans of folding if reraised by seat 1 or 2 and I will consider four-betting all-in versus the cutoff or button, depending on timing tells and whether or not I have folding equity based on the amount of their reraise.

I raise to 6,100, and everyone folds yet again. I collect another 4,680, my fourth uncontested pot in a row.

Hand 141

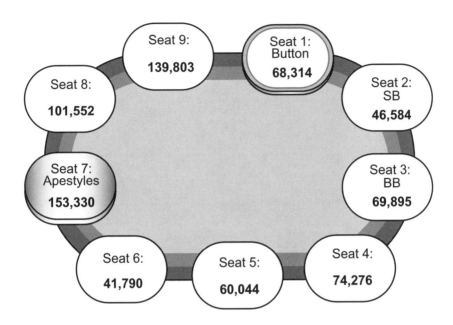

The blinds are 1,200-2,400 with a 120 ante.

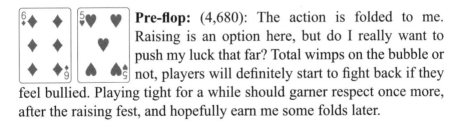 **Pre-flop:** (4,680): The action is folded to me. Raising is an option here, but do I really want to push my luck that far? Total wimps on the bubble or not, players will definitely start to fight back if they feel bullied. Playing tight for a while should garner respect once more, after the raising fest, and hopefully earn me some folds later.

I pause for a while so my open-fold doesn't go unnoticed, and muck.

Hand 142

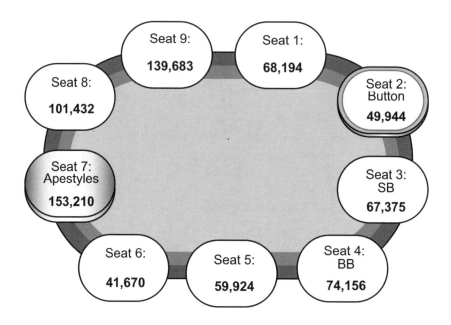

The blinds are 1,200-2,400 with a 120 ante.

  Pre-flop: (4,680): Seat 6 raises to 7,200. This is simply a terrible hand and position to make moves from. I fold.

Hand 143

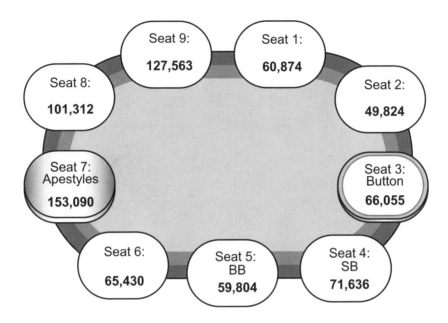

The blinds are 1,200-2,400 with a 120 ante.

 **Pre-flop:** (4,680): Seat 6 raises again to 9,600. I should take note of the fact that that this time he's raising four times the big blind, as opposed to his customary three times. Given the fact that he's under-the-gun and raising a rather large amount, he is likely to have a real hand that he's scared of playing either multiway or post-flop in general. Some amateur players will raise larger amounts with hands they perceive to be especially vulnerable post-flop. With hands like QQ-TT, and even sometimes KK in extreme cases, the threat of an overcard flopping looms large in their minds. This is often the case with A-K and A-Q as well. The larger raise serves to engineer as much pre-flop action as possible with hands they know are strong, yet for some reason they fear playing after the flop.

I fold my Q♠ T♥, as does everyone else. Seat 6 actually shows QQ while taking the pot down.

Hand 144

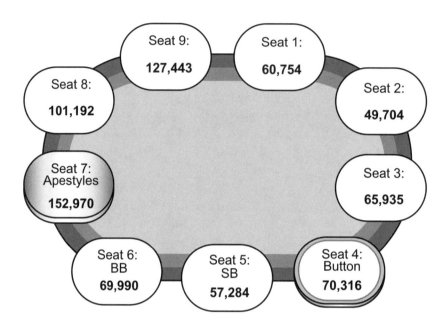

The blinds are 1,200-2,400 with a 120 ante.

 **Pre-flop** (4,680): This is an obvious fold for the same reasons mentioned earlier.

Hand 145

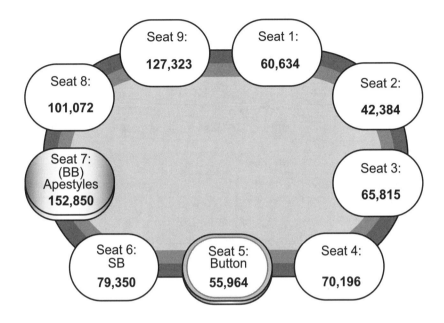

The blinds are 1,200-2,400 with a 120 ante.

  Pre-flop (4,680): Seat 5, an aggressive regular, raises to 7,200 on the button, and Seat 6 flat-calls. There's currently 17,880 in the pot. I am not worried about Seat 6 because he has consistently played weakly and also has been bragging about investing only $10 in a satellite. I'm nearly positive he's not trapping but rather just playing scared, and the $2,000 payout obviously means a lot to him. Seat 5 is aggressive; either his good hands seem to be coming to him on the button, or he just loves to steal from there.

Considering I have only Q-To, calling and folding are both fine options. Based on my reads, though, I prefer a re-shove in this situation to continue to apply pressure on my opponents. I usually don't try to abuse regulars on the money bubble, but I do have the last bet to put in here, and he's been consistently raising the button. By shoving, I am only giving Seat

5 about 1.5-to-1 pot odds to call, so I have enough fold equity here to force my opponent to fold a good portion of his raising range.

Let's do some rough math: He's raising around 20 to 25 percent of the time on the button, and I expect him to call my shove roughly 50 percent of the time. To make the math easy, let's say he's raising 22 percent of the time and calling my shove with the top 11 percent of hands. The top 11 percent of his hands is more or less the following calling range: 66+, A8s+, KJs+, ATo+, and K-Qo. His calling range could be even tighter with the bubble approaching. Q-To has about 33 percent equity against this range.

Assuming Seat 6 never calls, my assumptions lead to the following:
50 percent of the time my opponents fold and I win 17,880.
33.5 percent of the time Seat 5 calls and I lose 53,444.
16.5 percent of the time Seat 5 calls and I win 66,524 (17,880 + 48,644).

Below is an approximated EV calculation.

0.5 x 17,880 = 8,940
0.335 x -53,444 = -17,904
0.165 x 66,524 = 10,976

Chip EV = +2,012

Keep in mind that all of the above ranges and frequencies are rough estimates. This looks like a +EV push, almost one big blind in equity. Even if the villain's opening range was tighter and his calling range wider, it would still be break even or be slightly -EV at worst. I generally don't mind taking slightly marginal gambles with fold equity when I have a big stack.

Strategically, it could be argued that this shove isn't wise. First off, from a math perspective, Seat 5's opening range could be much tighter considering his smaller stack size and my aggressive image. More important, ignoring the math of that single hand, if I lose this pot I double up the only really good player at the table and also go from chip leader to fourth in chips with two big stacks to my left. I would lose the leverage

I presently have that allows me to take pots with impunity.

On the other hand, if I win I'll be able to run the table to an even greater extent during the remaining bubble, because I've now proven that I have no qualms about getting my chips in the pot. Players will be more reluctant to raise my blinds in the future, which might allow me to pick up chips later, uncontested.

I reraise to 80,000, putting both players all-in. Seat 5 calls with A-Jo, and Seat 6 folds. My Q♦ T♠ spikes a T on the river, and I win a pot of 119,968 and eliminate Seat 5.

Hand 146

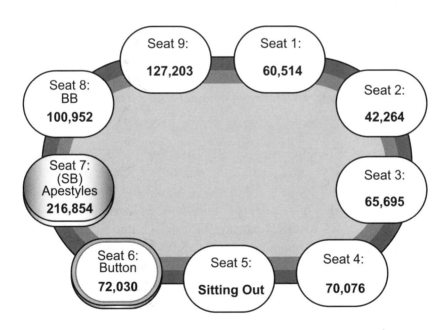

The blinds are 1,200-2,400 with a 120 ante.

Pre-flop (4,680): I was extremely fortunate to suck out in the previous hand, and I'm aware that my table image has declined. Everyone folds to me in the small blind. Despite my image, I am still going to put pressure on my opponents. I raise three times the big blind, to 7,200. Seat 8 reraises to 21,600 total, leaving around 80,000 behind. The only plays I have here are either to fold or to four-bet all-in.

Let's evaluate the reasons for four-betting: 1.) I am in a blind-versus-blind situation where it's commonplace to try to either steal the big blind or defend my big blind from steals. 2.) I've been extremely aggressive at the table and just got caught making a big play, making it very likely that he's playing back at me. 3.) Even though I am obviously aggressive, my image isn't necessarily maniacal or overly reckless by any means. 4) It is still the bubble and amateur players are still going to be uncomfortable risking being eliminated right before a $2K guaranteed payday.

I just got caught stealing in a very large pot, and usually after that happens, my opponents would expect me to slow down and not commit another big re-steal for a while. In the face of a four-bet all-in combined with this expectation, my opponent definitely has grounds to fear that I now have a real hand.

As a quick rule of thumb, you generally have four-bet all-in fold equity in a heads-up pot if your opponent has put in only a quarter or less of his chips pre-flop. Don't try to four-bet with a weak hand if your opponent has invested a third or more of his chips, because he'll usually be getting at least 2-to-1 odds to call. Learning little tricks like this will really speed up your decision making and help your multi-tabling abilities.

Just to demonstrate, let's look at the mathematics of this situation: There is 29,760 in the pot when I go all-in. My opponent has 79,352 remaining in his stack to win 123,512 (29,760 + 93,752). This only gives him about 1.5-to-1 pot odds, giving me plenty of folding equity.

I go all-in over the top of Seat 8's raise, and he folds after a little waiting.

Hand 147

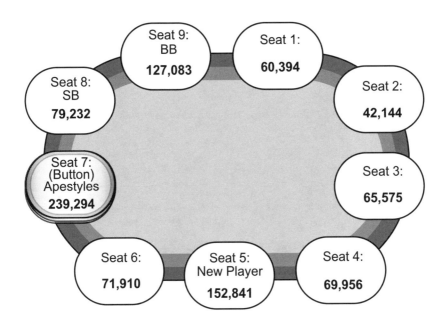

The blinds are 1,200-2,400 with a 120 ante.

 **Pre-flop** (4,680): Note that a new player is in Seat 5. Seat 6 raises to 9,600 from the cutoff. While I usually like to be aggressive against late-position raises, I've been extremely active at the table, and the last time Seat 6 raised four times the big blind he had QQ. I fold.

Hand 148

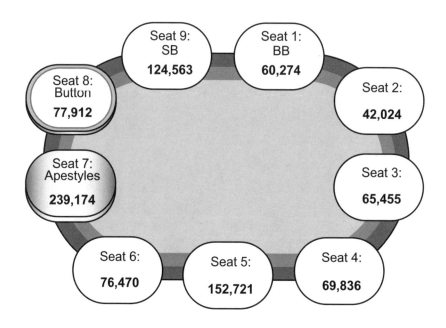

The blinds are 1,200-2,400 with a 120 ante.

 **Pre-flop** (4,680): Everyone folds to Seat 6, who makes a minimum raise to 4,800. Usually I would be tempted to three-bet here, as Seat 6 has shown a tendency to raise larger amounts with his big hands. Seat 6 also professed to be a satellite winner, and I've observed him making a lot of weak and scared plays. However, my image is tarnished right now, and I need to take some time to rebuild my credibility. I fold.

Hand 149

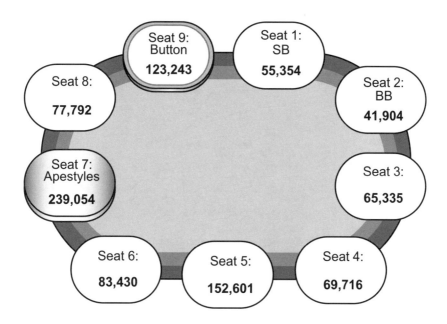

The blinds are 1,200-2,400 with a 120 ante.

 **Pre-flop** (4,680): Everyone folds to me, and I make my standard raise of 6,100. Seat 9 flat-calls on the button.

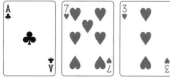 **Flop** (16,880): This is a fairly dry flop, and I am definitely going to make a continuation bet since it misses his most of his calling range. I bet 9,050, and Seat 9 quickly folds. I win another pot without a showdown, for 16,880.

Hand 150

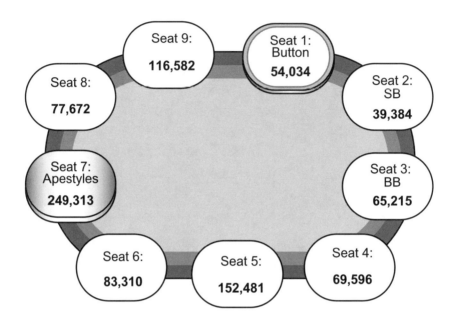

The blinds *increase* to 1,600-3,200 with a 160 ante.

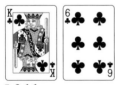 **Pre-flop** (6,240): The blinds have risen, and there's going to be 6,240 in the pot pre-flop from now on. Everyone folds to me, and I decide to muck since I've been so active recently and my hand is garbage.

I fold.

Hand 151

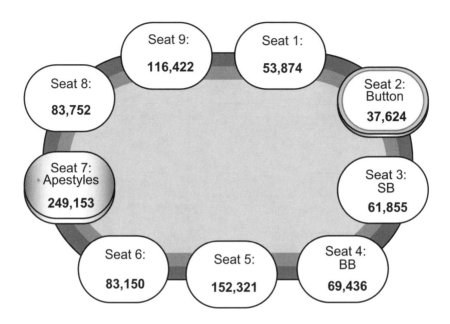

The blinds are 1,600-3,200 with a 160 ante.

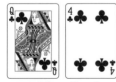 **Pre-flop** (6,240): Seat 5, a well-known professional high-stakes cash game player, raises three times the big blind, to 9,600, from under-the-gun. He has a big stack, and I am not happy that he was moved to my table a few hands ago. He knows how to play against my aggressiveness, and I expect him to do so. Regardless, this is an easy fold against anyone's under-the-gun raise. I fold.

Hand 152

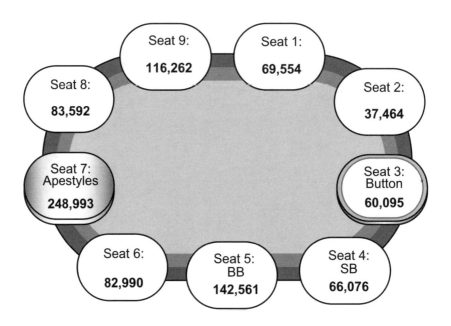

The blinds are 1,600-3,200 with a 160 ante.

 **Pre-flop** (6,240): This is almost always a fold, but since I've been quiet for a while, I decide to sneak in an unexpected early-position steal. Sometimes I do wacky and random stuff to mix up my play. I also choose to raise a small and odd amount of 7,373. A lot of players will interpret this as strong, and most of the time I actually am going to be strong when I make a smaller raise in early position. Objectively, this is one of the worst raises I've made on the bubble, but then again I am not going to get in a lot of trouble with a hand this bad.

I raise to 7,373, and Seat 3 shoves all-in for 59,935. I fold and feel like a donkey.

Hand 153

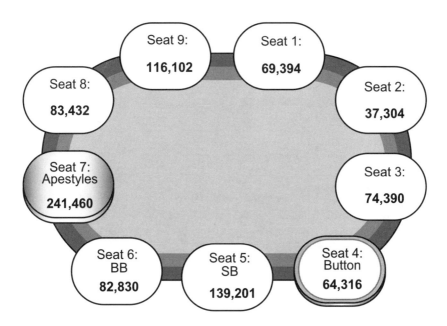

The blinds are 1,600-3,200 with a 160 ante.

 **Pre-flop:** (6,240): A-T isn't the greatest hand in the world, but it's pretty decent compared to the other hands I have been playing on the bubble. This is a marginal play, but given the bubble and my opponents' propensity to shy away from confrontation, I decide to raise the same amount I did last time, to 7,373. Many players tend to tighten up after getting re-shoved on, and this is what my opponents are expecting of me after the last hand. Instead I am going to raise here again to take advantage of this type of common psychology.

I raise to 7,373, and everyone folds. I collect 6,240 from the pot.

Hand 154

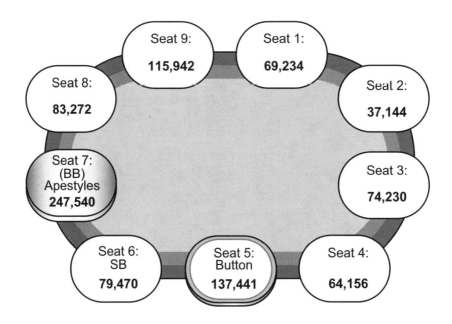

The blinds are 1,600-3,200 with a 160 ante.

 Pre-flop (6,240): Seat 8 raises to 7,777 under-the-gun, and everyone folds to me. Once again, there's absolutely no need or read that would qualify reraising an under-the-gun raiser with a junk hand out of position here. I fold.

Hand 155

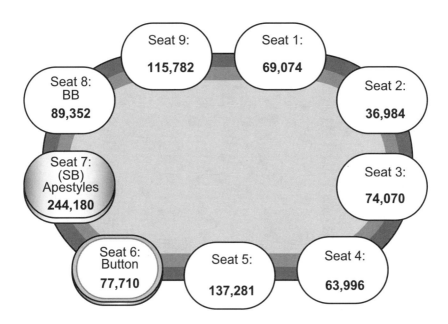

The blinds are 1,600-3,200 with a 160 ante.

  Pre-flop (6,240): Seat 2, who has been inactive during this entire bubble period, makes a minimum raise to 6,400. Seat 6 reraises to 22,400. A min-raise from a small stack is often a sign of strength, but since we're on the bubble, it might just as easily be a weak player on a steal. Besides this fact, Seat 2 has only about a 12 big blind stack, so I am obviously getting my chips in with queens against him regardless. Seat 6 hasn't been too active, but he can most definitely have 88+ and A-Q+ in his range here, which he could estimate as being ahead of Seat 2. If I shove he'll probably call with TT+ and A-K+. My queens are ahead of that range, so I elect to shove for value.

I four-bet all-in with Q♣ Q♠, and both players fold. I take down the 55,840 pot.

Hand 156

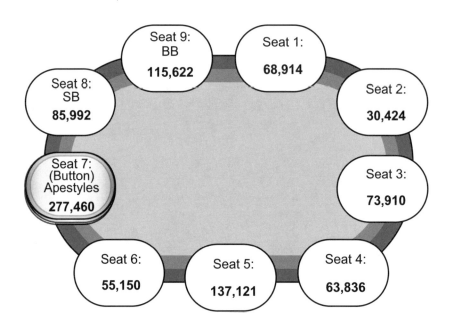

The blinds are 1,600-3,200 with a 160 ante.

 **Pre-flop** (6,240): Seat 6 raises to 9,600. I just took a big pot and decide it's probably a good time to get some folds in before firing up the steals again. I fold.

Hand 157

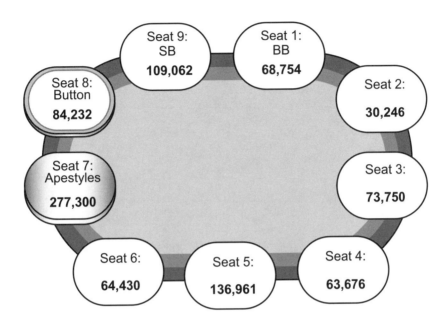

The blinds are 1,600-3,200 with a 160 ante.

 **Pre-flop** (6,240): Seat 5, the strong pro, raises to 9,600. I am not really looking to tangle with players capable of playing back hard at me, especially with T-2o. I fold.

Hand 158

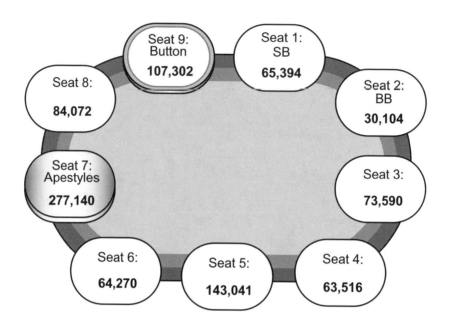

The blinds are 1,600-3,200 with a 160 ante.

 **Pre-flop** (6,240): Everyone folds to me, and I make it 8,134. I'd be most satisfied with just taking it down, but I intend on calling an all-in from the big blind because I'll be priced in. The cutoff or button will probably need a decent hand in this spot for a re-steal because any raise they make will end up committing them as well. I raise to 8,134, and the small blind just calls my raise out of position.

 Flop (20,098): An uncoordinated flop with one high card and a flush draw, this is a great flop to make a continuation bet on, as there aren't many K-x hands in his pre-flop range. Against a good player, I might be suspicious of a flat-call out of position with a 20 big blind stack. With a stack of this size, it is almost always a bad play simply to call pre-flop, unless you're trapping with a big pair or plan on check-raising all-in without a lot of fold equity on flops regardless of whether or not you hit. There's no reason to think this player is that sophisticated, and I likely will just take the pot down with a continuation bet as usual. Since this player is most likely to have missed and will probably fold to an assortment of bets, I decide that around half the pot is respectable enough to get the job done. It should be noted that betting less than half the pot here is acceptable considering the stack sizes. Any bet basically forces Seat 1 to play for his entire stack. However, I don't really want to induce a bluff check-raise by betting too little.

I bet a little more than half the pot, 12,503, and Seat 1 folds.

Hand 159

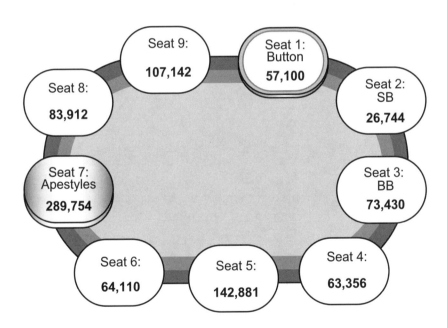

The blinds are 1,600-3,200 with a 160 ante.

Pre-flop (6,240): I was active last hand, and I'd also be forced to call the button's all-in if he did end up shoving over my steal-raise. I fold.

Hand 160

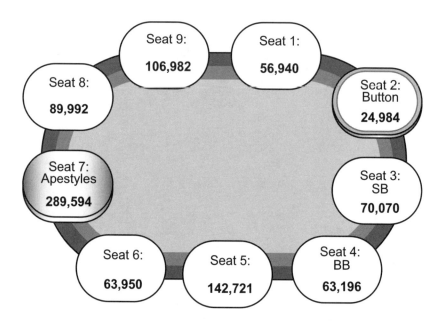

The blinds are 1,600-3,200 with a 160 ante.

  Pre-flop (6,240): I have a garbage hand, and a lot of the players ahead of me have perfect re-steal stacks of about 15 to 25 big blinds. I fold.

Hand 161

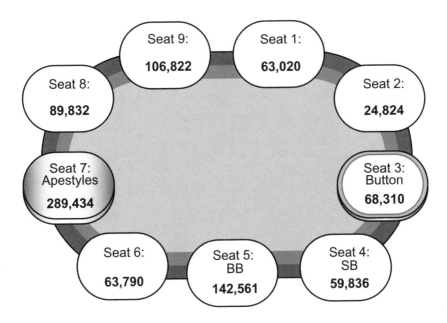

The blinds are 1,600-3,200 with a 160 ante.

Pre-flop (6,240): It's painful to fold so much, especially considering the stack I've amassed, but J-3s is just terrible. I am also in early position, and the table dynamics have changed because of the larger blinds. I fold.

Hand 162

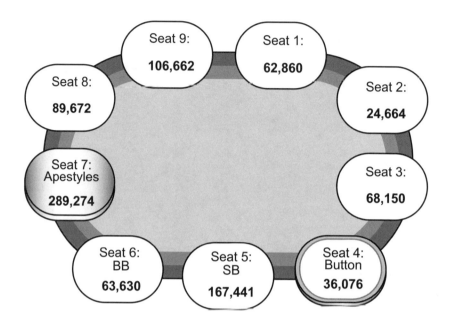

The blinds are 1,600-3,200 with a 160 ante.

  Pre-flop (6,240): The same factors from the previous hand apply. I fold. Note that Seat 3 knocks out Seat 4 and increases his stack to over 100,000.

Hand 163

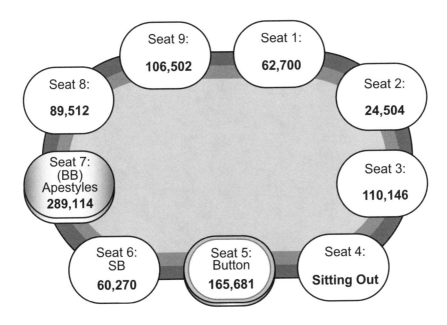

The blinds are 1,600-3,200 with a 160 ante.

  Pre-flop (6,080): The action is folded around to the small blind, and he folds to me, too. Another advantage of having a big stack and an aggressive image is that I get more walks (when the small blind folds to my big blind rather than attempts a steal). My big blind Q-T push earlier might have helped me out on this particular hand.

Hand 164

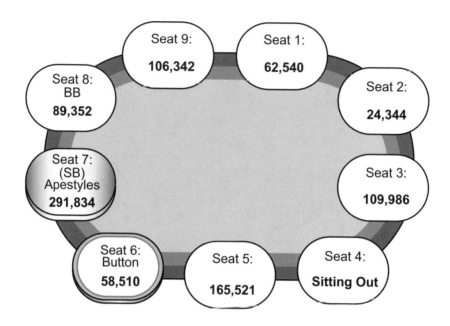

The blinds are 1,600-3,200 with a 160 ante.

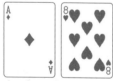 **Pre-flop** (6,240): Everyone folds to Seat 5, who raises to 9,600. This particular player plays the nose-bleed (very high stakes) cash games and wins or loses hundreds of thousands daily, so I can't exploit the fear that satellite players have. I also haven't observed much activity or any steal plays from him, and because of this, he's likely to be ready to get his chips in here in the event of a reraise. I fold.

Hand 165

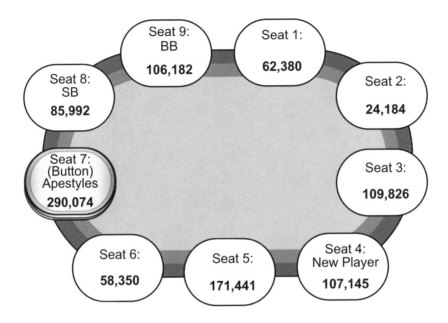

The blinds are 1,600-3,200 with a 160 ante.

 **Pre-flop:** (6,240): I haven't open-raised for a while, and I've been itching to do so again. Everyone folds to me, I raise to 7,999, and both players fold. I almost never fold this hand on the button on the bubble, especially since both stacks ahead of me are too big for re-shoving with weak holdings.

Hand 166

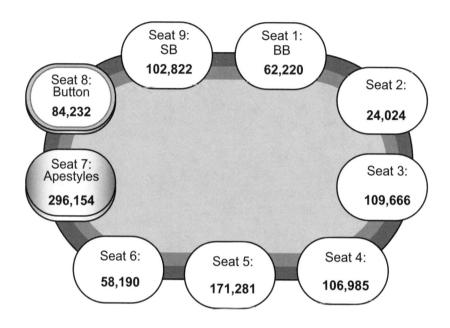

The blinds are 1,600-3,200 with a 160 ante.

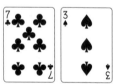 **Pre-flop** (6,240): Seat 6 min-raises again from the hijack. It's very tempting to reraise him even with this hand because I happen to know his min-raise is generally not a strong hand. But if I three-bet, I might be committed to call an all-in. This proves to be a miscalculation, however, as 7-3o is a bad enough hand that I can actually fold and get a little more than 2-to-1 on a call pre-flop if he goes all-in. Regardless, it would be a pretty marginal and probably reckless play. I fold.

Hand 167

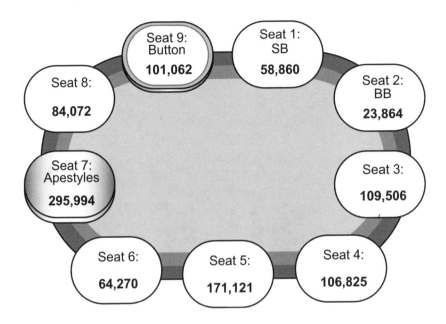

The blinds are 1,600-3,200 with a 160 ante.

 **Pre-flop** (6,240): Seat 5, the strongest player at the table so far, who also happens to be only second to me in chip count, min-raises to 6,400. I mentioned earlier my desire to avoid this player, but at some point I have to assert my dominance. I decide this is a great spot to three-bet for a couple of reasons. First, I have position with a hand that flops well. Next, reraising from the hijack looks a lot less like a steal than from the button, small blind, or big blind. With the extra players to act after me, this play is generally riskier than from a later position, and consequently, it is perceived as stronger in the eyes of my opponents.

I raise 8,600 more to 15,000 straight. This raise is much smaller than my usual raise of three times the bet for some very specific reasons. Due to betting rules, if I were to raise 12,600 to 19,000 and the big blind were to go all-in for 4,864 more, Seat 5 will have the option of reraising or calling while I'll only have the option of calling if Seat 5 calls. This is because Seat 2 has not made a legal raise. You may have heard people refer to this as a dead raise. Now, by raising 8,600 to 15,000, if Seat 2 goes all-in for 8,864 more and Seat 5 calls, I will still have the option of calling or raising to isolate. Making this smaller raise also serves the dual purpose of not committing me to an all-in from Seat 1 since I will be getting less than 2:1 odds versus his very tight range.

I reraise to 15,000 and everyone folds.

Hand 168

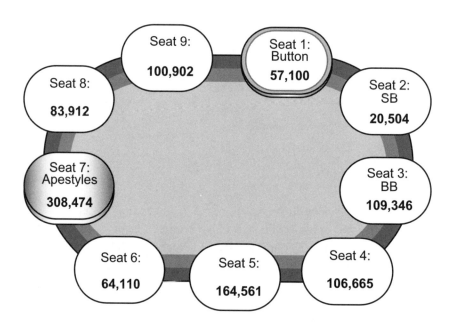

The blinds are 1,600-3,200 with a 160 ante.

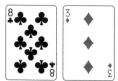 **Pre-flop** (6,240): Seat 5 raises again. I assume that like me, he's being aggressive on the bubble to pick up chips, and there are only two players left until the bubble bursts. I hate him being here, but I can't really fight back with 8-3o. I fold.

Hand 169

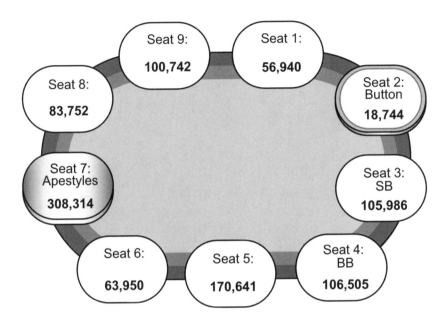

The blinds are 1,600-3,200 with a 160 ante.

 **Pre-flop:** (6,240): Seat 5, the aggressive pro, raises yet again. Again, it's just too reckless to three-bet Q-7o from middle position, even though I know what he's up to. We'll just both have to be table captains! I fold.

Hand 170

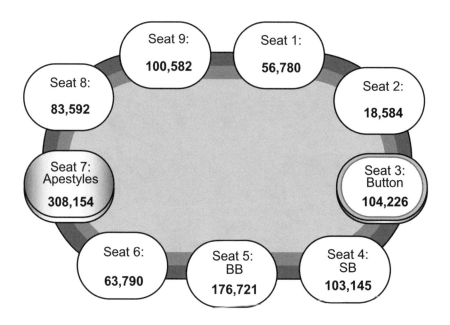

The blinds are 1,600-3,200 with a 160 ante.

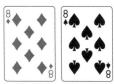 **Pre-flop** (6,240): Seat 6 min-raises to 6,400 under-the-gun. I choose to flat-call because I think I'm ahead of his opening range and also because I don't usually reraise directly behind under-the-gun raises with 88. That being so, this isn't a standard situation. I'm one person away from the money now, and it might be a stronger play to reraise. Players ahead of me would probably fold anything but QQ+, and Seat 6 is almost always folding. In retrospect, it probably would work, but I choose to call instead. Seat 5 calls the extra 3,200 as well out of the big blind.

   Flop (22,240): This is one of the worst flops possible for me. Seat 5 leads out for a very strong 19,200, and Seat 6 folds. Obviously, I have to fold.

Hand 171

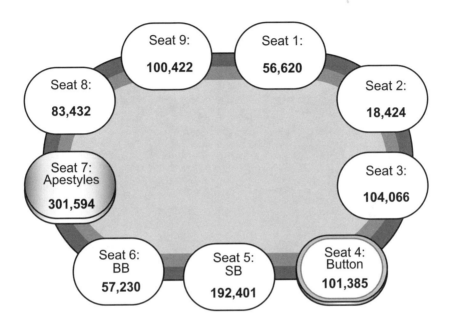

The blinds are 1,600-3,200 with a 160 ante.

 **Pre-flop** (6,240): I raise to 8,313 with the intention of folding to anyone's reraise except Seat 2's. Seat 5, the aggressive pro, calls out of position in the small blind.

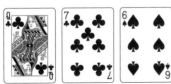 **Flop** (21,266): I pretty much missed this flop, but it's a decent board to make a continuation bet on. Seat 5 has been very active, so it's hard to put him on an exact hand range. He should give my under-the-gun raise respect since I haven't shown down any garbage and have been playing more tightly over the past few hands. I decide to make a continuation bet of a little more than half the pot, 12,505. I'll be forced to fold if he ends up check-raising me, which he is very well capable of doing.

I bet 12,505, and Seat 5 folds. I collect 21,266 from the pot.

Hand 172

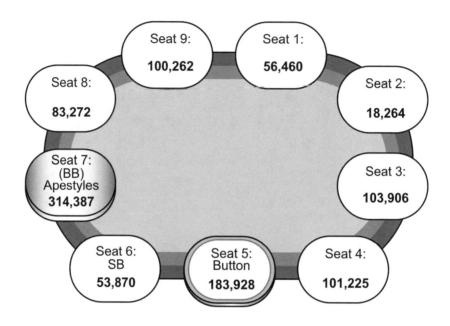

The blinds are 1,600-3,200 with a 160 ante.

 **Pre-flop** (6,240): Everyone folds to Seat 6, who completes the small blind for 1,600 more. Usually I would check behind because Seat 6's stack is perfect for limp-reraising all-in. The circumstances are a lot different here, though, since there's only one player left until the money and we're playing hand-for-hand. Seat 6 has been playing weak and tight while also bragging about his satellite earlier. I know there is very little chance he'll call an all-in. In fact, I suspect the chance is close to zero, as I would have expected him to raise any decent holding.

I put him in for his remaining 50,679. Seat 6 folds, and I collect 7,840 from the pot.

Hand 173

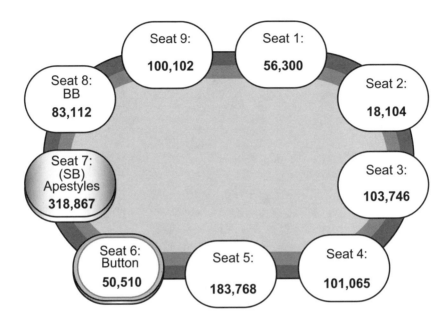

The blinds *increase* to 2,000-4,000 with a 200 ante.

 **Pre-flop** (7,800): The bubble still hasn't ended yet. The annoying aggressive player in Seat 5 raises to 12,000. Against almost any regular player I would strongly consider reraising, as it takes serious guts to risk such a huge stack right on the money bubble. However, from what I know of Seat 5, he is entirely capable of doing so, and I am definitely putting myself at risk of a four-bet if I do reraise. I hate sharing the table with other strong big stacks, but I need to be selective about my spots, too. I fold.

Hand 174

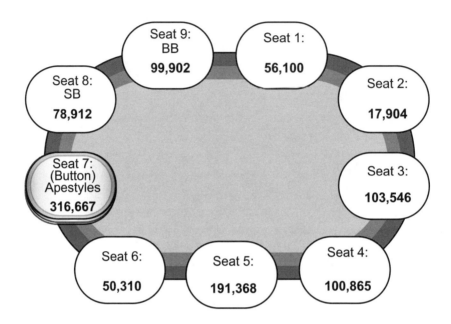

The blinds are 2,000-4,000 with a 200 ante.

 Pre-flop (7,800): The action is folded to me. One player is still left until the bubble bursts. The blinds are weak and obviously just want to cash before making any plays. What do you think I am going to do? I raise to 9,999, and both players fold. I collect 7,800 from the pot.

The Bubble Ends

Analysis: When I began to notice the table tightening up on the bubble, I immediately changed gears from tight-aggressive to very loose-aggressive. It was controlled aggression, though, as almost every play had a point and a purpose. I was not just maniacally throwing chips around without solid reasoning behind every decision. At the start of this hand series, I had a stack of 136,380, and I ended the bubble with 324,467. I added 188,087 to my stack by exploiting the increased tightness and fear that my opponents had during the bubble.

Admittedly, I did get lucky when my Q-T won against A-J, but even if you subtract the 66,404 gained in that pot, I still nearly doubled up without a showdown. You'll often hear players whining about how they can't win races in the latter stages of tournaments, but most of them don't know how to use fold equity and situational awareness to accumulate low-variance (low swings/less risky) chips.

Note also that the strong player in Seat 5 also increased his stack significantly during the bubble once he sat at the table, going from 153,000 up to 191,000. The bubble is the time when strong players make their moves up the leader board.

Be aware that bubble exploitation doesn't always go this smoothly. I definitely got lucky in terms of timing and the fact that I was rarely played back at. Like almost everything else in poker however, there are going to be times when I repeatedly fail despite playing well. Hopefully this series of hands offers some insights into the strategies used during big-stack bubble play in major tournaments.

20 Collaborative Hands

These are real hands where all three authors explain how they would have played the hand. The authors did not see each other's answers when responding to these questions.

Hand 175

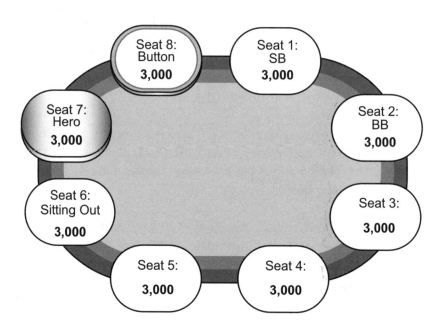

Setup: The Hero is in a $320 weekly tournament on Wednesday nights. This is the very first hand of the tournament with blinds of 10-20.

 Pre-flop (30): Seat 4 raises to 60, and it is folded to the Hero, who is in the cutoff seat holding pocket jacks. What do you do?

PearlJammer

Although I have been dealt a very strong hand at the start of the tournament, I do not want to build a big pot in the early going with it. If I reraise and the original raiser or another player four-bets, I would have to fold unless the four-bet is extremely small, allowing me to call with implied odds. I usually like to focus on controlling the size of the pot in the early stages of a tournament, and therefore lean toward the call. I call.

Rizen

This early in the tournament, I just call. I don't want to be forced to play a big pot post-flop when it's very likely there will be an overcard on the board.

Apestyles

While it's certainly fine to three-bet JJ pre-flop, I also like to flat-call with it when deeper-stacked. I really disguise the strength of my hand, and I can get a lot of value post-flop against opponents not expecting me to have it in my range. Since I am just flat-calling pre-flop, I definitely have to exercise post-flop skills and play carefully.

The Hero calls, and the big blind calls.

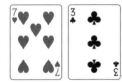

Flop (190): It is checked to the Hero. What do you do?

PearlJammer

Both the big blind and the raiser checked on a rather raggedy flop. With 190 in the pot and not wanting to give any free cards, I will almost always bet approximately two-thirds of the pot. I bet 120.

Rizen

I bet. I probably have the best hand, and there are a lot of turn cards I don't want to give to my opponents for free.

Apestyles

I like to make a good-size bet here of around 2/3 to 3/4 of the pot. If my opponent has a flush draw, he's almost certain to call any reasonable bet from me, considering I am still deep-stacked. If I get check-raised, I'll probably just call and reassess on the turn, depending on what it brings. If I'm check-raised, going all-in wouldn't be terrible either, as I might get called by draws and lower pairs.

The Hero bets 125, and the big blind calls.

 Turn (440): The big blind checks. What do you do?

PearlJammer

I still have an overpair, and my opponent is most likely drawing to a flush, perhaps with two overcards. Therefore, betting about two-thirds of the pot again to make him pay for his draw and maintain control of the pot seems like the most logical play.

However, sometimes in the early stages, I will check in a spot like this so as not to build too big of a pot. If I were to bet and get check-raised on the turn, I would be in a very awkward position and probably choose to let go of my hand. My opponent would be representing a set and would most likely bet strongly again on the river. I do not want to be involved in such a big pot at the early stages with only one pair, even though it is an overpair on a board where two pair is unlikely.

My opponent might have hit the T on the turn and decide to raise with a hand such as A♥ T♥, truly believing he is ahead. However, I believe I would be paying off a stronger hand much too often to justify making a call. In order to avoid facing such a decision, and to keep the pot small during the early stages of the tournament, I will mix up my checks and bets in this spot about half and half, leaning toward the check.

Rizen

I bet. I very likely have the best hand, and there are a lot of river cards I don't want to give my opponents a free chance to hit.

Apestyles

I bet again for value. Not much on the board has changed, and I can still expect to get called by flush draws and worse pairs some of the time.

The Hero bets 325, and the big blind raises to 980. What do you do?

PearlJammer

On the turn, the Hero bet 325 into the pot of 440. The bet was strong enough that it should have chased off any flush draws and should have boldly stated that I have a very strong hand. However, my opponent responded with a check-raise to 980! Because I bet even more than I normally would when I choose to bet in this spot, I can be fairly confident that my opponent has JJ beat with a set either on the flop or on the turn. It is hard to imagine him putting this many chips into the pot at the 10-20 level with a worse hand than mine. It is possible that my opponent is making a move or perhaps believes top pair and the flush draw to be the best hand. However, at this stage, I would rather risk making a bad laydown than calling off over 600 more chips, only to probably face another, even stronger bet on the river. I fold.

Rizen

This is a very strong line taken by the big blind, and it's still very early in the tournament. It is very likely that he has two pair or better. Even when I am ahead, he may well have a hand like Q♥ T♥ that has plenty of chances to improve on the river. It really doesn't make sense to play for what might easily be my whole stack here. I fold.

Apestyles

Right now, my hand looks very strong and my opponent has still chosen to raise. If he had a flush draw, he most likely would have bet or check-raised the flop rather than take a risky line of check-calling the flop with the intention of check-raising the turn. His equity is seriously diminished by waiting until the turn, and it would be pretty bold considering how strong he must perceive my hand to be at this point.

It really seems like my opponent has a set here. He flat-called out of the big blind like many do with a small pair, and then checked the flop, either to assess whether I have anything or to let me hit something on the turn so that he can get more out of the situation. Trying to bluff by check-calling the flop and then check-raising the turn is just too unlikely, although it's always possible. It's unlikely he would be playing a pair of tens this hard, not to mention the fact he would've had to float out of position with a T-x hand to get here in the first place. Everything points to a set, and I fold.

Results: The Hero folds.

Hand 176

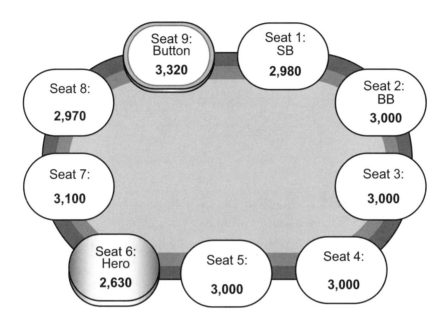

Setup: It is early in a $215 Sunday major tournament. The blinds are 10-20.

 **Pre-flop** (30): Seat 3 raises to 70, and the Hero reraises to 270. Seat 3 four-bets to 910. What do you do?

PearlJammer

In many tournaments, I will flat-call early position raises with QQ at such an early stage. However, in this example I choose to reraise, as I may get action from a wide range, especially with all the weak opponents in this particular field. Unfortunately, my opponent has come back over the top with a four-bet! At this stage of the tournament, unless my opponent is on a suicide mission, I should only be able to give him a range of three hands, AA, KK, and A-K. Two of these hands dominate me, and I do not have implied odds against them to call. The third, A-K, is less likely than AA or KK in this spot, as most opponents will choose to just call a three-bet instead of committing themselves to the pot pre-flop at such an early stage in the tournament. Even if I thought that my opponent would make this bet with A-K along with AA and KK every time, I should still fold. If I were to call or shove all-in, it would be with the hope that I am racing, and it is way too early to make such a move. I fold.

Rizen

Unfortunately, I can't call here for set value, and going broke this early in a tournament with QQ is a mistake as most players at this stage won't put in that third raise without aces or kings. Queens are a nice hand, but they're rarely good here, and I still have lots of poker to play. I fold.

Apestyles

This spot is incredibly borderline, and there isn't really a correct answer. With QQ, I prefer to flat-call pre-flop most of the time with these stack sizes, both to disguise my hand strength and to avoid having to fold a hand as strong as QQ before the flop if I am reraised.

Seat 3's play really reeks of aces or kings. He is raising from under-the-gun and then four-betting a little over three times my three-bet. It's unlikely (but possible) that he's playing A-K or JJ so hard this early when he has a stack of 150 big blinds. There is the whole random donkey factor, however, when some players show up with garbage a small percentage of the time. It is close, but I decide to fold, thinking my opponent holds AA or KK way too often here. Calling with the intention of getting it all-in on flops without an ace or king is OK, as well as just getting it all-in here. I lean toward folding because the average player only has AA or KK here, so I fold thinking I am a huge underdog to most player's ranges.

Results: The Hero folds.

Hand 177

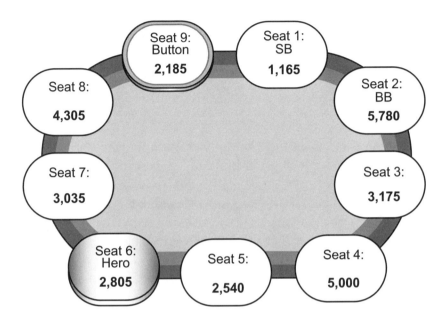

Setup: This is a $25 buy-in tournament. It is the second level with blinds of 15-30 and no antes.

 **Pre-flop** (45): Seat 3 raises to 120. What do you do?

PearlJammer

Unless I know that Seat 3 is an absolute maniac from previous experience, I should just call an early-position raise of four times the big blind, rather than reraise with A-K. In fact, I would rarely reraise a raise of this size from any position this early in a tournament with a hand weaker than KK, with both my opponent and myself having about the starting stack.

Rizen

Assuming that this is the typical $25 buy-in structure, which moves very quickly with very poor play, I would reraise here to 435 (one big blind more than a pot-size raise). In these faster structure tournaments with lots of weak players, the key is to play your big hands very strongly and very aggressively pre-flop. There is a good chance I'd even be willing to get all my chips in the middle here pre-flop in a typical $25 buy-in structure.

Ape

I usually three-bet about three times his raise to around 360 with the intention of getting my chips all-in if he four-bets. In a higher buy-in tournament with a better structure, I would fold to a four-bet after reraising A-K (or flat-call pre-flop more often), but this is a $25 tournament with weak players and a terrible structure. Occasionally, they even show up with A-Q and A-J. At this buy-in level with a faster structure, it is even more important to try and build a big stack early since the blinds and antes increase so fast. If Seat 3 flat-calls, I will make a continuation bet on most flops and play for stacks on ace- or king-high flops. Reraising also serves the purpose of isolating the original raiser with a hand that doesn't play that well in multiway pots.

Flat-calling is fine as long as I raise missed dry boards occasionally and take a few pots down that I don't hit. Also, I can't go broke multiway with one pair too easily either.

The Hero calls, and everyone else folds.

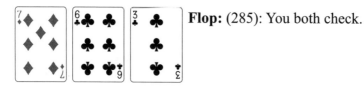 **Flop:** (285): You both check.

Turn (285): Your opponent bets 210. What do you do?

Pearl

I like my hand a lot at this point and could easily justify raising the turn. My opponent showed weakness on a flop of three rags but then led strongly at the ace on the turn. In conjunction with his pre-flop action, this almost surely means one of two things. Either he hit the flop very hard (flopped a set), or he hit the ace on the turn. A third, though less likely, possibility is that he is bluffing with a hand like K-Q, trying to represent the ace.

It is very difficult to believe that he flopped a set, as rarely does anyone raise four times the big blind, let alone raise at all, with a low pocket pair from early position at this stage in a tournament. If he did manage to raise with a low pocket pair and flop a set, he likely would have bet with a flush draw and three to a straight on the board. Therefore, I can safely assume that either he hit the ace on the turn or he is bluffing and likely to be drawing dead. If he is bluffing, I should just call, hoping he will fire another shot on the river. However, he most likely has the ace, probably A-K, A-Q, or A-J. His kicker range is wider than it really should be because this is a small, $25 tournament and he has opened for four times the big blind. Given this information, I usually expect my opponent to be a fairly weak player. Against this type of player and this range, I should raise for value, as I beat two of these hands and split with the other.

Rizen

Given the pre-flop action, I flat-call here. Seat 3 was under-the-gun, so his most likely hand range is some sort of big ace or middle pocket pair. This is something of a way ahead/way behind situation. Your opponent also will often bluff the ace with something like K-Q, and you'd like to give him a chance to bluff again. Most players would have made a continuation bet if they had a flush or a straight draw here, so I would not be overly concerned about either of those yet would remain aware of them. I can reevaluate based on the river action.

Ape

Regarding the flop, I don't necessarily check if checked to in position on the flop. Usually, my opponent has either a monster or whiffed-over cards; it's best just to try to take the pot down on the flop and fold to a check-raise. If he is slow-playing a monster, hitting one of my overcards could be a disaster.

Calling appears to be the best option because I don't get much additional value from A-x hands or bluffs by raising. Also, calling helps keep the pot small if I am against a set or the unlikely straight.

The Hero calls.

 River (705): The opponent bets 390. What do you do?

Pearl

My opponent's bet on the river is very much in line with his bet on the turn, and my read on his hand should be pretty much identical. I expect to split the pot much of the time, have my opponent beaten and likely get paid off some of the time, and only very rarely be behind. Therefore, I should raise for value. A raise to about 1,100 should get me paid off by A-Q and A-J.

It should be noted that against a strong opponent in a higher buy-in tournament, I would never raise on this river. A strong opponent will virtually never bet this river with any hand worse than A-K unless he is on a complete bluff. Therefore, if my opponent will never call with a worse hand on the river, a raise has no value.

Rizen

This bet looks weak to me. It's just a little more than half the pot, and with a strong hand here, most players would try to get a little more value out of it. Some players are tricky here, but this really smells like a blocking bet. I would make some sort of small raise to 900 or so, and try to extract a little extra value and a crying call out of an opponent with A-Q or A-J (or even weaker aces sometimes). This puts me in an awkward position when my opponent comes back over the top, but more often than not, I think I squeeze some extra value out of my holding here.

Ape

His bet size seems like a clear value bet that is typically a hand like A-Q or A-J, although he could have two pair, a set, or an unlikely straight. There is 705 in the pot. I am getting nearly 3-to-1 odds; this means I have to have the best hand around 1 in 4 times for a call to be correct. He is betting A-Q and A-J in this exact same way, enough to make a call mandatory if not a raise.

If he were deeper-stacked, I would consider raising to around 1,200 and folding to an all-in, but that would be ridiculous as short as he is. One option to consider is min-raising, or making a bet a little over two and up to two-and-a-half times his bet, with the intention of folding to an all-in bet. I usually just call but can definitely see the merits of raising to extract value from hands like A-Q or A-J.

Results: The Hero raises to 1,000 and is called by A♣ Q♠.

Hand 178

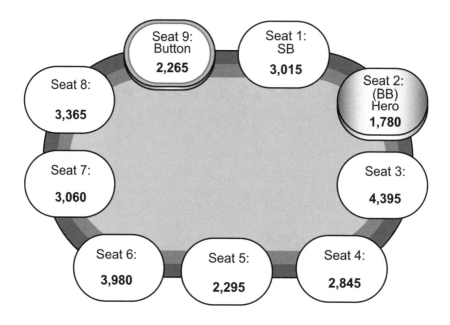

Setup: This is a nightly $150 buy-in, $100K guaranteed tournament. The Hero is at the second level and does not have any significant reads. The blinds are 15-30.

 **Pre-flop** (45): Seat 3 limps, and Seat 8 raises to 120. What do you do?

PearlJammer

I am out of position with an under-the-gun limp and a raise of four times the big blind in front of me. I can also assume the raiser is fairly strong to be raising after this limper. I could actually justify folding my hand here as A-K is not a great hand to play post-flop out of position, especially against two opponents who are both likely to be very strong. The under-the-gun limper still has the option to reraise. If I call and he reraises, I will have to fold as he will show up with AA or KK most of the time and will virtually never be holding A-Q or worse. Nonetheless, it is difficult to let go of A-K to a single raise, and folding is not necessarily the correct play, so I make the call.

Rizen

I flat-call. This tournament has a reasonable structure, and I am going to be out of position the remainder of the hand. If I make a raise here, I'll be creating a large pot out of position with an unmade hand. With the limper in this hand being under-the-gun as well, it's not very likely that the raiser is just isolating here with a weaker-than-normal hand.

Ape

I will generally just flat-call pre-flop because stack sizes would be awkward on the flop if I make a standard three-bet. For this reason, if I were to reraise I would make a larger bet, to around 550, which would enable me to make a pot sized shove on the flop after seat 8 calls. If the limper were to go all-in after my reraise, I would fold as he nearly always has AA, KK, or QQ. Flat-calling is the best option here.

The Hero and Seat 3 both call.

   Flop (375): It is checked to Seat 8, who bets 240. What do you do?

Pearl

If I raise this bet to approximately 650, I must be prepared to play for my whole stack against Seat 8, and I am likely to be pot-committed even if Seat 3 came over the top. With no flush draw on the board, I should be more inclined just to call the 240 bet and then reevaluate on the turn. Just calling will give me the opportunity to get away from the hand if Seat 3 were to come over the top and Seat 8 still liked his hand even after this action. Assuming Seat 3 folds, which he most likely will, I will check-raise all-in on the turn against Seat 8. It is important to note that on this board, there is no turn card to really worry about as the only overcard that could hit would improve my hand and it is very unlikely that Seat 8 could have any draw on this board. I call the bet of 240.

Rizen

I raise to around 800. Since I flat-called before the flop, it's going to be very tough for my opponent to put me on A-K. He could easily commit himself with K-Q or even K-J here (if he would raise with that pre-flop, that is). This board texture is such that I really don't want to slow-play top pair, top kicker. Any additional broadway cards bring in lots of two-pair and straight combinations. If my opponent comes back over the top all-in here, I'll be faced with a tough decision, but most likely will have to commit the rest of my chips.

Ape

There are two reasonable lines. Check-raising with the plan of calling the villain's all-in or check-calling are both fine. I am torn because there are good reasons for both. I check-raise to around two-and-a-half to three times the size of his bet (600ish) with the intent to call his all-in. By flat-calling pre-flop, I have disguised my hand, so he may go broke with K-Q, K-J, QQ, and worse.

The other option of flat-calling the flop is perfectly acceptable. There aren't that many actual scare cards. Q-J and J-T are unlikely gutshot-straight draws. 8-7 makes an open-ended straight, but that usually isn't in Seat 8's hand range. Check-calling disguises the strength of your hand while also keeping the pot small. When I take this line, I plan on check-raising all-in on the turn since check-raising the flop on such a dry board looks very strong and will fold out most hands I can get value from. However, many turn cards will put some kind of draw on the board that I can represent. If my opponent checks behind on the turn, I will value bet the river.

Results: The Hero calls. The turn is the J♣, and the Hero checks. His opponent bets 570, and the Hero pushes all-in. His opponent thinks for a long time and then calls the 850 with A♦ Q♠!

Hand 179

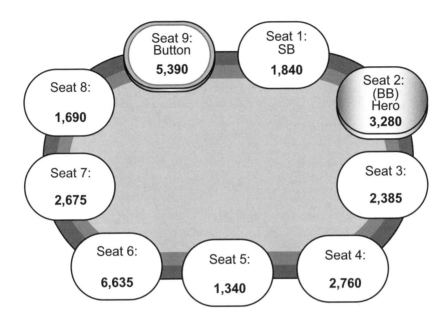

Setup: This is a nightly tournament with a $50 buy-in and $50K guarantee. The blinds are 20-40.

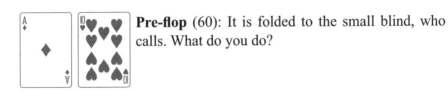

Pre-flop (60): It is folded to the small blind, who calls. What do you do?

PearlJammer
I check my option, as I would prefer just taking a flop with a disguised, semi-strong hand rather than building a pot this early in the tournament.

Rizen
I raise to 160 for value. I have the best hand here and position, so I should make the pot bigger.

Ape

This is an easy raise. I usually raise around three-and-a-half to four times the big blind in blind-versus-blind situations because players seem to be a little more stubborn and "defend" their blinds with light holdings. I raise for two reasons: First, I raise for value to build a pot with the best hand since my hand is almost certainly ahead of the range he is generally limping in with from the small blind. Second, I raise to take the initiative and to take control of the pot. Generally, if I raise pre-flop, the small blind will check to me on the flop, letting me bet and take down the pot the majority of the time.

The Hero checks.

 Flop (80): The small blind checks. What do you do?

Pearl

I could check this flop, as I do not yet have a made hand and I do not want to be check-raised. However, I should bet this flop some of the time as well because my opponent may or may not choose to call with one pair, against which I have eight solid outs to the straight and three probable outs to the ace. Most important, if he does call, and I hit my straight, my hand will be very well-disguised!

Rizen

If I raised pre-flop, I would make a continuation bet here. Given that I didn't, I would check behind because this particular board hits an awful lot of hands.

Ape

After I check pre-flop, most opponents will bet the flop if they catch a piece of it so I bet around 60-70 looking for a fold. If he calls, I still have a ton of equity versus nearly any reasonable holding and I'll have position on later streets. If he check-raises, I will probably just call and reevaluate on the turn.

The Hero checks.

Turn (80): The money card! The small blind bets 40, and the Hero raises to 200. The small blind calls.

 River (480): The villain is sitting on A♥ 7♥. What would you do in his shoes?

Pearl

In his shoes, I would lead out on the river. He has made the nuts, and he should be aware that I probably have a very strong hand but would be scared of the flush. Therefore, if he checked to me, I would usually check behind. In order to get value out of his hand, the villain should bet out for approximately 300, or two-thirds to three-quarters of the pot.

Rizen

The villain should make a pot-size bet here. Because the flush came backdoor, it's going to be tough for me to put him on it. Also, since it's the 9♥, it really looks like he is betting with a T here; and when I have a hand like A-T, the villain wins a lot more money. Also, when I have a hand like K-x, I am likely to check behind if the villain checks the river with that particular card. By betting, the villain basically wins additional bets from hands that I would call with but not bet with. The value of these additional calls more than makes up for those situations where the villain might lose out on a chance to check-raise when I have a T.

Ape

Because there is a four-straight on the board now, the only play is to make around a pot-size bet and hope to get paid off. As the villain in this example, I can't expect my opponent to bet on the river with such a scary board, and I allow him to check behind with two-pair and one-pair hands. If the river was a 2♥ or another non-connected heart, I would probably go for a large river check-raise as my hand is fairly well-disguised.

Results: The villain bets 200, and the Hero calls.

Hand 180

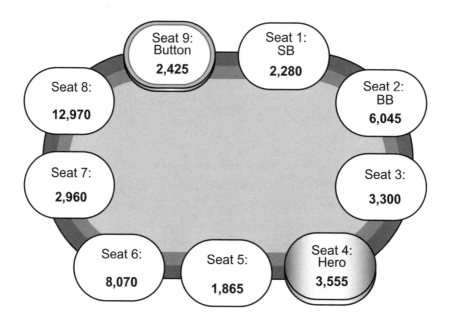

Setup: This is a $50 buy-in tournament. It is the third level with blinds of 25-50.

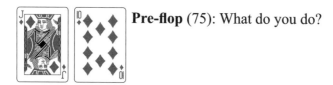 **Pre-flop** (75): What do you do?

PearlJammer
With a stack of approximately 70 big blinds, I can limp in with middle to low pocket pairs and strong suited connectors looking to hit big hands and win big pots. However, I should be open-raising with these hands at least as frequently as I am limping, so as not to become too predictable.

Rizen

I raise to 150. This creates some deceptive value for my hand and allows me to take control of the pot. Since I am in early position, players will often put me on a far different hand than I actually have, so I can win the pot frequently without a showdown. And when I hit, my opponents are not likely to put me on the type of hand I have.

Ape

I generally fold or raise with this hand. Since I am in early position with these stacks, I lean toward folding. To limp, you need a good read on the rest of the table; it's only correct to limp if the table is loose-passive with lots of multiway pots.

The Hero limps, and Seat 8 raises to 150. Everyone folds, and the Hero calls.

   Flop (375): The Hero checks, and his opponent bets 300. The Hero calls.

 Turn (975): What do you do?

Pearl

Often the best play is to check to the bettor upon hitting a draw; however, in this hand, I should lead into my opponent. With such a coordinated board where only a jack is needed for a straight, my opponent will probably be checking strong hands such as KK, QQ, K-Q, or A-K behind me. Therefore, in order to prevent him from getting a free card, I should bet my hand, making him pay to outdraw me. The only hand I lose to is A-J, which is unlikely given my opponent's bet of 300 on the flop.

Rizen

I lead into the pot for about 500. A little over half the size of the pot should get my opponent to **_look me up_** with a holding like two pair, and it also keeps him from taking a free card and filling up (when he has two pair or a set), hitting the backdoor flush, or hitting the river jack when he holds an ace.

Ape

On the flop, no option is really good even though it's a decent flop for me. To be more specific, this is probably a top 25 percent flop for this hand, and I have no clue how to proceed. Raising doesn't work because I'll have to fold to a reraise, so I have to call or fold. This is why folding hands like J-Ts out of position is optimal. Being the raiser is also advantageous, as playing pots without initiative is generally difficult and undesirable.

On the turn, I almost definitely have the best hand. I can't check here because the villain will usually check behind with two pair, overpairs, and sets. I could bet around half the pot, or 500. If I am raised, I have a tough decision. If I get it all-in on the turn against a competent villain, I'll almost always be a split at best and he could have me drawing dead with A-J. Also, I don't have the J♥, so there is a slight possibility that he has J-x of hearts and will be freerolling me with a flush draw and a straight. Freerolling means that he can't lose the pot but can win. I am very unhappy if raised but will call since there is a decent chance of him bluffing.

The Hero bets 600, and his opponent calls.

 River (2,175): The Hero bets 800, and his opponent pushes all-in. What do you do?

Pearl

I have now invested 1,850 in this pot, and I only have 1,705 left, so I should call this all-in, right? Wrong! I must fold.

My opponent should recognize from my betting that I have a straight and am likely to be committed to calling his all-in. Therefore, it is extremely rare for him to ever bluff in this spot. The 9♠ was a terrible card for my hand as it may well have completed my opponent's full house. I can be sure that he had a very strong hand on the turn to call my bet with, most probably a set. If he had a straight, even A-J, he usually would have just called my bet on the river instead of raising with a similar fear that I may have filled up. Given my opponent's actions throughout the hand, I can be very confident that folding my straight is the correct play.

Rizen

Well, first off, I never lead here! Once the board pairs and none of the other draws come in, I just try to get to a showdown. When you check, you give them the opportunity to bluff when they miss, and you're probably not getting too much value out of hands like K-Q here anyway. I also probably never make a blocking bet like this. The pot is 2,100. I think a blocking bet here puts my hand pretty much faceup. If my opponent is a thinking player and recognizes my bet for what it is, a blocking bet, he can make a bluff raise here and put me in a really bad spot. When he does fill up, it's also going to make it very tough for me to fold. I'd rather check and let him bet more than 800 the times he fills up than have to make the decision to call or fold when he pushes; not to mention the fact that I gain lots of equity against his bluffs this way, or if he's bad enough, he might even be thinking that he is value-betting two-pair or worse.

Since I did bet 800 and he pushed, the effective pot (because he has me covered) is 5,130, and I have 2,005 left. That's pot odds of slightly better than 2-to-1, but most of the time my best-case scenario is that I am looking for a chop (although I will pick off the occasional bluff). So if we say 5 percent of the time he's bluffing, 60 percent of the time he has just another dry jack, and the other 35 percent he has A-J or better to scoop me, my equity in the pot is just under 1,800. Calling 2,005 to win 1,800 (on average) is a losing play, so I think it's best to fold here. My opponent would need to be bluffing more than 10 percent of the time here and/or have a dry jack a lot more often to make this call profitable. Even so, I'd also have to balance out the fact that 30 to 35 percent of the time I'd be out of the tournament here, and at this stage, 2,005 is still a very playable stack to work with. I fold.

Ape

Generally, small river bets are tricky since they can possibly induce bluffs. However, in this case, the 800 bet is perfect. His flop bet indicated strength, and his call on the turn implied fear of the four-straight but a strong hand nonetheless. Based on the action, my opponent usually has a strong hand that he will not turn into a bluff. He will almost definitely call with K-Q, A-K, AA, and J-x but will raise if he has a boat or A-J. Not very many players would make such a sophisticated bluff or turn a hand with value into a bluff by raising. He has a boat here the majority of the time. As played, I fold and fairly quickly.

Raising or folding pre-flop makes this hand a lot easier to play. Generally I fold pre-flop to avoid spots like this.

Results: The Hero folds.

Hand 181

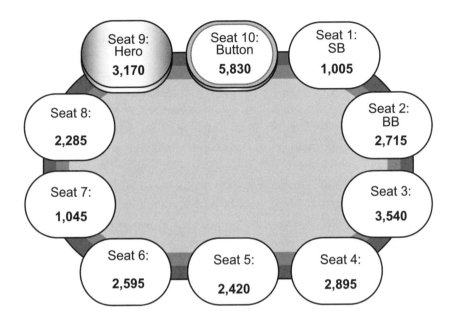

Setup: This is a $150 tournament with blinds of 20-40.

Pre-flop (60): Seat 3 limps for 40. Seat 4 raises to 140. Seat 5 reraises to 240. It is folded to you. What do you do?

PearlJammer

In the very early stages of tournaments, I am happy to be able to open a pot with A-K. If a player opens from late position, I am also happy to reraise with it pre-flop, especially in position. However, when faced with a raise and a reraise at this stage, I usually just want my A-K to shrivel up and die! Because I will have position throughout the hand, I consider cold-calling both bets, although reraising here is generally not an option. The stacks are all too deep relative to the blinds to want to get all my money in pre-flop. I will either choose to take a flop for 240, praying the original raiser does not reraise, or toss my A-K into the muck.

When faced with such a decision, most of the time I opt for the conservative route and muck my hand, as I have no money invested and two players are showing considerable strength. This conservative route is especially appealing at a ten-handed table such as this one as opposed to the more common nine-handed tables. I may be in a heap of trouble if I call and connect with the flop by hitting an ace and/or king. Also, if I do decide to cold-call, I will be prepared to surrender to any further pre-flop action from the original raiser or another player. My hand would become virtually worthless to a second pre-flop reraise. If, however, the reraiser has proven himself to be a maniac and is very likely to be making the reraise with a less than super-premium hand — an A-Q or A-J, for example — then I will gladly cold-call and take the flop in position, or I may even choose to reraise. Strong enough evidence to count on a reraiser being this reckless is very rarely available at this stage of a tournament. Therefore, I will usually fold my hand now before I invest any money in the pot. I fold.

Rizen

Fold. Seat 3 limped under-the-gun, which often scares players. The fact that Seat 4, the player immediately to his left, raised and the player immediately to Seat 4's left reraised indicates some very strong hands. If I do manage to flop an ace or a king, I am not likely to get involved in a big pot because I may be dominated. This is a situation where the reverse implied odds I offer my opponents when I hit a second-best hand are just way too high to play this hand profitably.

Apestyles

I fold here. When there's a significant amount of action from the early-position players, especially minimum raises and three-bets, A-K is often way behind and will be very difficult to play since we will not know where we are if we flop top pair. Also, we don't close the action if we flat-call and seat 4 could put in another bet forcing us to fold.

Results: The Hero folds. Seat 4 flops a set of tens, and Seat 5 loses with KK.

Hand 182

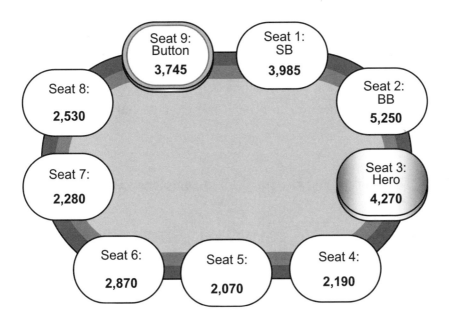

Setup: This is a major $200, $750K guarantee tournament on Sunday with thousands of entrants. The blinds are 30-60.

 **Pre-flop** (90): What do you do?

PearlJammer
Under-the-gun in the early stages of a tournament, I need a relatively strong hand to play. I'm going to fold hands as strong as A-Jo, A-Ts, K-Qo, and K-Js. Stealing the blinds is virtually worthless at this stage, and I don't want to get unnecessarily involved in a pot out of position. A-Js is borderline, but given that we are in a large field full of satellite winners, I will choose to open-raise to approximately 150-180 with it. I am much happier to get involved with this hand in this particular tournament than in a tougher, tighter field such as that of a daily $100 freezeout.

Rizen

Early on in these tournaments I often like to limp with A-Js and even A-Qs sometimes. Note that if it were A-Jo, I would probably muck here, but A-Js plays much better in multiway pots. I would also occasionally raise here to mix up my play. I call.

Apestyles

I always raise or fold here but lean towards a fold. A-J isn't a good hand at a full ring table in early position. However, the fact that it is suited makes me more inclined to play; it has the potential to flop well and make a big hand.

The Hero limps, and the small blind completes. Three players see the flop.

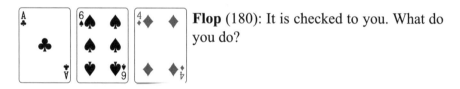

Flop (180): It is checked to you. What do you do?

PearlJammer

Although I would have preferred an open-raise or fold, I am happy the limp resulted in being able to play the pot in position against the blinds. I have flopped top pair with a strong kicker, and I should bet for value even though most likely I will only get action from A-x or a straight draw. I will charge the blinds to see the turn, not allowing them to hit two pair or a straight for free. I bet about 120, two-thirds of the pot.

Rizen

This is a good flop for me. Both of the blinds could be on quite literally any two cards, but I have to believe my hand is good here. Due to the fact that it is very difficult to put my opponents on a range of hands here, I would bet both for value and to help my opponents define their hands for me a little more clearly. I bet 120.

Apestyles

I bet between half and three-quarters of the pot to get value from worse aces, straight draws, and perhaps middle and bottom pair. I will be unhappy if check-raised but will most likely call and reevaluate on the turn. I would have preferred a raise pre-flop to be able to define my opponents' hand ranges more accurately and also because A-J does not play well in multiway pots.

The Hero bets 105, and the small blind calls.

 Turn (390): The small blind checks. What do you do?

PearlJammer
It is very unlikely that the small blind would call my flop bet with a 6 in his hand. It is much more likely that he has either A-x or a straight draw. With either of these hands, he will probably call another bet on the turn. I could check to keep the pot small and induce bluffs from missed straight draws on the river. However, I should be able to get value out of my hand, and I want to charge my opponent to draw, so I will bet about 250 or approximately two-thirds of the pot again.

Rizen
The 6♥ completes the rainbow board. I think there is a chance the small blind has a 6 in his hand. It's also possible he has a smaller ace, or hands like 8-7 or 7-5 for draws. I must weigh the value of checking behind and turning my hand into a "bluff catcher" on the river or value-betting again to get value out of the smaller aces. This early in the tournament, I think I'm more likely to check behind here to induce potential bluffs on the river, keep the pot small, and get to a showdown.

Apestyles
Either checking behind or betting around half the pot is acceptable. I generally am checking behind because a tricky player could check-raise, representing a 6 on the turn here, forcing me to fold even if he is holding a straight draw or bottom pair. Also, checking behind induces bets from worse hands on the river. The line I choose really depends on the reads I have on the player.

The Hero checks.

 River (390): The small blind makes a pot-size bet of 390. What do you do?

PearlJammer

In this example, I checked the turn to keep the pot small and perhaps induce a bluff on the river. My opponent led out for a pot-size bet on the river. Although I might be paying off a full house if he slow-played two pair on the flop or an A-T that improved to beat me on the river, I must make this call. He could be value-betting any ace, believing that he had the best hand when I checked the turn. He could also be bluffing a missed straight draw, as several hands fit this bill and could not win at showdown otherwise. There is also a slight possibility that he made trips on the turn and is betting his hand for maximum value; however, I still think that most likely he would have folded a 6 on the flop. Raising is not an option because it is extremely difficult to get paid off by a worse hand here and it would open up the action again if I am beaten. I gladly call.

Rizen

This bet looks very much like a value bet with a 6 or A-T. The turn check was designed to induce river bluffs, though, and he might feel like he's value-betting the best hand with A-9 or something. I would grudgingly call here.

Apestyles

I call his pot-size bet fairly quickly. With the line I played, he may well be betting a worse ace or a missed straight draw. You simply cannot check back the turn with the intention of folding on the river where your kicker still plays. For the most part, raising only makes worse hands fold and better hands call. I can definitely be beaten here a good percentage of the time. His pot-size bet seems fairly strong, but there really isn't any other play but calling here.

Results: The Hero folds.

Hand 183

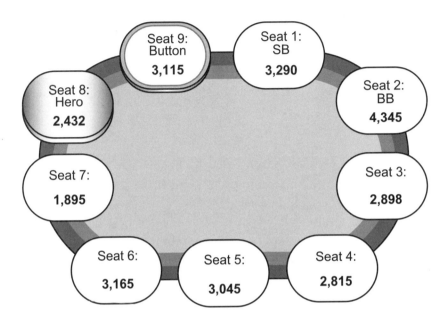

Setup: This is the first event of a major online tournament series. The buy-in is $200, and there are more than 5,000 entrants. The blinds are 30-60.

 **Pre-flop** (90): Seat 7 raises to 220. What do you do?

PearlJammer

In a major tournament series such as this, there are thousands of satellite winners and thus plenty of weak players. I am put in a tough spot when the hijack raises almost four times the big blind to 220 and I have TT in the cutoff. If I thought that Seat 7 always had a higher pocket pair here, I wouldn't have the necessary implied odds to chase a set with TT. However, much of the time, Seat 7's bet is indicative of a middle pocket pair from 99 to 77 along with A-K, A-Q, A-J, K-Q, and perhaps even other broadway hands or weaker aces. It is very difficult to narrow down the range of a complete unknown, especially when there are so many inexperienced players in this particular tournament field.

Reraising pre-flop with TT seems to be too aggressive, as I would commit myself to the pot with a reraise. With 2,432 at 30-60, I definitely do not want to be committed pre-flop with a hand as weak as TT. Folding to a single, late-position raise would be too weak with TT, so given my positional advantage, I will usually call in this spot and reevaluate on the flop. I call.

Rizen

Given that my opponent raised from the hijack seat and only has 30 big blinds, I think a reraise is in order here. If the stacks were deeper, I would prefer a flat-call, but the stacks are short enough that it makes more sense to reraise with what is probably the best hand. I should reraise an amount that makes my opponent think he is going to be all-in the hand, but not so much that I am committed to the pot no matter what happens. Typically, if a player has to put around one-third of his chips in pre-flop, he thinks he is all-in, so I would raise to 640 here. If someone besides the hijack reraises me, I will fold, but I am prepared to play for the hijack's stack if necessary.

Apestyles

I flat-call. With my stack I am not looking to get in significant pre-flop action with just tens at this point.

The Hero calls.

The button moves all-in for 3,115. It is folded to Seat 7 who thinks close to 15 seconds and then calls. What do you do?

PearlJammer

The button moved all-in for 3,115, an overbet considering the 530 in the pot, but very common in a tournament like this. Seat 7 made the call for all his chips after thinking for a bit. The action is back to me with TT. Normally, at the 30-60 stage, there would be virtually no chance that my TT was the best hand pre-flop with two players already all-in. However, in this spot, there is a legitimate chance that it is good. The button easily could have squeezed with a middle pocket pair or A-K or A-Q.

Seat 7's "thinking" could have been a ploy with AA, looking to get action from me, but most likely he was truly considering whether to call or fold. This time "tell" generally indicates a middle pocket pair such as JJ or 99 or maybe a hand like A-K or A-Q. I doubt he would call off with a small pocket pair or worse broadway cards, but you can never know for sure, especially in a minefield like this. Although there is a legitimate chance that I could be folding the best hand pre-flop, I don't believe that it is worth the gamble at this early stage to have to beat two all-in hands to survive. I take the conservative route and fold.

Rizen

I fold as quickly as possible. In this situation, I am looking for a perfect storm of being up against either two A-K combinations or A-K and a lower pair. It is highly unlikely that I am up against two lower pairs, and it is more likely that I am against at least one higher pair. This is part of the reason I would have reraised my hand pre-flop. As long as I don't make a full-pot reraise of 750 or more pre-flop when a raise to 640 would accomplish the same thing, I will get much more information about the hand while often taking down the pot right there.

Apestyles

I fold. With the strong action that has been taken already, and especially considering the slow overcall Seat 7 made with me left to act (which is often a sign of a monster trying to induce a call rather than a weak hand with a serious decision), my tens aren't going to shape up very well in a three-way all-in. I still have a fine stack to play with and can accumulate chips in much better spots than this one, so I opt to fold.

Results: The Hero in fact calls. The button shows A♠ K♠, Seat 7 shows 5♣ 5♠, and the Hero's hand wins a pot of 6,849.

Hand 184

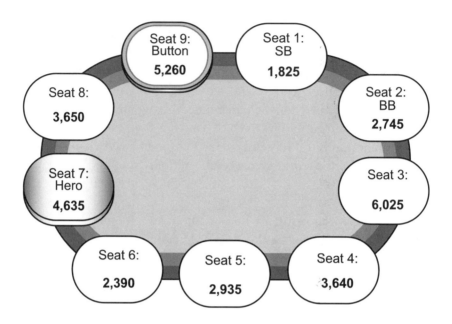

Setup: This is a $320 nightly buy-in tournament, and the blinds are 50-100. Seat 8 has been calling a lot of the Hero's pre-flop raises.

 **Pre-flop** (150): The Hero raises to 250. Seat 8 in the cutoff calls, and two players see the flop.

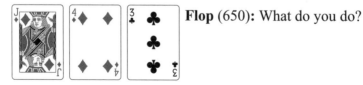 **Flop** (650): What do you do?

PearlJammer

With 650 in the pot and an overactive opponent, I should follow up my pre-flop aggression with a stab at the pot on the flop. My opponent is likely to fold any unpaired hands, and he might fold a middle pocket pair as well. If my opponent calls, I will shut down on the turn unless I hit a king or queen or pick up a draw. I want to bet about half to two-thirds of the pot.

Rizen

I make a standard continuation bet. While there is a flush draw on the board, this particular board is very unlikely to have hit my opponent. The pot is now 650, so I bet 400.

Apestyles

I definitely make a continuation bet on this fairly uncoordinated board.

The Hero bets 400, and his opponent calls.

 Turn (1,450): What do you do?

PearlJammer

I'm happy to have hit a king; however, this particular king completes a possible flush. If I check, I invite my opponent to bet hands such as a middle pocket pair or a jack that he most likely would fold if I followed through with another bet. Because my opponent is calling so many of my raises, I am probably resigned to paying him off if he has made a flush. If I were to bet, and my opponent raises all-in, I would have a hard time folding top pair and the second nut-flush draw. By checking, I help to control the size of the pot. If my opponent checks behind, I will value-bet most rivers. I check.

Rizen

I bet again. There is 1,450 in the pot, and I have 3,085 left. If I check and my opponent bets, I'll be in a very precarious position of potentially facing both turn and river bets for my whole stack with only top pair. If I bet 900 here, most likely my opponent will define his hand for me and I can make a good decision. It will be tough (although not impossible) for him to bluff-raise me here, giving me those kinds of pot odds to call his raise. If he just flat-calls, he'll often have a hand like

Q-J or J-T with maybe a single diamond, and I can value-push most non-diamond river cards.

Apestyles

This is a tough hand. Reads are really important in this spot. If I bet and he raises, my hand is probably in serious trouble and I will probably have to fold. If he just called with a jack on the flop, most likely he would call a turn bet rather than turn his hand into a bluff by raising with the king on the turn. However, he could be bluffing with gutshots and straight draws here. He also could have definitely flat-called K-J, a set, and a flush draw here, all of which absolutely dominate me on the turn.

While I do have the Q♦, I will not have the odds to draw to it if my opponent raises me all-in, especially based on the range of hands I put him on. I'd hate to fold my hand as well, since I have top pair, second kicker and a decent flush draw. Check-calling seems like the best option considering all this together; check-raising all-in isn't terrible either, as I get a bet out of worse draws. I check, hoping he'll check behind so that I can value-bet the river.

The Hero checks. Seat 8 bets 1,100 and the Hero calls.

 River (2,550): The Hero checks. His opponent pushes all-in for 1,900. What do you do?

PearlJammer

At this point, I am regretting having made a continuation bet in the first place. However, there is a lot of money in the pot, and my opponent has been playing too many hands. Also, the way I played the hand, he probably believes that I am relatively weak, perhaps with a hand like TT, or A-J at best. He might also think that I called on the turn with the naked ace of diamonds and cannot call his river bet. Nevertheless, he might have me crushed with a flush, set, two pair, or even a miracle straight on the river. It is a close decision; however, I choose to make the call given the size of the pot and my opponent's overactive play up to this point.

Rizen

This is why I bet the turn. Now I am getting nearly three-to-one pot odds to call, but it represents a majority of my remaining chips. Most opponents are not capable of calling the flop and then bluffing both the turn and the river here, so my opponent has to think he's betting for value. There aren't a whole lot of hands he can bet for value that I can beat, and folding leaves me enough chips to take some time and pick my spots in future hands. Calling and losing here leaves me with a nearly unplayable stack. I would fold and be mad at myself for not betting the turn!

Apestyles

My opponent has shown a ton of strength in this hand. The only way my hand could really be good is if he pulled some sort of extremely insane bluff line, or floated K-T and is now being overly greedy for value. If you compare the number of realistic hands that crush me to the very unlikely chance he's just doing something insane here, it seems really clear that I am beaten the vast majority of the time. I fold.

Results: The Hero folds.

Hand 185

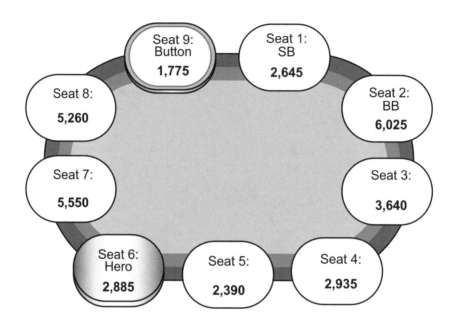

Setup: This is a $320 buy-in tournament, and the blinds are 50-100.

 **Pre-flop:** (150): Seat 3 limps, and the Hero raises to 400 with pocket queens. Only Seat 3 calls.

 **Flop** (950): The opponent thinks for quite some time and then checks. What do you do?

PearlJammer

I made a standard raise of four times the big blind with QQ after a limper to 400, and the limper called. Unfortunately, an ace has flopped, putting me in a tough spot. I could bet, hoping to take the pot down now. However, with no flush draw on the flop, I am unlikely to get any action unless my opponent has an ace. I should check in this spot and reevaluate on the turn based on my opponent's turn play.

Rizen
Most of the time when players think for a while and check, it's actually a sign of weakness, although sometimes it's also just a sign of them playing multiple tables, so I'm careful not to read too much into these sorts of "timing tells" without more information. That being said, I raised pre-flop, and this is a good flop to represent an ace on. With a 950 pot, I should bet 600.

Apestyles
For the most part, I actually advocate checking behind in this spot because you rarely make better hands fold or worse hands call. Occasionally a 9, 7, or lower pair peels off though, so the bet isn't too bad. Also, there is something to be said for just taking down the pot immediately and causing hands that have equity to fold. This generally isn't one of those spots, but betting isn't all that bad since it maintains the initiative, is what I would normally do if I missed, and occasionally gets value. Betting here also allows me to narrow down Seat 3's range somewhat. That being said, I prefer checking.

The Hero bets 500, and his opponent calls.

 Turn (1,950): His opponent bets 100. What do you do?

PearlJammer
My opponent has taken a very strange line in this hand by leading out for the absolute minimum on the turn. This bet is often representative of a draw or an otherwise weak hand looking to get to the river cheaply. My opponent could have picked up a flush draw on the turn or called with a straight draw on the flop. He could also be betting a weak ace or a 9, trying to see where he is in the hand. I should raise to about 500 or 600. If I were deeper-stacked, I would probably raise to about 800 to

1,000 based on the size of the pot, but with my current stack, I cannot afford such a bet. Hopefully, my opponent folds, but if he calls, I should be able to check behind in position on the river.

Rizen

With the "timing tell" from the flop combined with this super-weak bet on the turn, my impression is that my opponent has some sort of weak made hand at this point, maybe A-xs where he has picked up a draw and wants to set his own price for the hand. I actually like raising here even though it turns the pocket queens into a bluff. I think taking the pot down right now and preventing him from drawing cheaply to a better hand is more valuable than letting him bet again with a worse hand. I raise to 900.

Apestyles

Calling is the only move here. Folding a hand of this strength for this little seems kind of silly. Raising here would accomplish nothing in most cases; I am not going to be getting better hands like aces to fold to my raise. The only merit a raise might have is to get value from a lesser pair, a straight draw, or backdoor flush draw, which would be extremely unlikely in the face of a continuation bet and turn raise. My opponent is clearly inexperienced or too tricky for his own good based on his bet sizing. He has an ace more often than not here, but the significant odds I am offered make this a call.

The Hero calls.

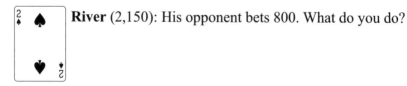 **River** (2,150): His opponent bets 800. What do you do?

PearlJammer

The backdoor flush hit, but all straight draws, J-T, T-8, and 8-6, missed. Because I just called on the turn, my opponent may attempt to bluff a missed draw on the river, assuming I do not have an ace and cannot call. It is tempting to call, hoping to pick off a bluff attempt. However, I cannot beat anything but a bluff or a very oddly played single pair such a TT or 9-8, and my opponent has made a relatively strong bet on the river. I am too short-stacked to consider raising on a bluff. It is a close decision whether to call or fold; however, I lean toward folding.

Rizen

The fact that I just called on the turn probably emboldened my opponent to think his small ace was good, or he tried to set his own price on his turned flush draw and just got there. After the first two streets, I have 1,885 chips left. While these represent very favorable pot odds, I can really only beat a complete bluff here. He might be making a blocking bet with a 9, but maintaining reraise fold equity on future hands with 1,885 chips is probably more important than hoping I can pick off a bluff. I fold.

Apestyles

I fold. This less than half-pot bet really screams of value, particularly with the lines he's taken on previous streets. I might look him up if I were deeper-stacked, given the odds as well as the chance to gain information, but that 800 is a significant portion of my stack and really limits my options in the upcoming hands. I reluctantly fold.

Results: The Hero folds.

Hand 186

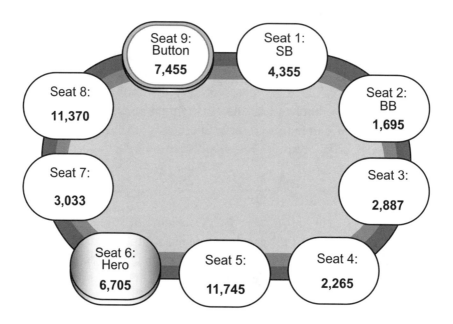

Setup: This is a $650 satellite tournament for a major live tournament event. The Hero is in the fifth level with 75-150 blinds.

 Pre-flop (225): The Hero raises to 400 with pocket jacks. The small blind reraises to 1,650. What do you do?

PearlJammer

Facing a rather large reraise from an out-of-position player, I must decide whether to fold or move all-in with JJ. Calling 1,250 more, creating a pot of 3,450 with my opponent only left with 2,705, is not an option. I can assume my opponent will make this raise with AA, KK, QQ, A-K, and perhaps TT, 99, and A-Q. In a tournament with a buy-in of this size, I should not expect an opponent with 40 big blinds to commit himself to a pot with worse than this range against a middle-position raise.

My opponent's rather large reraise is most typical of QQ or A-K, as he does not appear to want action. Nonetheless, he is clearly willing to commit his stack to this hand. If I somehow knew that my opponent had A-K, I would be willing to take my chances to accumulate a stack with my marginal edge. However, given my opponent's range, I should lean toward folding as I am more than likely in a coin-flip situation or in deep trouble against a higher pocket pair.

Rizen

With the stack sizes and the position I raised from, I would usually just flat-call the raise and then get it all-in on any flop with a single overcard or less, as long as it's not an ace. Given that this is a satellite (payouts aren't specified, but I'm assuming there are 9+ seats rewarded), I actually don't think folding is a bad move, and I don't like pushing much here at all. If it were a standard freezeout, I'd probably think a little differently, but in a satellite that awards multiple seats, value is often skewed toward staying alive with a reasonable stack versus trying to accumulate large amounts of chips.

Ape

This is a marginal spot. Knowing the payouts and how many are left would be helpful. Assuming I am not very deep in the tourney, I elect to go all-in. Usually players make smaller reraises with AA or KK, although without any reads I really don't know. In general, I assume he is making this raise with 99+, AQo+, although that might be a little loose. JJ plays well versus this range. Even if he is only reraising me with TT+ and A-K, I think he has A-K a lot more than he has QQ-AA because of the size of his raise. Folding isn't terrible here, though. However, if you fold JJ every time someone reraises you online, you become very exploitable.

Results: The Hero folds.

Hand 187

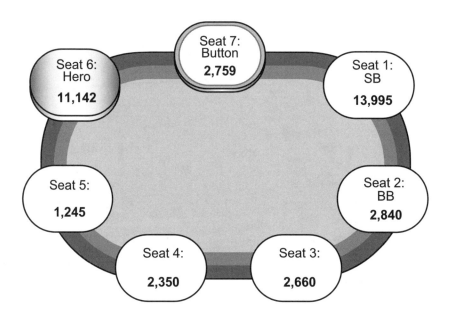

Setup: The Hero is in a $150 buy-in nightly tournament. A total of 63 players remain, and the tourney is paying 27 spots. The blinds are 80-160.

  Pre-flop (240): You raise to 400, and the button pushes all-in for 2,759. What do you do?

PearlJammer

I have made a standard opening raise in late position with A-Q. The cutoff, with a relatively short stack, pushed all-in on top. He should reasonably and correctly assume that I am raising a very wide range of hands in this spot, due to three factors: I am very deep-stacked relative to the blinds, I am also deep-stacked relative to most of the players at this table, and I am in late position. Thus he will reraise all-in here with a fairly wide range. His range should be A-8+, K-Q, any pocket pair, and perhaps even a few weaker hands such as weak suited aces, K-J, Q-J, or

J-T. He correctly assumes that he has fold equity; however, I have a very strong hand given the situation. I call.

Rizen

My image is very important here. Did I build my chip stack by playing aggressively or have I hit solid hands and been paid off by second-best hands? Do I know anything about the button's level of aggression? I have to call 2,359 to win 3,399 chips, or pot odds of roughly 3-to-2. I would have to assume that the button would only push with A-Q+/JJ+ in order to make this a proper fold from a chip-equity standpoint. Only the tightest of players would have that sort of reraising range with fewer than 20 big blinds.

The other consideration is how this affects my stack if I call and lose. In this case, I have 10,742 chips left after my raise. Calling and losing would leave me with 8,383 chips, which would still make mine the second-largest chip stack at the table. Calling and winning would put me at 14,141 and make me the chip leader at my table, which could potentially be a huge benefit going into the bubble. There is also the added benefit of players at the table seeing me call the all-in push when raising from late position, which might make them more hesitant to reraise me in the future and enhance my ability to steal as the blinds escalate. I call the all-in raiser here.

Apestyles

Call after high-fiving the monitor! I am ahead of pretty much any decent range. I have a strong hand, and the button is shoving over a late-position raise for less than a total of 20 big blinds. Here, 15-25 big blind stacks are perfect for shoving a wide range of hands over aggressive players raising in late position. I can definitely expect the button to be shoving with a lot worse than A-Q. I dominate A-x hands and broadway cards like K-Q, and I am a coin flip against most pairs that probably comprise a decent part of his range. I would have to have a strong read to fold here. I am ahead of his reraise range and call quickly.

Results: The Hero calls and wins against 99.

Hand 188

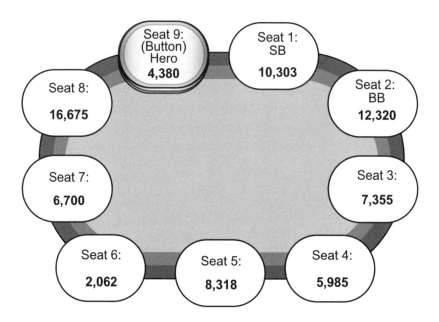

Setup: This is a $650 online satellite to a major live tournament event. It is still early, with 100-200 blinds. The event pays out 18 seats.

Pre-flop (300): The Hero raises first-in to 600. The small blind calls, and two players see the flop.

Flop (1,400): The small blind checks. What do you do?

PearlJammer

I have picked up a huge hand on the button and made a standard raise of three times the big blind, to 600. I would like to see one of my deep-stacked opponents in the blinds reraise, in which case I would gladly put my money in pre-flop. Although neither opponent obliges, the small blind calls, and I see the flop heads-up in position.

If I bet the flop, I will be in a very difficult position if my opponent raises. If I know my opponent is a maniac who would often check-raise or shove over the top with air on the flop, I should make a continuation bet of about 800, planning to go all the way with the hand. However, against most opponents, I would certainly have to fold to a check-raise. I could only be ahead if my opponent were semibluffing with a flush draw, or an open-ended straight draw such as Q-T or T-9, or over-playing a hand such as A-J. In order to avoid being put to this decision, I check and take a free card.

Rizen
This is a dangerous flop for many reasons. Obviously the king overcard is a potential problem, but I also have a multitude of flush and straight draws out there that my opponent could easily check-raise me all-in with, given my stack size and the pot size. Even if he doesn't check-raise, check-calling will put me in a precarious position, as any reasonable bet, when called, will make the amount in the pot roughly equal to the amount remaining in my stack. I should check here and try for a cheap showdown.

Apestyles
While betting is an option, I like to check behind here for a few reasons. First of all, there's an overcard on the board as well as a flush draw and some straight draws. On this type of board texture, I am at risk of being check-raised all-in. This is because my continuation bet would have to be around 1,000, and I'd have only 2,780 left, which is the perfect stack for my opponent to check-raise. This puts me in a really tough spot, because my stack is small and he could easily be check-raising with worse hands.

Second, by making a continuation bet, small-pair hands like TT, 99, and 88 will most likely fold. By checking, I might very well get some value out of them on the turn; after checking behind on the flop, a turn bet will look like I am sensing weakness and taking a stab. I give hands like Q-J and J-T confidence in their worse pair and can probably extract a decent amount of value from them. Also, I might be able to induce bluffs on the turn if my opponent thinks my check indicates weakness and takes a stab at me.

The Hero checks.

Turn (1,400): The small blind checks, and the Hero bets 800. The small blind raises to 1,800. What do you do?

PearlJammer

Ugh, I am in an absolutely gross spot. The turn was seemingly very good for me. With two kings on board and a check from my opponent, I became pretty confident that my opponent does not have a king. My bet should get action from a jack and also charge my opponent for a draw. Unfortunately, I get a lot more action than I bargain for!

By check-raising with a small bet instead of going all-in, my opponent appears to be begging for action. His line throughout the hand would make perfect sense with JJ or 77, and it would be reasonable with K-Q or K-J as well, perhaps even A-K. I can usually discount A-K in this spot, as most opponents would reraise with it pre-flop. A tight opponent, however, especially a satellite winner, may choose to just call with it pre-flop. My opponent's raise indicates that he is going all the way with his hand since I would be left with only 1,980 if I were to call.

My opponent could be over-playing a jack or making a move, as he probably does not put me on that strong of a hand, so I have a close decision to make. I should lean toward a fold, as my opponent's bet size shows enormous strength and there are many legitimate hands in this spot that beat me. I fold.

Oftentimes in this spot, after checking the flop, I should check the turn as well. Then, if my opponent bets the river, I will call, often picking off a bluff but costing me about the same as my turn bet if I am beaten. If my opponent checks the river, unless it is an ace, I should bet for value. I will often get a call from a jack or even a lower pair, as he would be very suspicious that I was trying to pick up the pot with a bluff.

Rizen

In this sort of satellite, I would grudgingly fold. I don't need to accumulate all the chips to get the maximum prize; I simply have to finish in the final 18. Proper satellite strategy is to fold here. Sure, I am sometimes folding the best hand, but when I am behind I am drawing at best to two outs. In these satellite situations, the seat is much more valuable than the chips, so I need to fold.

Apestyles

I reluctantly call. His raise seems pretty strong, and he has a king a decent percentage of the time. Also, most hands that would semibluff this board are unlikely because they contain a queen. However, now that I've checked behind and underrepresented my hand strength, besides the fact that he would now have to have aces or trips to beat me, I really don't have any other options but to play for stacks. If I call the turn, I am pretty much committed to calling a river all-in. It allows my opponent to bluff the river with air, and if he checks to me on the river, I will probably check behind as I doubt I will get value from worse hands since he usually either has a K or air after raising the turn.

Results: The Hero pushes all-in, and his opponent folds.

Hand 189

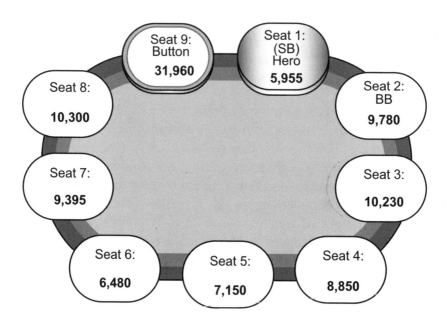

Setup: This is a $500 major Sunday tournament. The blinds are 150-300. The Hero has recently been moved to the table, so he has no reads.

Pre-flop (450): Seat 8 raises three times the big blind, to 900. What do you do?

PearlJammer

Having fallen well below the starting stack in a major Sunday tournament, "Bullets" are a sight for sore eyes! The cutoff has opened for 900, three times the big blind, and the action is on me. My only concern is figuring out how to get all of my opponent's chips in the middle. Reraising, shoving all-in, and flat-calling are all viable options. With no read on my opponent, I should consider how he would respond to each action.

My standard reraise out of position would be to approximately 3,000 at this level, or half my stack. This reraise would clearly commit me to the pot and probably represent immense strength to my opponent. If I lowered my reraise to approximately 2,300, it would probably represent even more strength and still clearly commit me. Any such reraise would allow my opponent to get away from his hand if he is not prepared to risk over half his stack with it pre-flop.

What if I were to shove all-in instead of making my standard reraise? My opponent would most likely assume that I do not have a super-premium hand because I am applying maximum pressure and do not appear to want a call. Many opponents would snap-call this shove with 7-7+ or K-J+ and might even call lighter if they incorrectly sense that I am weak. If I get called, then all of my opponent's money is in the middle, and my work is done.

If I choose to flat-call the raise with AA, I run the risk that the board will scare my opponent off his hand cheaply. I might lose out on action from a hand with which he would have put his money in pre-flop. On the other hand, if he catches a piece of the flop, he might give me action with a hand that he would have mucked pre-flop to a shove. Of course, he might also outflop me with a garbage hand, but that is a risk I must be willing to take. Flat-calling also gives the big blind a chance to make a mistake. If he calls as well, I will probably lead out on somewhat scary flops so as not to risk both opponents taking a free card. However, if I am heads-up, I will check to my opponent, looking to check-raise either now or on the turn, depending on the size of his bet and the coordination of the flop.

Re-shoving and flat-calling are both viable options in this spot. If my opponent were deep-stacked, I would lean toward re-shoving as he would be more likely to take a gamble and call pre-flop. However, because calling my all-in would cost this particular opponent over half his stack, I tend to prefer flat-calling. I call.

Rizen

There are really several viable ways to play this, in my opinion. I can smooth-call and slow-play for deceptive value to try to squeeze more chips out of the pre-flop raiser. I can raise to 2,500 or so with the hope that the original raiser will feel like he's getting a good price to call, then hit a piece of the flop and stack off. I can also just straight shove here, and try to make it look like I'm stealing the pot in the hopes that he might call me with some marginal hands. Given that I have no reads on the table, I have a stack that can do a lot of damage to the original raiser's stack, and I have fewer than 20 big blinds, I think this is an appropriate spot to smooth-call with the intention of check-raising all-in on most flops. With fewer than 20 big blinds, I'll take a chance that my opponent might outflop me in order to increase the chances of doubling up. If I had appropriate reads, though, this could easily change. Some of the more-aware players are actually more scared by the smooth call than if I had just open-shoved and made it look like a re-steal. Others are slaves to the math and would call a small raise, justifying it with pot odds. Against the average Sunday tournament player, though, I think the smooth-call will usually be the best play.

Apestyles

There are a ton of fine options here. I call versus some players, mainly aggressive, inexperienced ones, as they will make a continuation bet on most flops and I get an extra bet. However, this play is transparent to good players since I don't often flat-call raises pre-flop with a stack of this size, and they may shut down. If I flat-call with AA pre-flop with this stack, my reraises get less respect, and I usually reraise a lot with this stack size. Calling might be the best option if you're an unknown player because it doesn't matter if your play is exploitable or not. However, as a well-known player, I have to vary my play more and try to play in a way that cannot be easily exploited. Honestly, min-raising isn't that terrible either, especially if it's an instant min-raise that looks like a mis-click. Really, it doesn't matter as long as you don't fold!

Results: The Hero calls pre-flop. The flop comes Q♥ T♠ 7♣. The Hero checks, his opponent bets 1,200, the Hero pushes all-in, and his opponent folds.

Hand 190

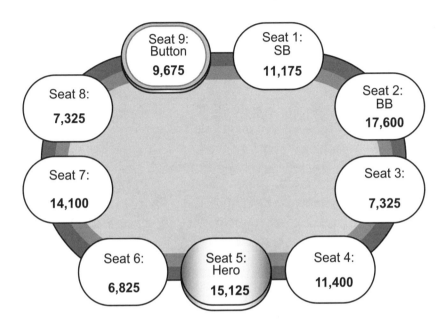

Setup: This is a major Sunday tournament with a $200 buy-in. The blinds are 150-300.

 **Pre-flop** (450): Seat 4 raises to 900. You act right behind him and are sitting on pocket sevens. What do you do?

PearlJammer

Playing low and middle pocket pairs to a raise where the stacks are approximately 40 to 50 big blinds can be tricky. Often the decision to call, fold, or reraise pre-flop hinges on position, knowledge of the raiser, both his and the whole table's image of you, the overall aggressiveness of the table, and precise implied odds. Sometimes the decision can be so close that all three choices are fine. The particular hand in question is one such multifaceted decision.

Seat 4 opens for 900, three times the big blind, with 10,500 chips behind. I am in the next seat with 77. If I were to call here, I would have about 12-to-1 implied odds against the raiser. Although this is short of the 15-to-1 odds usually needed, I often open up to about 10- to 12-to-1 against unknown or presumably weak opponents (as most players are in a Sunday major). I am more likely to get paid in full when I flop a set against a weak opponent. I also have position in the hand, so I may be able to take away the pot on the flop if I sense weakness.

Although it seems like these are certainly good enough reasons to call, I am aware that there are six players left to act behind me. If one of them reraises, the hand becomes a clear fold. Thus, if I am at an overly aggressive table, this point alone would probably convince me to fold.

One final option in this spot is the reraise. I might consider this if my opponent and I were closer to the button, but given that we are both in early position with a lot of players left to act behind us, I would not consider a reraise.

All in all, this hand is a close decision between a call and a fold, but I lean towards calling.

Rizen
Given the fact that the initial raiser is in early position, it makes sense just to call here. I wouldn't hate folding either, but early-position raises tend to have a freezing effect on the table, so it's unlikely someone will reraise without a very big hand. My call might entice several other callers, allowing me to play the hand to hit a set and win a (hopefully) big pot.

Apestyles
Because I have an effective stack size of 38 big blinds with Seat 4, I like to flat-call pairs here for a few reasons. While I am calling to flop a set here and win a big pot, I am not going to neglect good post-flop situations where I can outplay my opponent. I am in position and intend on floating or raising Seat 4's continuation bets if the board is right. Raising is a bad idea, as I am forced to fold to a four-bet if I reraise. I call.

Results: The Hero folds. The player behind calls, and the big blind calls. The board comes A♦ 9♣ 7♦. Two players get all-in and the Hero would have won a huge pot.

Hand 191

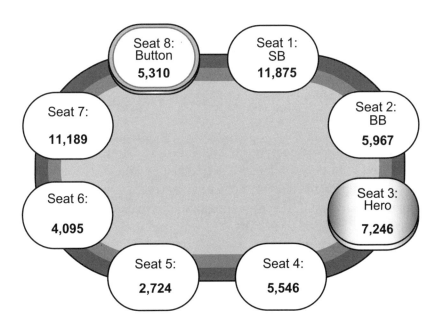

Setup: This is a $25 buy-in tournament, and the blinds are 150-300 with 25 antes.

Pre-flop: (650): The Hero raises under-the-gun to 800. Only the small blind calls, and two players see the flop.

Flop (2,100): The small blind checks. What do you do?

PearlJammer

I see the flop heads-up in position against a deep-stacked opponent. Because my opponent might call with a wide range pre-flop and my raise came from under-the-gun, I should continue to represent strength and bet the flop. With 2,100 in the pot, a bet of about 1,100 to 1,200 should suffice. If my opponent calls, I will probably check any turn card, looking to get to a showdown and hopefully pairing up by the river. However, my position should give my continuation bet some added respect and earn me the pot much of the time.

Rizen

This is a very coordinated flop with many flush and straight draws. These sorts of flops can be very dangerous to make continuation bets on, and with 2,100 chips in the pot, any bet would represent a significant portion of my remaining stack. There are also a lot of turn cards that potentially gives me the best hand or allows me to win by betting if he checks to me a second time. I check.

Apestyles

This board is a good one for making a continuation bet on. I bet more often than not here.

The Hero checks.

 Turn (2,100): The small blind bets 600. What do you do?

PearlJammer

My opponent leads out with a very small bet of 600, giving me 4.5-to-1 pot odds to call. The board is draw heavy, and my ace high may be ahead, yet my opponent most likely has at least one pair. When facing such a small bet with two overcards and a double gutshot-straight draw, calling and raising are both viable options. If I have seen my opponent lead out and then fold to a raise before, then I could argue for a raise to about 2,200. I could represent a jack or a slow-played set with such a bet. Tight opponents might fold a hand as strong as K-J to such a bet; however, one-third of my stack is a lot to risk on such a play at this point in the tournament.

My opponent has given me such good pot odds that just calling is certainly a better option. I would keep the pot small by calling, looking for an ace, king, queen, or 9 on the river. If I hit the ace or queen, however, I may have a very difficult decision if my opponent bets big. He would have to be suspicious that either of those cards could have helped me, so he might be able to bet a very strong hand such as a straight or set for value. Due to excellent pot odds and a chance to win a big pot if I hit, I call.

Rizen
I would call. Potentially I have a lot of outs here, and if I raise I may get reraised off my hand. Also, since I checked the flop, the small blind could be on a complete bluff, and I could win the hand either with a showdown or by betting the river as a bluff when checked to, even if I don't make my hand.

Apestyles
I call. This is a really tiny bet, only about a third of pot. I have a double-gut straight draw, possibly two overcards to draw to, and I might very well have the best hand some of the time. The odds I am getting right now are too good to fold, and I can probably get value when I hit my outs. My stack size is way too awkward to semibluff. If I raise to 1,800 to 2,400, I have to call off my stack with marginal odds if he goes all-in. I also have direct odds to hit if the majority of my cards are live. The clear choice here is to call.

The Hero calls.

Results: The river is the A♠. The small blind bets 600, and the Hero calls. His opponent takes down the pot with K♦ Q♠.

Hand 192

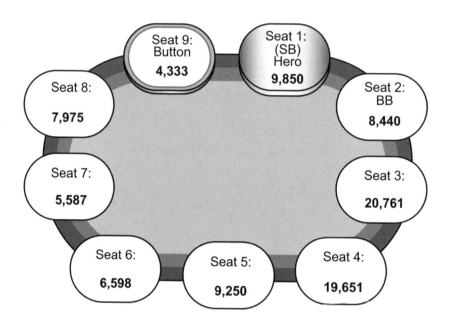

Setup: This is a $100 buy-in tournament. The blinds are 200-400 with 25 antes.

 **Pre-flop** (825): It is folded to you in the small blind, and you complete. The big blind checks.

 **Flop** (1,025): What do you do?

PearlJammer

Blind-versus-blind hands are often very tricky to play "correctly" because both players usually have a hard time giving each other any credit for a real hand. Usually the line I take in hands such as this depends more on my history with the player in previous orbits than it does on the strength of my hand.

In this spot where I can assume that I am new to the table and have no previous history of playing against my opponent, I tend to take a more cautious, conservative line. I would check to my opponent, looking to call a bet on the flop and reevaluate based on the turn card. If my opponent checks behind, I will lead out for value on any turn other than a king, queen, or 8, the worst cards to see.

Rizen
I have a very strong hand and should bet here. There is 1,025 in the pot, so 700 should be fine.

Apestyles
Without question, I bet 60 to 70 percent of the pot. I have top pair and an open-ended straight draw in a blind-versus-blind situation. I gladly get it all-in here.

The Hero bets 725, and his opponent raises to 2,005. What do you do?

PearlJammer
In this particular example, I took a more aggressive route and led out for 725 into my opponent. He responded with a raise to 2,005.

It is very difficult to assign my opponent a range of hands in this spot. Hands such as Q-T, J-9, and T-9 are all possible. He may have flopped the straight with K-Q, Q-8, or 8-7. He probably would have raised preflop with K-Q, JJ, TT, or 99, but blind-versus-blind play is often unpredictable. Along with made hands, he could easily be semibluffing with Q-x or even J-x or T-x, looking to take the lead in the hand and perhaps get a free river card if called. His range is enormously wide in this spot, making it very difficult to play my hand profitably.

Because I initially took the aggressive route in this example by leading into my opponent, I am going to continue with aggression and move all-in. My opponent's similar stack gives me fold equity, and calling to play a big pot out of position seems too weak and passive. This is an unusual spot where I am unsure whether or not I am moving in with the best hand. However, I am using my chips to apply pressure and force my opponent into a decision, as opposed to him putting me to a decision on the turn.

Rizen

I push. There are a lot of hands I am ahead of. K-Q likely would have raised pre-flop, and most of the time would have slow-played the flop. He could easily have two pair or 8-7, but this is often a semibluff with a naked queen. If I had a relevant read, I would fold here against tighter, more passive players, but against most players I would push here. There's too much in the middle, though, and my hand is too strong.

Apestyles

I have too much equity to do anything other than shove here. Against a two pair J-T, J-9, and T-9 range, I have almost 40 percent equity. It's very likely that he can be doing this with similar hands to mine as well, like Q-T, Q-J, and T-8. He might have the straight already, but this part of his range is overwhelmed by all the combinations of pair and straight-draw type hands. K-Q is a possibility, although I would expect him to have raised pre-flop. Also, in blind-versus-blind situations, he could just be over-valuing middle or bottom pair or be on a complete bluff.

Overall I probably have around 40 to 50 percent equity (depending on whether or not we include K-Q or K-T here, etc.) against a tight calling range, and he folds a decent amount of the time. I am definitely shoving here.

Although this isn't possible in the heat of action, I can check my analysis afterward to see how close I was in determining my equity. Let's assume the following range: KJs+, Q9s+, J8s+, T8s+, 87s, KJo+, Q9o+, J8o+, T8o+, and 8-7o. J♠ 8♦ will win against this range 39 percent of the time and tie 7.5 percent of the time.

Results: The Hero pushes all-in to 9,425, his opponent calls with 8♣ 7♣, and the Hero does not improve.

Hand 193

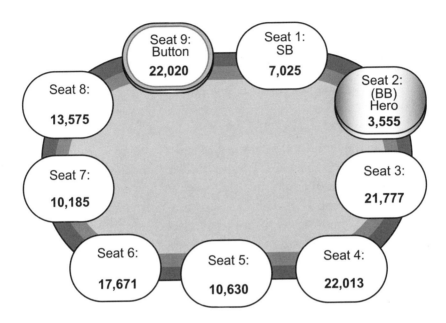

Setup: This is a $50 buy-in tournament, and the blinds are 300-600 with 50 ante. The Hero is very close to the money, with only a few players remaining to be knocked out before payday.

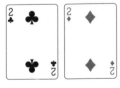

Pre-flop (1,350): Seat 6 raises to 2,000. The button calls. There is 5,350 in the pot, and the Hero is sitting on pocket deuces with only 2,905 remaining. What do you do?

PearlJammer

I am on the bubble with an extremely marginal hand. In another seat, especially late position, I should shove all-in with the deuces, looking to win a race and build my stack. In this spot, if the action was folded to the small blind and he shoved all-in, I should call, as his range would be virtually any two cards. With a raise in front of me and a call, however, I am very likely to need a deuce or hope I am against three or four over-cards and they hit blanks, right?

Wrong!

If I were playing for the win, not just to cash, I should see a third, very viable option given the stack sizes in this spot. Seat 6 raised to 2,000, or 1,400 more than the big blind. If I were to shove all-in, I would be raising an additional 1,505. Because this is a full reraise, I would open the action back up to Seat 6. At this point, Seat 6 is very likely to reraise, pushing out Seat 9 on the button. If this happens according to plan (and it will much of the time, given the stack sizes in this hand), then I will only have to go to a showdown against one player. I might find myself up against a higher pocket pair; however, more often than not, I will be in a coin-flip situation. I would also increase my stack from 2,905 (if I folded) to 9,760 if I win due to the dead money in the pot! It is this incentive of about a 3.3-to-1 increase to my stack that means I should lean toward a push.

I might actually get even better odds on my money in this spot. If Seat 6 open-raised with a marginal hand and Seat 9 called with a hand like A-K or A-Q, then Seat 6 might call my all-in, prompting Seat 9 to re-shove! If this scenario occurs and I end up heads-up against Seat 9, I will increase my stack to 11,265 by winning, a 3.9-to-1 increase to my stack. When given the opportunity, either player might be tempted to make an isolation play in this spot. It is a gamble and will lead to my exit from the tournament at least half the time; however, in the long run it should be very profitable.

Rizen

I would just fold. At this point, I don't have enough to make anyone fold if I push, and twos aren't ahead of anything. My best hope is that I shove here and Seat 6 makes an isolation play so that I can get heads-up with dead money in the pot against something like A-K. I am very likely to be called by both players, though, and a pair of twos is fairly horrible against two opponents in a showdown.

Apestyles

Pocket deuces, in general, is a very poor hand to get all-in three ways, and I like to avoid doing it. With around five big blinds left, I would much rather raise all-in first to act with any two cards where I might actually have some fold equity against weak opponents, or possibly find a premium hand to get my money in with.

Results: The Hero folds. The flop is A♣ 6♣ 4♦. Seat 6 bets 2,600 and is called. The turn is the 2♥, Seat 6 checks, Seat 9 bets 3,000, and Seat 6 folds.

Hand 194

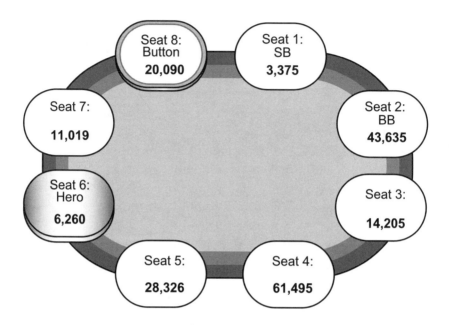

Setup: This is a $150 buy-in, $55K guaranteed tournament. There are only 58 players left, and 54 of them make the money. The blinds are 400-800 with a 100 ante. Your stack is about eight big blinds, but with an M of 3 given the antes.

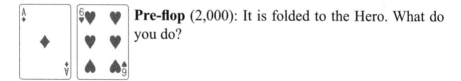

Pre-flop (2,000): It is folded to the Hero. What do you do?

PearlJammer

I am very short-stacked with an M of only 3, yet this is not quite short enough to need to shove with almost any two cards. A-6o is a very marginal hand to shove with in this spot, and given the stacks behind me, I believe that I am better off folding. If the big blind had a similar stack to mine, I would lean more toward pushing in this spot, as I would be much more likely to get a fold from him. However, with such a big stack, his range for calling opens up dramatically, and A-6o is barely favored over any two random cards. Of course, there is always a chance of someone waking up with a bigger ace or a high pocket pair behind me. I would be much more willing to push with a hand like J-Ts or K-Q than A-6o in this spot.

Rizen
In this situation, I would push. Seats 7 and 1 are both going to have a very hard time calling me without big hands. Seats 8 and 2 can afford to gamble a little more, but A-6 is a favorite here over four random hands, especially considering that Seats 7 and 1 will probably be folding all but their top 10 percent or so. My stack is at a point where accumulating chips will give me a chance to go deep into the tournament, which should be my primary consideration over just making the money. Longer term, the times I accumulate here and make a deep run to the final table will more than make up for the times I bubble and miss out on making my 150 back. If I had a bigger stack (say, 10,000 or so), I would probably fold, since picking up the blinds doesn't make quite the same impact on my stack and the results of getting called and losing would be more catastrophic. If I had a smaller stack (say, 4,000 or so), I would also fold because I am much more likely to get called at that point. Doubling up does not significantly enhance my chances of finishing deep in the tournament and getting to the "big money," so I'd wait for either a more significant edge or until I actually got into the money.

Apestyles
In general, when short-stacked on the money bubble, I tighten up a little bit. In tournaments, getting into the money isn't a huge consideration, but it is something to be aware of. For instance, to maximize my overall expectation, I might fold what is generally a marginal shove if I were very close to the money. However, this is not a marginal shove. I will increase my stack by around 32 percent if all four players ahead of me fold, and I might even have the best hand if called. The short-stacked small blind should be tighter than usual and might fold better hands, while the larger-stacked big blind might call me with worse hands like J-To+ and any pair. Overall, this is a favorable situation for me, and I shove, hoping to win the pot without a showdown.

Results: The Hero pushes all-in, and the small blind calls with J♣ J♥. The Hero doesn't improve.

Glossary

A-x – A hand which contains an ace and an unspecified card.

A-xs – A suited hand which contains an ace and an unspecified card.

Backdoor – A hand completed by both the turn and river card (same as runner-runner). A backdoor flush is a flush where you must use both the turn and river card to complete your flush.

Barrel – A bluff bet. Generally refers to a sequence of bluffs on consecutive streets.

Blocking Bet – A small bet designed to prevent your opponent from betting even more, should you be behind. The purpose is usually to control pot-size and get to a showdown.

Bounty tournament – A tournament where an additional prize is given whenever you knock out certain players.

Broadway – Any card ten or higher. A broadway straight is an ace high straight.

Cold call – Calling when there has been a bet and another opponent is also in the pot.

Continuation bet – Betting the flop after raising pre-flop.

Counterfeit – When a card on the board diminishes the value of your hand. For example, you hold bottom two pair and the board pairs the top pair.

Crying call – Calling when you know your chance of winning is small, but the pot odds make it worth a call.

Double belly buster – A two-way inside ("gutshot") straight.

EV – The expected value or the value of a play on average.

Float – A bluff which takes two streets to implement. Generally, a float involves calling a flop bet with the intention of bluffing on the turn or river.

Fold Equity – Refers to your ability to get your opponents to fold, and the associated value you have when they fold. When extremely short-stacked, you have little fold equity as you don't have enough chips to force players to fold.

Four-bet – Raising when there has already been a raise and reraise.

Freezeout tournament – A typical tournament where tables are combined as players are eliminated and there are no re-buys or add-ons.

Hijack – The position two seats to the right of the button (one seat to the right of the cutoff seat).

Look me up – When a player calls to make sure you have the hand that you are representing.

Post oak bluff – A bluff where you bet a small amount in the hope that your opponents will perceive your bet as strong.

Probe bet – A bet or raise with the primary purpose of gaining information to see where you are in a hand.

Re-buy tournament – A tournament where you are allowed to buy additional chips for a certain time period as long as you are under a certain stack level.

Reverse Implied Odds – Situations where your hand will either win a little or lose a lot.

Runner-runner – A hand completed by both the turn and river card (same as backdoor). A runner-runner flush is a flush where you must use both the turn and river card to complete your flush.

Satellite tournament – A tournament where entries to a larger tournament are awarded as prizes.

Three-bet – The same as a reraise.

UTG+1 – The position after the player under-the-gun, or the player two to the left of the big blind.

Other Books from Dimat Enterprises, Inc.

The Poker Mindset: Essential Attitudes for Poker Success
By Ian Taylor and Matthew Hilger

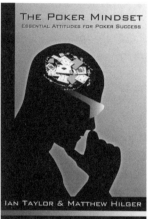

The Poker Mindset became a top-ten best-selling poker book at Amazon, largely as result of word-of-mouth. This book examines the emotional and psychological aspects of poker to help you bring your "A" game to the table every time you sit down.

What "secret" separates top poker players from poker wannabes?

Is it zen-like mind-reading skills, a computer-like brain or thousands of hours of play? No. It is a series of established approaches and behaviors that enables these experts to bring their "A" game to the table session after session, regardless of short-term results.

In this groundbreaking book, Taylor and Hilger lay bare the secrets of the Poker Mindset: seven core attitudes and concepts that ensure you have the optimal emotional, psychological, and behavioral framework for playing superior poker.

The Poker Mindset deeply explores vital topics that most poker books only touch upon:

- Tilt: What it really is, why and when you are most prone to it, and how you can avoid it.
- Bankroll: A complete examination of bankroll management from a technical, but more importantly, from a psychological and emotional viewpoint.
- Opponents: How to determine your competitors' mental and emotional processes so that you can dominate, out think and outplay them.
- Downswings: Every poker player experiences them, but you will truly understand and be armed against low ebbs when they occur.
- Bad Beats: *The Poker Mindset* will enable you to overcome the trauma of bad beats and losing big pots.

Poker is a fun game, but it is even more fun when you win. *The Poker Mindset* may be the most valuable poker book you will ever read. Embrace its concepts and you can overcome the unseen obstacles that are limiting your success at the table.

When you make the Poker Mindset your mindset, you will take control of your game and walk away a winner.

Texas Hold'em Odds and Probabilities:
Limit, No-Limit, and Tournament Strategies
By Matthew Hilger

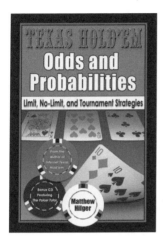

Texas Hold'em Odds and Probabilities has been a top ten best-selling poker book at Barnes & Noble for over two years. If you want to understand the math behind the game, this is your book.

- How often does each starting hand win against a specific hand or random hand?
- What are the odds of your opponent holding a pocket pair when he raises?
- What is the probability that an over-card will flop when you hold JJ?
- How do you determine if drawing is profitable or not?

Texas Hold'em Odds and Probabilities answers all of these questions and more. Every single decision you make at the poker table is in some way related to odds and probabilities. Whether you are deciding to bet, call, fold, raise, or even bluff, odds and probabilities are an integral part of the decision-making process.

Texas Hold'em Odds and Probabilities covers all forms of the game, including limit, no-limit, and tournament situations. This book does more than just show you how to calculate the odds – more importantly, the focus is on how to *apply* odds to make better decisions.

Hilger's approach shows that you do not need to be a math wiz to be successful in poker. Simple concepts and strategies that anyone can learn will have you matching wits with the top players in no time.

Some of the topics include: raising draws for value, backdoor draws, facing all-in decisions before the flop, protecting your hand, the impact of stack sizes, and much more. In addition, the most comprehensive collection of Texas Hold'em charts and statistics ever put in print is provided as reference.

Poker is a fun game, but it is even more fun when you win. Expert players understand the simple math behind every decision they make – now you can too.